Teaching Faith
with
Harry Potter

A Guidebook for
Parents and Educators
for Multigenerational
Faith Formation

Patricia M. Lyons

 Church Publishing
NEW YORK

To my Beloved Wife
Lisa Kimball
You form the world in faith.
You form my soul in love.

Church Publishing
19 East 34th Street
New York, NY 10016
www.churchpublishing.org

Cover design by Jennifer Kopec, 2Pug Design
Interior design and layout by Beth Oberholtzer Design

Library of Congress Cataloging-in-Publication Data
A record of this book is available from the Library of Congress

ISBN-13: 978-0-8192-3355-4 (pbk.)
ISBN-13: 978-0-8192-3356-1 (ebook)

Printed in the United States of America

Contents

Acknowledgments

To be an expert on Harry Potter requires only that you know that, like the Gospels, it is a story about the power of love and the presence of the resurrection in all creation. Everything else is trivia—true and transformative, but trivia.

This book is in so many ways a transcript of the life-changing conversations and relationships I have had with people who love Harry Potter, God, or both. I am grateful for all the students who have been my teachers over the past twenty years. I am especially grateful for the students of St. Stephen's & St. Agnes School in Alexandria, Virginia, who have inspired me with their passions for truth, understanding, justice, and lives of meaning. Thank you to every one of you who joined our chapter of the Harry Potter Alliance. Watching you wear Hogwarts robes and carry wands while designing and doing acts of service and social justice taught me without words the power of J. K. Rowling's epic to inspire justice, ignite courage, change lives, and heal a broken world. For nearly fifteen years, two former students, Maria Jones and Julian Wamble, have continued to teach me about love, God, and Harry Potter. May this book be a testament to your faith and its impact in the world.

The vision, wisdom, hard work, and grace of my editor Sharon Ely Pearson have been the gift and the gears to get this book written and finished. I am grateful for your guidance, humor, and profound knowledge of our shared loves, the Episcopal Church, and Harry Potter. I cherish too the Order of the Phoenix I gathered once I started this book project. Thank you to Harry Potter geniuses and genuinely powerful disciples Sam Faeth, Missy Green, Kimberly Lucas, Lindy Bunch, Samantha Gottlich, Maria Jones, Julian Wamble, Dawna Wall, Bronwyn Clark Skov, Dawn Alitz, Shannon Ferguson Kelly, Wendy Claire Barrie, and Day Smith Pritchartt.

I treasure the heart and mind of Chris Stewart, who, like Joanne Rowling, is a passionate person with a heart for Scotland and a heart for stories.

Your help in this book project was essential. I knew I loved you when I pulled a Golden Snitch out of my clerical robes and preached about Harry Potter at your wedding. There was no guarantee that you would love this choice as much as your Harry Potter fangirl bride did on that sacramental day, but your broad smile at that sacred moment sealed our friendship forever.

And to your Harry Potter fangirl wife, the Reverend Audrey O'Brien Stewart, I bear love and tenderness and gratefulness beyond words. You know more about Harry Potter than anyone I know. More important, you have walked bravely with God throughout your life in ways that continue to teach me, inspire me, console me, and form me into the person God has called me to be. You bring faith, hope, love, and glitter into my life. Faith formation is your palpable joy and contagious metabolism. Your life is an orchard of fruits of the Spirit, and your nourishment of my soul has made this book and so many of my words and deeds flow into the world. You are my priest and my best friend.

The Girl Who Lived

I remember exactly where I was when I decided to write this book. I was in room 210 in a hotel near a beach taking a two-day reading and writing retreat. I was sitting on the edge of the bed just a foot or two away from the large television crammed into a discount-size room. I was surfing channels trying to find weather reports for my day. I stumbled upon CNN. The anchor was introducing the next segment: a follow-up story to a horrific tragedy I had read about three days earlier.

The original story was gruesome and unthinkable. An armed and angry man went looking for his former wife. When he could not find her at her home, he went looking at her sister's house in the small town of Spring, Texas. He knocked on the door and was let in by his sister-in-law's fifteen-year-old daughter. He entered the house to find his sister-in-law, her husband, and their five children home. What followed was a bloodbath that still haunts me. He shot every family member execution-style and then walked out. He thought he had killed them all. But one of the children—the fifteen-year-old girl who had let him in—was still alive even though she had been shot in the head. She played dead among her deceased family members until the man left the house. When she was sure he was gone, she got to a phone and called the police. While the gunman had been shooting her parents, she heard him threaten to find her grandparents and kill them as well. She alerted the police, who were able to intercept the murderer outside the grandparents' home, just in time. Though shot in the head, Cassidy Stay was still able to save her grandparents' lives.

Among the dead were Cassidy's two brothers, ages four and thirteen, and her sisters, ages seven and nine. Also dead were her thirty-nine-year-old father, Stephen Stay, and her thirty-three-year-old mom, Katie Stay.

Just three days after the slaughter, the Spring community held a rally in a public park to support Cassidy and her surviving grandparents and to honor the young woman's heroic bravery. A live report from this loving rally was what I watched in my hotel room. As soon as I saw the story, I froze on the bed, waiting to see if the surviving girl would come out in public. I just had to see her face. Hundreds had gathered, prayed, and brought balloons to release at this rally. And then, right there on live television, Cassidy Stay appeared on the small rented stage. She stepped up to the microphone and looked out at the crowd, which went wild with cheers. Cassidy smiled. Her hair was pulled back in a ponytail, looking both sweet and purposeful while functionally covering shaved and patched parts of her head's bullet wound.

As the crowd continued to cheer, I listened to two child and family psychologists commentating live for the cable news channel. They were describing the ongoing scene of Cassidy smiling at those cheering for her. They practiced the all-too-common reductionism of psychological analysis. "Remember, she's in shock and isn't really present at this moment," "Yes, she's smiling right now, but remember, she is likely taking strong coping medications," "She's waving, but don't assume that she is really feeling anything right now," and so on. I am not demonizing psychological explanations of events, but too often these aggregated musings miss the unique, mysterious forces in a person's life that are distinctively spiritual. "She's just in shock," they said, again and again. Cassidy continued to wave, to smile, to bite her lip as she held back tears. She was clearly profoundly sad and simultaneously feeling the love of her community.

Then, amazingly, Cassidy looked at the microphone, cleared her throat, and started to speak. My finger landed firmly on the volume button of the remote control, prepared to blast her words across my room. What on earth was she going to say?

After a deep breath, Cassidy thanked the community with a young but strong voice. I tried to ignore the "experts" who were attempting to insert trained caution into this unusual event, explaining that this girl really had no idea what she was saying and that her condition would most certainly manifest and deteriorate in the coming hours and days. I am not a psychologist, but I saw a young woman naturally mixing tears with smiles, feeling desperately sad, yet embodied enough to feel the ocean of love in that community rally. And I will never forget what she said:

> I am really thankful for all the people that have been praying for me and keeping me and my family in their thoughts for the past couple days. And I'd like to thank all the first responders, nurses, and doctors who have taken care of me. I am feeling a lot better and am on a very straightforward path toward full recovery.[1]

The crowd cheered for her.

And then, after reading her scribbled remarks to doctors and first responders, she looked up from her folded sheet of paper and took another deep breath to speak, but this time without a script. After a pause and a renewed smile, she spoke words that took my breath away:

> I really love Harry Potter. In the *Prisoner of Azkaban*, Dumbledore says, "Happiness can be found even in the darkest of times, if one only remembers to turn on the light." I know that my mom, Dad, Becca, Zach, Brian, and Emily are in a much better place, and that I'll be able to see them again one day.[2]

Her voice cracked. She looked up and smiled once more at the crowd with sadness, confidence, and love. The news coverage then ended and went to a commercial. Sitting on the edge of my hotel bed, I muted the television and wept. Cassidy's honesty and vulnerability were astounding for a fifteen-year-old. I couldn't help imagining how hard her future might be as a sudden orphan from such a large, loving family. I have worked in education and faith formation with adolescents for twenty years, and Cassidy immediately became one of the most tragic and beautiful souls I have ever witnessed. She exhibited so much grace, faith, and strength, especially for someone so young. I wished I could rewind the clip. I swallowed the lump in my throat and heard myself say, "Did she just quote . . . from memory . . . in that impossibly heavy moment . . . *Dumbledore?*"

The girl whose story I had been watching for three days had finally spoken. The central role of a Harry Potter quotation in her first public utterance left me convicted. I found out later that she and her family were devout Mormons. She quoted Scripture often in the following weeks of interviews, clearly fluent in the formal language of her faith. Yet at that moment—to that crowd, when Cassidy spoke for the first time to the whole world—she quoted Albus Dumbledore as if he were her best friend. And when her voice spoke his name and his words, her face and eyes and posture were stronger than at any moment in that rally. A character created by J. K. Rowling had spoken to Cassidy and inspired her. At a rally marking the most critical threshold of her life, she shared Dumbledore's words with those she loved.

I knew it would take a few minutes or hours for the news clip to be posted on YouTube, so I had some time to think about Cassidy's words before I could hear them again (and again and again). I walked to the hotel window and stared as my pounding heart and spinning mind attempted to make meaning of what I had just witnessed.

In all my work with adolescents and their families, including a doctorate focused on adolescent faith development and ultimately writing a book on the subject, I have learned that we cannot shelter our children from crisis, suffering, and death. Life happens. And though it is our instinct to help those we love avoid pain, research and experience prove that when we develop habits of sheltering our children from suffering, we only stifle their spiritual growth. The answer is to form young people with faith so that when they inevitably face hard times, they will have a well within them of baptismal identity, community-modeled faith, and resurrection hope from which to draw. In addition to praying for them, equipping young people to discover and fill their internal wells is all we can do.

We form faith by fortifying the souls of people with testimonies and traditions from our Scriptures and sacraments. We model what lives look like that are rooted in the liberation of baptism and the presence of God. And then we wait and watch and pray that what is planted in them by God and the gathered communities of God will take root and be a stronghold for them to turn to when events good or bad rock their lives. That's the goal of anyone who works in faith formation—to help people find God in themselves, their neighbors, and their world. My goal is that they would know their faith tradition, know their own life story as an epic narrative of relationship with God since their creation, and be able to find and connect their experience of God with all the stories around them—finding God in culture, in films, in blogs, in Harry Potter. What does that actually look like in the life of an adolescent? Cassidy Stay.

From that day in that hotel room forward, Cassidy Stay has been my example of two things: what successful faith formation looks like and the power of the Harry Potter stories to teach a person how to connect one's faith with daily life. I don't know exactly what Cassidy's faith formation was, but I am confident it worked. She survived. And I don't just mean she physically survived the massacre of her entire family in her living room. I mean her hope survived—evidenced in her contagious smile that to this day survives. I have read much about her since the tragedy, and I can tell you that her tender, wounded soul survived. Her hope continued to heal her and others with each passing hour and month. The only way to describe Cassidy's resurrection is that her faith and the Harry Potter narrative formed her to be a Girl Who Lived.

NOTES

1. Elisha Fieldstadt, "Texas Teen Who Witnessed Murder of Her Family Speaks at Memorial," July 12, 2014, http://www.nbcnews.com/storyline/texas-family-killings/texas-teen-who-witnessed-murder-her-family-speaks-memorial-n154311.

2. Ibid.

I Ignored Harry Potter for a Decade

I confess to not having read the Harry Potter books when they first came out. I also skipped all eight films when they were in the theaters. I had no disciplined stance against the series. Unlike others, I did not take up the Bible against the series. I was vaguely aware that the Vatican had blacklisted the books, as did Focus on the Family and other prominent evangelical leaders. No, my posture was not from orthodoxy but from laziness and disinterest. I just didn't get it, though I also never sat down with any Harry Potter reader and asked them why they loved the series. I treated it the way I treat kale. I hear it's great. I know many people love it. I am happy that they are happy. But I have never tasted kale and feel whole and happy despite that choice.

Around 2001, while I was running on a treadmill next to a friend doing the same, she mentioned reading a British novel about wizards that a friend in England had sent her. I brushed off her book suggestion. By the time the second book came out, I was aware of the Rowling buzz. I vaguely remember hearing an interview on NPR with Rowling in which I learned that J. K. was actually a woman. I don't recall what she said, but whatever it was, it did not persuade me to order her books. By the time local news was covering long lines at bookstores, I knew I would need to read the first book before the second or third. But I never did. Then the first movie came out, and good friends said I should read the books before seeing the films, which meant I was now behind by five books. Somewhere in there, I gave up catching up.

I became defensive whenever Harry Potter references were made around me. By the release of the last film, I knew deep down that I had missed out on something culturally significant. But this was not enough to push me into the penance of reading seven novels of over four thousand pages. After the last film was released, I believed the craze would fade.

But then the high school where I taught chose Harry Potter as the Homecoming Spirit Week theme one October. The creativity was contagious. Our whole JK–12 school was transformed into Hogwarts. Students dressed up as wizards and witches all week. Their joy was palpable. So many faculty members, even those known to be the stiffest and shyest, were dressed up and caught up in a week of Pottermania. For the first time in my fifteen years as a high school teacher, I saw a Homecoming decorating theme become more important and more communal than any traditional Homecoming sporting or social event. I heard almost nothing in the halls about Homecoming kings or queens or even the usual gossipy buildup to the football game or dance. Every day of that week was about Gryffindor colors, stuffed owls on shoulders, wands in hands, and thunderbolt scars on the foreheads of girls, boys, and teachers alike. In one magical week, that high school saw so many of its walls of class, race, religion, and gender turn into bridges. When the week was over, I secretly rented all eight movies and watched them in three days. I realized that Harry Potter has become the Book of Common Prayer for this generation of young people, and I wanted to join the congregation.

My epiphany was and is that this series is a functional and contagious religion of words, rituals, and moral code for many young people from age five to twenty-five. Should it be? Who is to say? Are the religious police of many conservative religions right to agree with the Vatican's original condemnation of the series as sorcery and glamorization of the occult? The answers to these questions are, to some degree, irrelevant to this fact: a narrative of vocation, friendship, and fighting evil that is powerful enough to dethrone Homecoming kings and queens is now part of the DNA of the spiritual imagination of generations to come. I have seen it. And I am convinced that Harry Potter is here to stay.

What is most refreshing is that this is a story about learning in school and in life, not just youth socializing in front of the backdrop of a school or real life. Unlike blockbuster teen television shows in the past decade such as *Gilmore Girls, Gossip Girl,* or more recently, *Glee,* in which there is little or no homework, test taking, studying, or teaching, Harry Potter and his heroic friends stay up or sneak around at night, not to drink or smoke or cheat, but to read books under their bed sheets in order to know and hone their gifts and to practice their religion. They long to learn. The narrative is about being faithful to beliefs, friends, and the common good, and learning to understand the world and how to be an agent of change in it. And above all, it is about becoming a hero in one very particular way:

sacrificial love. The greatest act of victory and glory is not to win, but to die freely so that others may live.

This divine form of heroism heralded to half a billion readers is good news for those of us in religious education. And the role of sacrificial love at the core of these stories makes them more than a mere memorable galactic drama like *Star Wars*. Reading and loving Harry Potter appears to make millions of people . . . *better* people. Go online to the Harry Potter Alliance (HPA),[1] and you will see just one of thousands of social service organizations created by Potter fans to do justice work in the real world. The HPA is a global network engaging in registering voters; battling illiteracy, poverty, homelessness, and malaria; and even sponsoring three planes to travel to Haiti with disaster relief supplies one month after the massive earthquake. The names of the three planes sending volunteers and medical supplies? Harry, Ron, and Hermione. The cost of this trip? Nearly $150,000. How long did it take the HPA to raise this money? Two weeks. The motto of the Harry Potter Alliance? "The Weapon We Have Is Love."

Joanne Rowling's great epic is forming the faith and moral vision of millions of people. If you are reading this book, forming faith is at least part or maybe all of your vocation, as teacher, pastor, parent, godparent, roommate, sibling, spouse, or friend. In baptism, we vow to form our faith and the faith of others. To not use this modern epic in your sacred work is to leave on the table one of the most ubiquitous and enchanting tools of our time to awaken and baptize the imagination. Don't put this wand away.

NOTE

1. http://www.thehpalliance.org.

PART ONE

Why Does Harry Potter Work for Teaching Faith?

CHAPTER ONE

⋆ From Rags to Snitches

The Resurrection of
J. K. Rowling

She looked ordinary enough to be a mere Muggle, but as the woman moved respectfully but steadily closer to me in the church activities hall, I realized I was wrong. "I came to your lecture tonight to ask you one question. I could ask it now or at the end," she said softly. Her smile was so warm I could feel it. She clutched a purse knitted by hand, her moccasins dated from the 1980s, and she didn't seem to waste any time in her day on brushing her hair. She looked a lot like my image of Molly Weasley.

The church hall was festive for the lecture that night, titled "Harry Potter in Lent." Church volunteers had set up four long tables for their potluck dinner, each with a Hogwarts House banner above it, and the tables were piled high with British-themed desserts. An eagle picture hung on the podium set up for me to give my lecture on theological themes in Harry Potter. I had brought dozens of handmade Chocolate Frogs with Wizard Cards I'd made with faces from the church community directory. At the entrance to the hall, I placed my Hedwig puppet in an antique birdcage I had found online. The birdcage sat on top of a trunk with Hogwarts stickers on it, under a large sign in the hallway for King's Cross Station and a smaller sign for Platform 9¾. The church hall was lit by strings of electric candles hanging from the ceiling.

I usually bring decorations to any public lecture on Christian themes in Harry Potter. But this particular church had its own passionate Harry Potter fandom, a group including all ages from young children to retired seniors. They had worked for hours before the lecture to turn their activities hall into the Great Hall, and many had brought their own Harry Potter memorabilia to add to the decorations. As is often the case, individuals who were previously inactive or mostly unseen members of the church had volunteered to help out with the Harry Potter lecture. Nearly every volunteer was wearing something that looked like old Hogwarts-themed Halloween costumes: House ties or scarves, Quidditch robes, and more than one pair of eyeglasses held together with tape. But these Potter fan volunteers had to be shown where the bathrooms, lights, or outlets could be found in the church. Harry Potter–themed events at church have a way of not only bringing new people into the church but also reinviting and reconnecting inactive members, often with their (young or adult) children in tow.

But back to the woman. She had approached me in a way that was both shy and bold. Her eyes were twinkling. I told her I would be happy to try to answer her question before the event started. The lecture was being recorded, and unknown to me, the recording had already started. So I have her words in digital form, though I can't imagine forgetting them. She took a deep breath and then said these words: "I don't go to this church—or any church, really—but my neighbor does. I saw the flyer about tonight from her church bulletin that was hanging on her refrigerator." Her crouching posture and nervous rocking back and forth told me she was somewhat apologetic about not being a churchgoer, but not much. She continued:

> I am a total Harry Potter fan. I'm not a church fan. But I came here tonight hoping that you can explain to me *why* you think these books have changed my life. I know they did. I'm just not sure how, because I've read a lot of books in my life and not been so moved and changed by them. I've been a reader since I was four, and I'm seventy-one years old—my birthday was just last month. But very few things have ever moved me the way Harry Potter has moved me. I'll tell you this: these stories are too real to not be real. I don't believe in magic, but I'm here tonight to try to figure out what is different about these stories and why I'm different because I read them. So, that's my question before you even start talking: why does this story change people?[1]

There is a holiness about her words that has stayed with me as I speak to groups small and large, whether they be youth groups, adult retreats, clergy conferences, teacher conferences, secular parenting groups, book clubs, leadership seminars, or Harry Potter Bible studies. No matter where I go, I remember this woman's conviction and her question: "These stories are too real to not be real" and "why does this story change people?"

The woman's words resonate strongly with me because for years of teaching Christianity, I have often said the words "the resurrection is too real to not be real." So I recognized what the woman was trying to say about ideas that seem too good to be true and yet also so powerful in our lives that they can't be fiction. Keep in mind Harry's question to Dumbledore about the very nature of magic, life, and death in their final intimate exchange at King's Cross Station.

> "Tell me one last thing," said Harry. "Is this real? Or has this been happening inside my head?
>
> Dumbledore beamed at him, and his voice sounded loud and strong in Harry's ears even though the bright mist was descending again, obscuring his figure.
>
> "Of course it's happening inside your head, Harry, but why on earth should that mean that it is not real?"[2]

Often we are drawn to accept certain ideas or narratives into our definition of reality, not as propositions or arguments, but rather as explanations for our lived experiences. Of all the ideas, claims, and parables in the Bible that are hard to understand or even to accept, the resurrection is an event and an experience that makes sense to me and my lived experience. I see its presence and power in my daily life—in seasons, in relationships, in joy, and in suffering. I have simply never experienced a death of any kind that did not unfold in some form of resurrection—of new life, new identity, or new freedom. Resurrection is not the erasing of pain or grief, but rather a birth through pain and grief, pointing and powering toward new life. Resurrection is too real not to be real. And the specific account of the resurrection of Jesus strikes me as sharing the shape of my own experiences of death and resurrection in the human condition. The Gospels never introduced to me the reality of life after death. Rather, the life, death, and resurrection of Jesus affirmed and confirmed my own experience of liberation—in body and spirit—in all the areas of my life where I have accepted and passed through the limits, the losses, and the death inherent in human life and creation. When I have dared to embrace the promise of abundant life in Christ through many kinds of suffering and death in human experience, I have found every tomb empty, powerless over joy, and flooded with resurrection light. Resurrection is real to me because resurrection has happened to me. For me, the Gospels are not didactic as much as they are diagnostic. I do not believe I am unique in holding this conviction. I believe that at the core of every human person is both the hope and the expectation that we can and even will overcome death in all its forms. Grief is itself the evidence that death is a scandal to our imagination and our rational mind.

The reason the Harry Potter series is so powerful for teaching faith is that it is a story about resurrection, from the first page to the last word of the epilogue. And in this way, the epic corresponds to the deepest longings and dreams of any person. The stories do more than engage us with a story about the life, death, and resurrection of any one character. They brilliantly portray countless examples of folks living familiar and relatable versions of daily life, though living in a world infused with both the natural and the supernatural. Rowling has intentionally written an epic in which there are sufferings, deaths, and explicit resurrections in the lives of many characters, and the result is that the truths in her books correspond and call to the truths in our own experience. In lectures and teaching, I have learned from many a Harry Potter reader that often a voice in their head whispers things like "Me too" when they read Rowling's masterpiece.

It's crucial to consider that Rowling's epic is not just about the possible resurrection of Harry Potter after receiving a death curse from Voldemort in the Forbidden Forest at the end of the series. I want to be clear about this from the outset of this book: I do not believe Harry Potter ever died in the seven books, nor do I believe he was actually resurrected from the dead, as some have interpreted from the stories and specifically when Voldemort strikes him with the killing curse in the forest. These seven books are a resurrection story, but I do not believe they are a resurrection story about Harry Potter. If this were the case, then this epic is only a resurrection story about Harry, and that would not, in my opinion, explain the global appeal of these books and the millions of readers who say that the books affected them in unique and transformative ways. Such a narrow understanding of where and how resurrection happens in this narrative simply does not explain how these books are changing people's lives.

Hidden in the Snitch

I believe these books change people's lives because the resurrection at the core of this story is the real and lived resurrection of Joanne Rowling. Her story of resurrection in her lived experience is not fiction. It is the story and reality of her life. I have witnessed what happens to people when they experience the truth and grace in her life story, told through the narrative of Harry Potter.

The fact that these books tell the story of J. K. Rowling as much as the story of Harry Potter was not my first impression. The story was so compelling and engaging that I thought little of the author on my first viewing of the films or reading the series. I'd seen all the movies and read all the books more than once before I did any serious consideration of the life story and the spiritual journey of Joanne Rowling. But once I had sifted through documentaries and the awkward interviews (and gotten used to

Rowling's disconnection from, leaning toward disdain for, the press), it became clear to me that her actual life is woven into every chapter of the fictional books, the stories reflecting the dark depressions and miraculous resurrections she experienced as a child and young adult. And so powerful were those experiences and transformations in her life—coming from darkness to light in learning to deal with her depression, learning to deal with her independence as well as her need for other people, meeting with both success and failure—that the grace-full cycles of breaking, healing, and resurrecting in her life can be experienced by the reader. Her real resurrections—incarnate in Harry, Neville, Dobby, or Snape—arrest us because they remind us of our deep hope for our own. We love Harry Potter, not because Rowling wrote a great story, but because Rowling wrote our story with the ending we have longed for in our lives. How did I answer the question of the Molly Weasley–looking woman in the church hall? "When we read the truth, the truth will set us free."

It is predictable in our consumerist culture that many people simply admire the life of J. K. Rowling, calling hers a "rags to riches" story. But the story that is most remarkable about J. K. Rowling is not the financial success, not going from being on public assistance and living in public housing to becoming one of the wealthiest women in Britain and the world, though thanks to Oprah and *Time* magazine, that's the story many people know. The story I'm talking about is her personal experience of loss, failure, depression, and hopelessness, which did not destroy hope or creativity but allowed, perhaps forced, her to die to many things and find new life in writing the story of Harry James Potter. In a speech to Harvard graduates, Rowling put it this way:

> I think it fair to say that by any conventional measure, a mere seven years after my [college] graduation day, I had failed on an epic scale. An exceptionally short-lived marriage had imploded, and I was jobless, a lone parent, and as poor as it is possible to be in modern Britain, without being homeless. The fears that my parents had had for me, and that I had had for myself, had both come to pass, and by every usual standard, I was the biggest failure I knew.
>
> So why do I talk about the benefits of failure? Simply because failure meant a stripping away of the inessential. I stopped pretending to myself that I was anything other than what I was, and began to direct all my energy into finishing the only work that mattered to me. Had I really succeeded at anything else, I might never have found the determination to succeed in the one arena I believed I truly belonged. I was

set free, because my greatest fear had been realized, and I was still alive, and I still had a daughter whom I adored, and I had an old typewriter and a big idea. And so rock bottom became the solid foundation on which I rebuilt my life.[3]

For most of us, our greatest fear as human beings is death or one of the countless forms of death in our daily lives. Even Freud, haunted and left undone by his own thoughts of death, who wrote so many volumes to explain (and blame) all the fears in life that fashion human beings, spoke of the "painful riddle of death." But Rowling makes peace with death in a way that Freud never did, "because [her] greatest fear had been realized, and [she] was still alive." In more than one way, Joanne died. And yet she found that life was not a casualty of death. This resurrection transformed "rock bottom" into the solid foundation on which she "rebuilt [her] life." Tens of millions of readers have been inspired to seek similar transformations in their lives because J. K. Rowling left her tomb with a typewriter.

Defeating Dementors

I'll talk more about dementors in chapter 4, but a dementor is precisely the kind of character that is created by a person who has wrestled with real demons in her life. Who has not encountered something like a dementor at some point in life? I have lost count of the number of people—from children to adults in their eighties—who raise their hands in lectures or book groups to testify about their struggles against what they call the dementors in their lives.

One of my techniques to help group members flesh out these impressions is to have them each write down a list of their personal dementors—those things that suck the joy and every happy memory out of them—and make word clouds to project on the wall of the meeting space. Words leap out of the collections of daily dementors: *cancer, divorce, insecurity, loneliness, depression, failure.* One of my favorite ways to use these dementor word clouds is to collect them from different groups of people and show them to new groups, asking, "How old do you think the people are who made this dementor word cloud?" Folks are often shocked when I tell them that clouds speaking of *cancer, terrorism,* and *financial insecurities* are from eighth graders. Equally shocking to groups is when I read a list of dementors containing *insecurity, popularity,* and *awkwardness* and inform them that it's from a senior citizens' book group.

In years of talking to Harry Potter fans, I have never had a person say they haven't faced dementors. Not one. Varied are the ways we suffer as human beings, but Rowling's brilliance is inventing a potent and palpable creature that readers recognize and immediately associate with their suffering and struggle with death. Rowling's foul hooded joy-suckers put a particular face on our universal foes. "There is a whole burgeoning field of religion and popular culture . . . looking at these stories as a reflection of the spiritual or religious sensibilities of the culture," says Russell W. Dalton, an assistant professor of Christian education at Brite Divinity School in Texas and the author of *Faith Journey through Fantasy Lands: A Christian Dialogue with Harry Potter, Star Wars, and the Lord of the Rings*. Dalton goes on, "When stories become as popular as the Harry Potter stories, they no longer simply reflect the religious views of the author, but become artifacts of the culture, and they say something about the culture that has embraced them."[4] "Reading Harry Potter is like reading the diary I never kept for myself," one senior citizen in Pennsylvania told me. A young adult said to me in a Bible study, "Harry Potter books are the soundtrack of reality." In many ways, the series stands before each reader as a Mirror of Erised; in Rowling's personal and resurrection-focused narrative, we see our own longings for a resurrected life.

We have all been in the valley of the shadow of death. But not all of us are able to climb out. We can become incapacitated. And that too was part of J. K. Rowling's experience. She was diagnosed more than once as clinically depressed. Just a few months after Rowling had begun to write the Harry Potter series, her mother died, and the event nearly crushed her. Her mother never knew anything about Harry Potter. But J. K. Rowling has said in many interviews since finishing the books that the death of her mother figures prominently throughout the series. Joanne's grief multiplied after her father abandoned his relationship with his daughters. Add to that grief a rocky start to finding a career, what she called "a brief and catastrophic marriage," and single motherhood on welfare—all by her midtwenties.

A Personality

C. S. Lewis once said, "If anything whatever is common to all believers, and even to many unbelievers, it is the sense that in the Gospels they have met a personality."[5] He was trying to explain that for him, reading the Gospels was a different experience than with any other genre of literature. Page after page, parable after parable, he felt what he called "a personality" present in the text. He felt a person speaking to him, listening to him, persuading him, consoling him, rebuking him, inviting him, blessing him. He felt directly spoken to, not by the text, but by a person—Jesus Christ—speaking through it.

Many of the Harry Potter fans I talk to describe a similar experience of feeling known and addressed by a single person through the countless characters in the series. Since the book is written from the perspective of Harry, many people feel that they are developing the strongest and deepest relationship with Harry Potter. Others feel as if Dumbledore is watching and mentoring their reading of the story. But when I question readers about their frustrations with Harry or Dumbledore (for there are things to detest as well as to love about both of them), it is clear that there is a perspective or voice or person that comes through the text and guides the reader, beyond any one character we know by name, pulling us, touching our lives, coming off the page into our hearts.

I believe that this person is Joanne Rowling, whose agenda is potent and persuasive. She has said more than once that her books are different than the works of C. S. Lewis or J. R. R. Tolkien in that they are not intentional Christian allegories meant to convert or form hearts and minds into belief in God. I categorize Rowling's work as testimonial rather than apologetic. Rowling doesn't weave a story to teach the resurrection. Rather, her own experience of resurrection is so powerful that it rules the rhythm of the stories she tells. She is driven, not by the possibility of the reader's resurrection, but by the power of her own.

The Power of Love

Harry Potter helps people find, explore, and increase their faith because Rowling is not asking the reader to do anything other than witness the power of love above all else, even death. Throughout the series' more than four thousand pages, she crafts a community of contagious characters, some driven toward goodness and others toward darkness, and subjects them all to the power of love—specifically, sacrificial love that can conquer death. Her goal is the participation of the reader in the struggle between good and evil, not the persuasion of the reader to adopt Rowling's own convictions.

Like any student at Hogwarts or any adult witch or wizard contemplating sides in the war led by Voldemort, we can choose our path as we read the books. The lack of explicit religious claims, names, or norms in this series allows the reader to respond to the power of sacrificial love made manifest in the lives of characters without the allegorical aims found in authors like Lewis, Tolkien, Madeleine L'Engle, and others. Sirius Black says it best to Harry: "The world isn't split into good people and Death Eaters. We've all got both light and dark inside us. What matters is the part we choose to act on. That's who we really are."[6]

Words

"Words are the most powerful, inexhaustible source
of magic that we have." —Dumbledore to Harry[7]

Of all the interviews and documentaries I've seen on the life of Rowling, my favorite is a British documentary called *J. K. Rowling: A Year in the Life*.[8] In the documentary, filmed from October 2006 to October 2007, you watch Rowling typing the last lines of the epilogue to the *Deathly Hallows*. The independent filmmaker was a friend, so Rowling granted him unusual access to her private life. Many facts and personal stories from her life that now float around the internet or appear on the Pottermore website were first (and only) revealed in this forty-five-minute film. In one part of the documentary, Rowling is unexpectedly asked to do word association with the filmmaker. If the director is to be believed, Joanne did not know this particular sit-down would include word association. It makes for riveting viewing because it is clear as you watch that Rowling was speaking extemporaneously and with a rare authentic presence usually kept hidden when talking to journalists.

Consider carefully the questions the filmmaker asked her and Rowling's penetrating one-word answers. On screen, she takes no more than two to three seconds to offer her one-word responses. The one-minute clip is a tour de force, a peek into the vault of her deepest convictions. Here are his questions and her one-word answers:

Director: What is your favorite virtue? Rowling: Courage.

What vice do you most despise? Bigotry.

What is the vice you are most willing to forgive? Gluttony.

What is your most marked characteristic? I'm a trier.

What are you most afraid of? Losing someone I love.

What is the quality that you most like in a man? Morals.

What is the quality you most like in a woman? Generosity.

What do you most value about your friends? Tolerance.

What is your principle defect? Short fuse.

What is your favorite occupation? Writing.

What is your dream of happiness? A happy family.[9]

When you read this word list, it becomes clear that the Harry Potter series is as much an autobiography of Rowling as it is the epic story of the Boy Who Lived. Without trying, Rowling's one-word answers to these probing and poignant questions outline many of the major themes of her books and highlight many of the aspects of her central characters. In the seven-book series, we see the depth and breadth of Rowling's storytelling soul. In this list of single words, we glimpse the fingerprint of that soul at work in her one-million-word epic.

Brokenness and Death

"His job was to walk calmly into Death's welcoming arms."[10]

One of the more arresting quotations of C. S. Lewis is this: "Die before you die, there is no chance after."[11] This statement captures so many ideas and invitations we find in the New Testament and reminds us of so many promises that if we are willing to die in this life, we will be resurrected in this life. We find abundant life when we decide, as Galatians 2:20 says, that "it is no longer I who live, but it is Christ who lives in me. And the life I now live in the flesh I live by faith in the Son of God, who loved me and gave himself for me." This is, in a sense, the central message of the New Testament and the central message of Jesus Christ: that if we follow him—if we are willing, in his words, to die to ourselves—we will come to abundant and eternal life in him. We can, as Paul says in Romans 13:14, put on Christ.

But we cannot have this death and new life as long as we continue to trust or to serve things other than God. C. S. Lewis is correct that the gospel is an invitation to new life while you are alive—to become a new creation even as you walk the world in the flesh. For guidance in this resurrected living, we are given the narratives of Jesus after his own resurrection, when he walks to Emmaus or has fish and fellowship with his followers on a beach.[12] He is seen in the flesh, and through Thomas we are invited to touch the wounds in his hands and experience a resurrected person in the world.[13]

In the Christian faith, we believe that these postresurrection narratives teach that Christ offers us his life—a life that doesn't end at the crucifixion or in the tomb. Christ shows up on the other side of death to walk with us, talk with us, feast with us, and incarnate the message that we can be resurrected in this life, freed from "death's sting."

This is precisely why Harry Potter is not a Christ figure. I part company with many people who have interpreted the series by saying that Harry is a Christ figure. I say he is not a Christ figure because if that is true, he becomes less of a role model for any of us. If he were anything near perfect as his Father in heaven is perfect, then he would not be a good example of a normal person trying to live a faithful life. Harry does Christlike things. Dumbledore does Christlike things, and for this reason he too is often labeled a God-figure by interpreters of the series. But both Harry and Dumbledore also do humanlike things, including cruel and selfish things. They both have in their history manipulation, lying, and pride leading to the suffering of others. For all these reasons, I would never describe Harry as a Christ figure. But what is so much more exciting, inviting, and inspiring is that Harry can be Christlike, as can we. One of the reasons these books work so well in inspiring acts of faith, hope, and love in readers is that the central heroes of the stories are as broken as they are blessed.

Despite Harry's brokenness, he chooses to follow love to the moment when he can kiss the Snitch and say, "I am about to die."[14] The whole series to that point is the process of Harry learning what it means to die to himself. He finally decides to reserve nothing for himself or for revenge, to withhold nothing from his friends or family, but instead to walk straight into death knowing that others would live. Harry's drama is the drama of every baptized Christian. We are sealed on the forehead in baptism into the gift of self-sacrificial love that makes abundant life possible for us. How do we become people who, like Harry, take responsibility for fighting evil and protecting the common good? How do we fight evil without becoming evil? How do we become people capable of laying down our lives for others? When faced with death, which of the Three Brothers will we be?[15]

No one forces Harry to die. Rowling doesn't force the reader to agree that death is the only path to freedom for Harry or the world. Rather than be explicit about her own Christian convictions, she gently shows her hand and heart in the words of Dumbledore when he speaks to Snape about the need for Harry to give up his life to Voldemort:

> "So the boy . . . the boy must die?" asked Snape quite calmly.
> "And Voldemort must do it, Severus. That is essential."[16]

The Seeds of Faith

Occasionally I have led workshops or clergy conferences where it was my challenge to help church folks evangelize or develop faith formation programs in their communities. A favorite opening activity of mine is to break up the gathering into small groups and hand them each a paragraph describing a nameless person. You might call this a case study exercise. I challenge the groups to read the description and discuss how they might minister to the person. What kind of sermon, rituals, or social justice initiatives might speak to her? For what is she longing? What might her struggles be—socially, economically, and spiritually? What might push her away? What kinds of liturgies might reach out to her and engage her heart?

If she came to visit their church on a Sunday, would she even stay through the end of the first service? Here's a sample of the paragraph I hand out:

A woman in her forties arrives to your church on a Sunday. She was born into a hardworking, middle-class family with educated parents. In her teens, her mother was diagnosed with MS and died slowly throughout her teenage years. Her mother eventually died when this woman was in her early twenties. She is now, and has been for a long time, estranged from her father, who was mostly absent during her adolescent years. She grew up without any religion practiced at home, but from the age of ten she hung around the Anglican church on her street and presented herself for baptism when she was only eleven. Her faith has come and gone through her college years and since, though she continues to attend church as often as she can. An early and short marriage, a miscarriage, and more than a year of living on welfare and in public housing as a single mother eventually stabilized into a fruitful romantic and economic life in a second marriage. She had two additional children. She is creative, progressive, and skeptical. She has worked for nonprofits and schools, caring deeply about social justice action. She is a writer.

I watch small groups go to work to set up ministry plans or analyze their church programing and liturgies, all with an eye to share the gospel and offer discipleship to the hypothetical woman. Folks often put together wonderful plans to reach out to this woman. Many realize through the exercise that they don't have social justice activities that would inspire or engage her. They realize they don't have formation programs that would address both her intellectual curiosity about faith and her childcare needs. They wonder how on earth they could get a woman like this to commit to their church or faith community. It is always a crowd silencer when I finished the activity by saying, "And by the way, this is a real person and her name is J. K. Rowling."

Rowling wrote fantasy stories and read them to her younger sister, Dianne, as they grew up. Her childhood home in Tutshill, Wales, was named Church Cottage and sat alongside a graveyard near the Forest of Dean. At age nine, she started working on Saturdays for one British pound a day, cleaning the pews of St. Luke's Anglican Church.

When I first discovered this piece of information about her Saturday hours in an old church, I smiled and thought of the priest or staff at that church. They obviously did not need a nine-year-old girl and her seven-year-old sister to clean their pews, but they saw two young souls who had moved to the neighborhood and were looking for something to do, people to know, and relationships outside their home. I believe the church that hired those two children to do simple work was up to something—a sacred scheming to introduce or engage their spiritual curiosity.

You can go to the church to this day and find that the two of them signed their names in the guest registry every week. We know that J. K. Rowling would sit in the pews in the colorful streams of light coming through the stained-glass windows. We know from her that she played and maybe even prayed among the dusty candles and tired wood structures of an old and small neighborhood church. Joanne was curious about Christianity and its sacraments, though her family did not share this curiosity.

Called by Name

How many children seek out a priest for baptism at such a young age? I have always thought it significant that magical children in the Harry Potter series get their Hogwarts letter at age eleven—the same age at which Joanne received the baptism she passionately sought. A fruitful connection for teaching faith can be made between J. K. Rowling's baptism and receiving a Hogwarts letter. The letter doesn't make one magical, nor does baptism make a person into the image of God. Our sacraments do not create our identity, but they name and feed our identity and direct us toward our destiny to be one with God as Christ is one with God. At Hogwarts, the name of each magical child is written, on the day they are born, by a magic quill into a book of names, housed at the Ministry of Magic. The Hogwarts letter is no more and no less than a ritual to deliver and declare that fixed identity to the person who is already magical. The letter begins the journey to learn how to develop one's identity. This is as good a definition of a sacrament as you can find.

The first chapters of *The Philosopher's Stone* demonstrate the truth that one's identity is only named by the letter and not created by it. [17] Vernon Dursley did not understand this, trying to save Harry from wizardry by destroying every letter. You can stop the letter, but you can't stop the invitation that calls a person to live and learn into their true identity. The letter is the baptism into the wizarding world.

In many of the retreats or lectures or classes I've taught about Harry Potter and theology, I always try to begin the gathering by having a Hogwarts letter written to each person in the room. I've developed my own Hogwarts stationary. I use the same color ink as in the movies. I found a font for Professor McGonagall's handwriting. Each person who comes into the lecture hall, parish, retreat center, or classroom has the opportunity of receiving a Hogwarts letter. And I use wax seals as well. I can't tell you how many times I have stayed up late in my living room preparing for a lecture, class, or retreat, burning the candle, melting the wax, and putting the Hogwarts seal on the back of each acceptance letter. I do this because I always intend, as the classes unfold, to let people know that in baptism we say that you are sealed as Christ's own forever. And I make the connection between being sealed with oil at baptism and receiving a Hogwarts letter, something that lets you know who you are and what is ahead for you, with a wax seal. In time and through study, Rowling learned the meaning of the ritual of Holy Baptism: that we lose our lives in the water only to rise up from it into the life of Christ and into his body, the church. Death is drowned in the water of the open font—ever a symbol of the open grave. Perhaps not at eleven years old, but in time, Rowling came to know that the font is a sign of dying to self and rising in Christ. Harry's Hogwarts letter on his eleventh birthday symbolizes Rowling's own journey into the font whose welcoming waters whisper that the last enemy to be defeated is death.

Resurrection

Many people say the Harry Potter series is primarily a story of the battle between good and evil. J. K. Rowling has made comments like this herself. This observation is true but imprecise. I believe these stories also play out the battle between two worldviews in Western civilization: immortality versus resurrection. In a first-world superpower, we play with and peddle in immortality all around us. As the baby boomer generation marches on in years and into retirements that are lasting longer than those of any generation before it, we are drowning in commercials for pills to combat every sign of aging. Anyone in ministry knows that people of all ages in our faith communities are often terrified by death, despite our sermons, creeds, hymns, prayers, or liturgies. As a high school chaplain, it never ceased to amaze me that some of my twelfth graders had never been to a funeral. Some families go to great lengths to shield their children from experiencing death. When I was a child, families in our community brought pets into their home with the precise aim of teaching children to handle building relationships and dealing with death in childhood. Nowadays you can pay to clone your favorite pet.

When we think of Voldemort, we think of someone who does spectacular acts of cruelty and murder. But at the core of Voldemort's life is not necessarily a desire to hurt other people. His enemy is death, and he does and dares anything to avoid it. Voldemort is the embodiment of the quest for immortality at all costs. This makes him both terrifying and tragic. He is the extraordinary version of a desire in all of us to somehow avoid our inevitable descent in body and mind as we approach our death and the deaths around us. Voldemort does not seek the Deathly Hallows to use them in life, but rather to empower him over death.

Contrast that drive for unending life with the sacrificial love of Lily Potter or Harry Potter, who decide that they would rather die than live if it means that the lives of others can be protected or saved. Voldemort would rather kill than die. So the battle rages on between Voldemort, driven by the desire to escape death, and Harry, driven by the desire that others might live. Harry's very existence is preserved until becoming an adult only because he is bathed in his mother's sacrificial blood. Harry was made an orphan by an act of love; Voldemort was made an orphan by lack of love. Harry was raised with the reality that his life was so precious that others would die for it; Voldemort was raised with the reality that his life was so worthless that others would disown it. Harry is able to face death in ways Voldemort cannot because he comes to understand the ongoing and ever-present love and care of the people who died for him at key points in his life, as in the graveyard or the forest when he sees visions of his parents pledging their presence in the battles with Voldemort. When holding the Resurrection Stone, Harry sees his parents, Lupin, and Sirius in the Forbidden Forest before giving himself up to Voldemort, and he asks, "Why are you here, all of you?" His mother's answer teaches the communion of saints in three words: "We never left."

A Choice to Live

I have always been taken by the fact that Rowling began writing Harry Potter stories not because her life was falling into place, but precisely at the time when her life was falling apart. She describes herself as having been deep in spiritual and psychological darkness, but her passion for writing the story in her heart about a boy who went to wizarding school allowed enough light in her life to start a flame. Rowling explains her climb out of depression as a combination of fear, adrenaline, and hope. Having failed, in her estimation, at many endeavors in her young adult life, Joanne felt there was nothing else she could do but write. She wasn't sure anyone would ever publish her book, but she decided to write for herself. She made a choice to live, to find the words for the story in her heart. She believed writing her story might begin to heal the brokenness in her life. This is the beginning of the resurrection experience. Through hope, however faint, death in any form can be faced, endured and defeated by resurrection. Rowling wrote her way to new life, and I believe that there is a residue of her resurrection on every page in the Harry Potter stories.

"I Open at the Close"

In one of the most significant scenes for those interested in Christian theology or for those wanting to share or teach faith with Harry Potter, we see Harry walk into the Forbidden Forest during the last Battle of Hogwarts. He pulls out the Snitch, kisses it, and says, "I am about to die." And at that moment, the words written on the Snitch become clear to him in a way they had not been before: "I open at the close."[18] And the Snitch indeed opens. The Resurrection Stone appears to him—a resource and reward for his vow to die for others. This moment of receiving resurrection power from a decision of sacrificial love is a powerful symbol for those of us that want to use Harry Potter as we share and teach the Christian faith. Harry's willingness to die unlocks the Stone, which makes possible the experience of seeing those who loved him to death. But his experience of that great cloud of witnesses is limited. Harry realizes that full communion with them comes only after death. So he drops the Stone and puts his faith in resurrection over immortality.

In Harry's dramatic walk toward death, one might miss the subtle message of the Stone buried in the Snitch. Consider the Snitch as a handful of gold, something highly prized for its value. We are all Seekers of peace and safety and often look to material goods that promise wealth or security. Who among us has not sought after a golden Snitch in the form of some promise of safety or wealth in the material world? But in contrast to that drive to gather and gain, consider the message of the buried Stone. Even if we try foolishly to seek safety or freedom in the empty but sparkling trinket treasures of the world, we can nonetheless find resurrection buried in the heart of all things. Where can we find the freedom and new life of resurrection? Rowling answers: even in idols unworthy of our search, God plants the experience of resurrection. No matter where or what we are seeking, God finds and feeds our longing to overcome death.

Every Easter we hear the gospel story of the faithful women going to the tomb to clean and properly bury the dead body of their leader and Lord. Since my childhood, I have pictured these women walking and weeping at sunrise, waking from the Sabbath having to face the reality of death. I see them falling down on their knees in exhaustion and confusion when they see that the stone sealing the tomb is rolled away. The first time I read the passage of Harry's Snitch opening to reveal the Stone, I began to reimagine this familiar gospel narrative. What if those women had looked up at the tomb and seen something written above the entrance, carved deep into the stone? What do you think it would say that might explain what happened there? I know what I think should be written: "I open at the close."

NOTES

1. Attendee at "Harry Potter for Lent" lecture series, Meade Memorial Church, Alexandria, Virginia, March 2016.

2. J. K. Rowling, *Harry Potter and the Deathly Hallows* (New York: Scholastic, 2007), 723.

3. J. K. Rowling, "The Fringe Benefits of Failure, and the Importance of Imagination," Harvard Commencement Address, June 5, 2008.

4. Michael Paulson, "The Book of Harry," *Boston Globe*, August 16, 2009, http://archive.boston.com/bostonglobe/ideas/articles/2009/08/16/how_the_boy_wizard_won_over_religious_critics/.

5. C. S. Lewis, *Readings for Meditation and Reflection* (New York: Harper-Collins, 1996), 20.

6. David Yates, "Harry Potter and the Order of the Phoenix" (Warner Bros. Pictures, 2007), film, 01:15:40.

7. David Yates, "Harry Potter and the Deathly Hallows, Part 2" (Warner Bros. Pictures, 2011), film, 01:34:57.

8. James Runcie, "J. K. Rowling: A Year in the Life" (Glasgow, UK: IWC Media, 2007), film.

9. Ibid.

10. *Deathly Hallows*, 691.

11. C. S. Lewis, *Till We Have Faces: A Myth Retold* (New York: HarperCollins, 1956), 291.

12. Luke 24:13–35; John 21:4–14.

13. John 20:24–29.

14. *Deathly Hallows*, 698.

15. Ibid., 406–9.

16. Ibid., 686.

17. J. K. Rowling always intended for the first book to be called *The Philosopher's Stone*, but the American publisher came up with the title *The Sorcerer's Stone*. In this book, I use Rowling's intentional title, calling the first book of the series *The Philosopher's Stone*.

18. *Deathly Hallows*, 698.

CHAPTER TWO

✦ The Bible Tells Me So

Teaching Faith with Harry Potter Is Biblical

S orcery is against God," the well-dressed and mild-mannered man said to me as he walked into my classroom. I was his daughter's high school religion teacher, and it was parents' night at school. At the time, I was teaching an elective religion class called Christian Themes in Harry Potter. I had heard about this dad. His daughter was a huge Harry Potter fan, and she had told me on the first day of class that her parents had argued over whether she should be allowed to take this course. Her parents were both postal workers and lay preachers in their nondenominational African American Bible church. In the end, the daughter was given permission to take the class as long as she didn't miss a single youth group meeting at her church that year. I could tell by the father's skeptical demeanor that his daughter was in my class because he had lost that argument.

"I assume you are referring to Galatians or perhaps Revelation?" I said quietly as he hovered at the doorway and waited for me to answer his statement about sorcery before entering the room. "In any case," I continued, "I wholeheartedly agree that biblical texts are no friend of sorcery, nor am I. Sorcery is an attempt to bypass God's wisdom and power and give glory to Satan instead. I can assure you that as an Episcopal school, we teach against such things. Stick around for a few minutes, and you'll see that no one is practicing sorcery in here. Some silliness for sure on our way into the gospel, but no sorcery." I forgive him to this day for taking a seat slowly despite my attempts to disarm his alarm before our session began. After all, I was wearing a Gryffindor robe and House tie and directing parents to their seats with my wand. The entire classroom was decorated as a Hogwarts classroom, with House banners hanging from the ceiling, faux torches on the walls, jars of colored jelly beans hanging on the wall in four colors to keep track of House points, a perch near the window with photos of owls carrying notes for students, a broom hanging on the wall over the door, and pens at every seat with a long white feather connected to each so that everyone had a quill and parchment ready to write. The street preacher and concerned parent was correct that I was up to something in this space.

I couldn't wait to start the class and declare out loud that I teach faith in a Hogwarts classroom and a Harry Potter robe for one reason: I believe in the moment and the miracle called Pentecost.

A Pentecost Pedagogy

The Acts of the Apostles tells us that there was a miracle at Pentecost—a very particular miracle—and it is crucial to reflect on what that miracle is and how it worked in the biblical narrative before going any further. The skeptical man in my classroom was asking all the right questions, and his faith-based fears deserve an answer.

I believe the biblical account of the first Pentecost presents a Pentecost way of sharing or teaching faith: a pedagogy that blesses, encourages, and commands us to use theological fiction—to use anything that is good and just—in order to preach the gospel. Paul also blesses a Pentecost pedagogy when saying in 1 Corinthians 9:20–22:

> To the Jews I became as a Jew, in order to win Jews. To those under the law I became as one under the law (though I myself am not under the law) so that I might win those under the law. To those outside the law I became as one outside the law (though I am not free from God's law but am under Christ's law) so that I might win those outside the law. To the weak I became weak, so that I might win the weak. I have become all things to all people, that I might by all means save some.

My use of Harry Potter to teach faith is something I do in obedience to the Great Commission in general and to the dictates of the Pentecost story in particular. The connotation of sorcery—not at all an obvious or clearly defined concept or practice, if you ask any biblical theologian or historian—is often a cause for concern for believers, and those of us who teach faith with Harry Potter need to be crystal clear about why such a concept has no connection to our use of the Rowling series for sacred purposes.

If you are reading this book, you are probably familiar with the biblical Pentecost story—in fact, you might be too familiar with it. If we misinterpret the miracle depicted in the narrative, in my experience, we get all the wrong kinds of reasons and rules for ministry.

The story of the miracle at Pentecost depicted in the Bible begins in the first chapter of the Acts of the Apostles. Jesus is with his disciples after his resurrection and reassures them of God's presence in their midst to the end of the world. He states, "John baptized with water, but you will be baptized with the Holy Spirit not many days from now" (Acts 1:5). Jesus goes further in describing the impending arrival of the Holy Spirit to the disciples, saying, "You will receive power when the Holy Spirit has come upon you; and you will be my witnesses in Jerusalem, in all Judea and Samaria, and to the ends of the earth" (Acts 1:8). After delivering these prophetic promises, Jesus ascends to heaven in their sight.

The next chapter of Acts says that after choosing a replacement for Judas, the disciples were "all in one place" in a room in Jerusalem. What happened next is the familiar but miraculous account of the arrival of the Holy Spirit as tongues of fire in their midst and above each of their heads, a vision depicted in tens of thousands of windowpanes, paintings, and poems for nearly two thousand years of Christianity.

> And suddenly from heaven there came a sound like the rush of a violent wind, and it filled the entire house where they were sitting. Divided tongues, as of fire, appeared among them, and a tongue rested on each of them. All of them were filled with the Holy Spirit and began to speak in other languages, as the Spirit gave them ability.

The noise caused a wave of wind and words that flooded beyond the house, and a crowd gathered to discover the source of the sound. The passage emphasizes the wide diversity of the people who came to investigate the group of followers, "devout Jews from every nation under heaven living in Jerusalem." What the wondering witnesses found was more than a loud crowd of disciples telling stories:

> And at this sound the crowd gathered and was bewildered, because each one heard them speaking in the native language of each. Amazed and astonished, they asked, "Are not all these who are speaking Galileans? And how is it that we hear, each of us, in our own native language? Parthians, Medes, Elamites, and residents of Mesopotamia, Judea and Cappadocia, Pontus and Asia, Phrygia and Pamphylia, Egypt and the parts of Libya belonging to Cyrene, and visitors from Rome, both Jews and proselytes, Cretans and Arabs—in our own languages we hear them speaking about God's deeds of power.[1]

In this extensive list of nations, we watch the author of this text paint a picture of the whole world of the time coming together to witness an arrival of something supernatural—the coming of the Holy Spirit to a house and to the world. But at this point in the story, a crucial dynamic of the miracle is made clear, and it's something that many people neglect to notice: the curious listeners from cities and countries abroad were able to understand the storytelling of the Galilean disciples in languages foreign to those disciples.

The miracle celebrated by the church since that day is that a small group of Aramaic-speaking Jews were able to share their accounts and convictions about Jesus and be understood by a crowd of people who spoke in foreign tongues. The message is not that a miracle happened that allowed the gathered folks to speak Greek or Aramaic, though often I witness people teaching the faith as if that misconception were true. Too often those of us with faith stories to share seem to be waiting for others to learn our language, understand our rituals, appreciate our liturgies, or treasure our Scriptures. These folks live as if the miracle at Pentecost were that the one or two languages of the disciples were miraculously understood, instead of what really happened, which is that the disciples were able to speak in the countless other languages present in the crowd.

Too often I meet with faithful people who are burned out in sharing their faith, teaching their faith, or ministering in faith communities. As we talk, it becomes clear that many are trying to teach "the world"—teenagers, peers, senior citizens—to value the faith, rather than the message of Pentecost, which is to teach the church to value the languages, cultures, and trends of the world around us. We are not called by what happened at Pentecost to ape the culture or adopt its values and trends as our own rule of life. However, Pentecost does promote the mission of growing our literacy for the world around us—a high level of literacy that would make our peers and people of all ages say along with those in the original Pentecost gathering, "And how is it that we hear, each of us, in our own native language?" (Acts 2:7b).

The miracle at Pentecost is that the disciples were spared the cost and effort of something like Rosetta Stone or some other difficult and comprehensive language course. And unless and until the Spirit comes again in this way, teaching faith in the Pentecost tradition means that we all have to become literate in the languages around us. Until a tongue of fire appears over your head, it is up to you to start learning the meaning systems around you and learn them so well that you can then translate your lived experiences of faith in God into that language. According to our Scriptures, this Pentecost pedagogy for sharing our testimony of the gospel is how the church started and how the church was sent forth into the world on fire from the Spirit.

So you might want to reread the Pentecost story today or tonight and think about your methods of sharing your faith. Some of the exhaustion and frustration you may have might actually stem from the fact that you are praying for the conversion of others to your way of thinking, speaking, acting, or praying, instead of spending your time in the joyful learning of how others think, speak, act, or think about spiritual things. Learning and living into the diversity of ideas around us can spark creativity, compassion, and growth. Waiting for and wanting others to learn about and take on your habits and your preferences, cultural or religious, can lead to impatience, judgmental thoughts, and defensive postures.

There is more than one passage in the New Testament that demonstrates a Pentecost pedagogy. Consider Paul in the Areopagus. One of the open forums in Athens, the Areopagus was actually a court, a place where one gave testimony or made appeals for justice. It had statues of all the gods because it was thought that a person should swear to the truth of their case in front of both men and gods. The statues were a divine jury, a check to be sure a person spoke the truth, the whole truth, and nothing but the truth. The statues stood for the same reason we have people swear on Bibles in our own culture. There were statues for as many gods as could fit in that space so as to make an impressive showing of authority and accountability. Witnesses would then offer their stories in the presence of this pantheon of the people's religion.

The story of Paul in the Areopagus sharing his belief in the life, teaching, and resurrection of Jesus is another one of those familiar biblical stories that perhaps we need to revisit, lest we miss the Pentecost pedagogy at work. Paul looks around and sees all the faces of the divine according to the culture he is visiting. Paul sees this monument to their beliefs and their gods, central not just to their legal system, but also to their entire understanding of what is true. He does not share these beliefs, but he notices the essential role they play in the culture of those to whom he seeks to preach the gospel.

Paul surveys each of these treasured statues and finds one attributed to the Unknown God. In the creation and placement of this mysterious sculpture, Paul sees his opening to preach the gospel: "Men of Athens, I see you are religious in every way" (Acts 17:22). And then he begins to tell them that the god that is unknown to them is known to Paul as the one, true, living God.

Like the Pentecost story, this narrative is a good test of our ministry methods. Paul could have shown up with just as much bravery and launched into his testimony about Jesus from the start. But notice he did not say, "Your religion is untrue." He did not declare that there was no Mount Olympus, no Zeus, no god of this or that. He looked at the religion that they had, and rather than waste energy on speaking against their religion, he found a way to use their religious language and bring his convictions about the incarnation into that polytheistic system. Onto the skeleton of polytheism, he brought the life and flesh of the incarnation of Jesus. Paul could do this only because before he opened his mouth to the Athenians, he was already fluent in their religious symbols and meaning. Fluency in what and how Athenians think and believe allowed him to share his story in their terms.

So the question for anyone who wants to teach their faith to others is, what are the languages—literal languages as well as cultural ideas, symbols, and trends—spoken in your communities? Where do you need to increase your fluency in order to speak the gospel in languages natural to those you want to reach?

Teaching faith with Harry Potter is biblical because to do so is a powerful Pentecost pedagogy. Considering that nearly eight hundred million books in sixty-eight languages have been sold, it is hard to find a larger community with one shared language system of meaning and symbols than Harry Potter readers. There are only a handful of nations on earth with a larger population than the Harry Potter fandom. These numbers alone justify Christians seeking fluency in Harry Potter in order to share the gospel. I wear Harry Potter robes and write Hogwarts letters as I teach faith because I believe and obey the Pentecost story. I make no idol of any one human story or cultural trend, but the Bible and the Christian tradition depict and celebrate that on the first day the church began it did so with disciples speaking the languages of the world around them and not their own. Teaching faith with Harry Potter is nothing more or less than sharing the gospel precisely as the Bible commands.

The Stickiness Factor

In Malcolm Gladwell's bestseller *The Tipping Point*, he introduces the term "the stickiness factor" to identify the characteristics of an idea or product that allow it to spread rapidly or gain popularity. According to Gladwell, "The specific quality that a message needs to be successful is the quality of 'stickiness.' Is the message—or the food, or the movie, or the product—memorable? Is it so memorable, in fact, that it can create change, that it can spur someone to action?"[2] Gladwell does not offer a generic list of attributes that will create a stickiness factor. Rather, every idea or product is different in the way that it might stick in people's minds. His point is that when creating an idea or product, one ought to consider how to tailor it such that it is accessible, understandable, and immediately relevant to people's lived experience. The Harry Potter series has obvious stickiness. Practitioners of any faith or philosophical tradition envy the stickiness factor of Rowling's epic. But let's consider what exactly it is about Harry Potter that makes it so memorable in order that we might understand how to share the gospel using similar stickiness.

Why Harry Potter Sticks

Atheist Hemant Mehta has a YouTube channel called the Atheist Voice. Across many platforms of social media, he has many followers who like and share his cheerful millennial attitude about the most serious moral and philosophical questions in life. He is also a huge Harry Potter fan. In 2014, one of his most popular posts was a list worth consideration: "16 Reasons Harry Potter Is Better Than the Bible." True to his style, this list weaves irreverent sarcasm and penetrating truth. This is an important list because it is a brief explanation of the stickiness factor of Harry Potter, as well as the lack of stickiness of the Bible for multiple generations in our contemporary context. Here is his list:

1. Harry Potter has better writing.
2. The story is much more interesting.
3. When there's mass genocide, it's committed by the villain.
4. If you don't think the books are worth reading, you're not going to Hell.
5. The moral lessons are much less ambiguous.
6. It's openly fictional.
7. The movies about Harry Potter are so much better than God's Not Dead and Left Behind.
8. In Harry Potter, parents sacrifice themselves for their children. They don't make their children die for other people.
9. The books celebrate diversity. They don't condemn people for being different.
10. When characters do condemn others, by calling them "mudblood," they're presented as awful people. Meanwhile, lots of pastors will use homosexuality as a slur and they're applauded for it.
11. At Hogwarts, most of the professors like it when you ask challenging questions. Good luck challenging your Sunday school teacher.
12. The books aren't used as justification for slavery; in fact, they condemn it.

13. Harry doesn't ask people to worship him.
14. People aren't killing each other because they have different interpretations of Harry Potter.
14. No one expects Hermione to be submissive to her husband.
15. The majority of Harry Potter fans have actually read the books.[3]

Anyone who has tried to share their faith with others has run into some of this humorous but truthful skepticism about the Bible or about "religious people." But what the Atheist Voice is railing against is claims or even crimes of Christianity throughout history that many present-day followers of Christ would also reject. This list explains quite well why Harry Potter sticks in modern minds and hearts. What it also shows is that perceptions of Christianity—built from sad but true actions and agendas of the Christian community over centuries—have dulled the imagination and curiosity of many regarding the gospel. The Bible that the Atheist Voice has no use for is a caricature and has lost its stickiness. It is hard not to hear the words of Jesus in the fifth chapter of the Gospel of Matthew: "You are the salt of the earth; but if salt has lost its taste, how can its saltiness be restored? It is no longer good for anything, but is thrown out and trampled under foot" (Matt. 5:13).

Sticky Parables

The reality is that for many modern minds, the Bible has lost its stickiness—its relevance, its wonder, its invitation. Jesus faced a similar culture in the Israel of his time, a nation worn down by war, poverty, and military occupation. His response to this religious but not spiritual culture was to speak in parables. In his own words, he declared, "I did not come to change a single word of the Law." But he did choose often to speak in parables, so that "those with ears might hear." You could say he used a parable pedagogy—not to introduce completely new ideas, but to unfold the meaning of the Law and the love of God in new ways.

Parables have high stickiness factors. The parables of Jesus stuck because they were constructed on the words and the ways common and immediately relevant to daily life. They relied on the grammar of farming, carpentry, politics of the day, religious laws, and social justice concerns. Parables stuck because they spoke like and to the people listening.

We have a stickiness problem in teaching faith with the Bible. However, Jesus is an example of using a parable pedagogy to revive nonstick Scripture. So it follows that those who want to share the Bible with others today ought to consider relying on parables that stick. Finding the Christian themes in Harry Potter links the Christian faith and Rowling's fables. When we teach faith with Harry Potter, we are borrowing the stickiness of Rowling's stories to revive the relevance of biblical truths. Her writing about biblical truths concerning love, suffering, and sacrifice has a stickiness that reading the Bible alone does not, or at least so say the Atheist Voices among us. Rowling intended that we do so. Connie Neal, a prolific Christian commentator on Harry Potter, gives us this wise insight: "The Harry Potter phenomenon was the greatest evangelistic opportunity that the church has missed."[4]

Of All That Is, Seen and Unseen

Biblical theologians often explain that the Bible has both distinct parts and a coherent whole. There is, in a very real sense, one story being told across all sixty-six books of the Bible. Archbishop Rowan Williams states it this way: "The Bible traces God's way into human history, a story culminating in the coming of Jesus. If you try to deduce the whole picture from one 'frozen frame' you will have a very odd picture of God's activity."[5] The "whole picture" of creation found in the Scriptures is that the world is both natural and supernatural—realities seen and unseen. This world has a Creator and creatures. The Creator loves and forgives, while the creatures are free to find their own rhythms of independence and dependence on the Creator. The creatures come in and out of relationship with the Creator, but ultimately the Creator enters creation to restore all broken relationships. In becoming a creature, the Creator shows the creatures a way into right relationship with the Creator and with each other. This is the whole picture.

Unfortunately, individual Bible verses are held up at baseball games or stuck on bumpers, and rarely do they speak of the whole picture. Political candidates are famous for saying in debates that their favorite book is the Bible or their favorite person or philosopher is Jesus, with few details or concrete examples as to why. The presentation of Christianity that comes from bumper stickers and disingenuous political leaders leaves many unchurched folks at best uninterested in the gospel and for good reason.

Losing the "Whole Picture"

Attendance at religious services is down dramatically, and people stating "none" for their religious identity constitute the fastest-growing "religion" in America. The whole picture of the world and God found in the Bible is becoming ever more distant from culture. We are losing our collective understanding that the world is both natural and supernatural. It doesn't matter what age people are; I have been a chaplain with both children and senior citizens. I have seen what we all know: we are losing a collective cultural belief in a supernatural world and God.

Even among those who attend religious services, my time spent in small groups or Bible studies and at bedside visits has proven to me that many "religious" people do not even have a supernatural belief within their practice of religion. They name a God but do not pray or believe in any intervention from the Creator in the events of daily life. They don't take Scripture seriously, if they read it at all. They attend the sacraments but do not hold any expectation that anything is actually happening at the altars or in the pulpits at church. I do not say this with judgment. It is an observation. We are losing touch with the mysterious and the miraculous. Our deepest longings have often been detoured into consumerism. For many, life is a struggle of economic and social survival in the cruel weather of a class-stratified superpower, leaving our imaginations tame or lame. Sadly, the Bible is both too foreign (how many have actually read it?) and too familiar (because of its ambient presence in American culture). I dare say that it requires modern midwives for its meaning.

In a sermon titled "The Weight of Glory," C. S. Lewis confronts a culture steeped in war. It was delivered from an Oxford University pulpit in June 1941, when all of Britain and the world were uncertain as to whether Hitler could be stopped by anyone. For reasons different than our own, his pews were full of people who were also losing or who had lost that "whole picture"—the basic notion and assumption that despite any drama or brokenness in life, there is a Creator and a chance to be in relationship with that Creator and for that relationship to transform life on earth in ways impossible without God. Lewis's congregation had unique challenges. Many were too frightened or too grieved at the losses of war to focus on the supernatural or even the possibility of a supernatural reality. In this single sermon, Lewis sought to wake up the imagination—to awaken a consideration or perhaps a belief in the supernatural. His words to do this are many but worth reading:

> In speaking of this desire for our own far off country, which we find in ourselves even now, I feel a certain shyness. I am almost committing an indecency. I am trying to rip open the inconsolable secret in each one of you—the secret which hurts so much that you take your revenge on it by calling it names like Nostalgia and Romanticism and Adolescence; the secret also which pierces with such sweetness that when, in very intimate conversation, the mention of it becomes imminent, we

grow awkward and affect to laugh at ourselves; the secret we cannot hide and cannot tell, though we desire to do both. We cannot tell it because it is a desire for something that has never actually appeared in our experience. We cannot hide it because our experience is constantly suggesting it, and we betray ourselves like lovers at the mention of a name. Our commonest expedient is to call it beauty and behave as if that had settled the matter.

Wordsworth's expedient was to identify it with certain moments in his own past. But all this is a cheat. If Wordsworth had gone back to those moments in the past, he would not have found the thing itself, but only the reminder of it; what he remembered would turn out to be itself a remembering. The books or the music in which we thought the beauty was located will betray us if we trust to them; it was not in them, it only came through them, and what came through them was longing. These things—the beauty, the memory of our own past—are good images of what we really desire; but if they are mistaken for the thing itself they turn into dumb idols, breaking the hearts of their wor-shipers. For they are not the thing itself; they are only the scent of a flower we have not found, the echo of a tune we have not heard, news from a country we have never yet visited.[6]

We are wired for a supernatural world. Augustine said it best: "[God,] you have made us for yourself, and our heart is restless until it finds rest in you."[7] Lewis is correct: we excuse our longings away because they are evidence that we are dependent, at our core, on something or someone other than ourselves. Dependence often breeds defensiveness in the hearts of people who live in a bully-or-be-bullied culture such as ours. We fear being seen as fools. So getting people to believe anything is difficult, because belief represents the acceptance of something real and worthy outside and beside ourselves. It is hard to make commitments in a culture of defensiveness and self-protection. One of the most common acronyms swirling around the internet to voice the reticence in our culture to make decisions or commitments is FOBO: fear of a better offer. There's too much to fear, too much to choose from, and too much to lose in a society where scarcity is the dominant paradigm. Belief in the unseen and the mysterious is difficult to sell to a culture obsessed and obese with the seen and sold.

And yet, more fiction is being published on pages and directed on screens than ever before in American history, despite the increasing prices to enjoy either. Lily Tomlin is famous for declaring the truth that "the trouble with the rat race is that even if you win you're still a rat."[8] The rat race breeds the need for escape, and fiction lets us pause the pull of this Darwinian world.

Real Fiction

But for those who want to teach faith, it is good to remember that fiction can be more than escape. Consider Tolkien's "On Fairy Stories" and Lewis's "Sometimes Fairy Tales Say Best What Must Be Said."[9]

Fiction need not be a distraction from any reality in the Bible but a wider path into the whole picture of the Bible for the seeker. Fiction is precisely that place where we enter a different world and assume that our rationality must be tamed in order to enjoy and engage the story. We meet new realities and have fresh eyes in pretend worlds because there are no rules for reality demanding our obedience. And in those worlds where we have suspended our rationality, we can pretend to be different people and perhaps believe different things.

Consider this question: what was the most common book found in the homes of Puritans and other colonial religious households? You might be tempted to say the Bible, but you would be wrong. One of the most published books in the seventeenth and eighteenth centuries in this country was not the Bible, but John Bunyan's 1678 Christian allegory, *The Pilgrim's Progress*. Benjamin Franklin wrote of the book in his autobiography, saying, "I have since found that it has been translated into most of the languages of Europe, and suppose it has been more generally read than any other book, except perhaps the Bible. Honest John was the first that I know of who mix'd narration and dialogue; a method of writing very engaging to the reader."[10] To this day, this book has been translated into over two hundred languages and has never been out of print.

Why would Puritans own more Bunyan than Bibles? Because even the biblical literalists knew that the Bible does not teach itself. To teach the Bible—to communicate the whole picture of its message and meaning to humankind—it is crucial to create a simpler but no less supernatural narrative that introduces the complex themes of the Scriptures. John Bunyan tells the story of a protagonist named Christian who is trying to live a moral life. The reader follows Christian on an epic journey to heaven. Turns out the Puritans used the same parable pedagogy that Jesus did: do not change one word of the Law and Divine Love you are trying to teach, but find a contemporary grammar of meaning to weave a story that speaks to the listener.

Pretending Our Way to Biblical Truths

The first section of Lewis's *Mere Christianity* argues gracefully and forcefully for the existence of God. Most of the C. S. Lewis quotations you see on calendars or in memes on the internet come from the first half of this apologetic masterpiece. The later parts of *Mere Christianity* take up smaller matters than theism versus atheism. Tucked into that often neglected second half of the book is a very short chapter titled "Let's Pretend." In this, the shortest chapter of the book, Lewis makes the point that there are two types of pretending:

> There is a bad kind, where the pretense is there instead of the real thing; as when a man pretends he is going to help you instead of really helping you. But there is also a good kind, where the pretense leads up to the real thing. When you are not feeling particularly friendly but know you ought to be, the best thing you can do, very often, is to put on a friendly manner and behave as if you were a nicer person than you actually are. And in a few minutes, as we have all noticed, you will be really feeling friendlier than you were. Very often the only way to get a quality in reality is to start behaving as if you had it already. That is why children's games are so important. They are always pretending to be grownups—playing soldiers, playing shop. But all the time, they are hardening their muscles and sharpening their wits so that the pretense of being grown-up helps them to grow up in earnest.[11]

Lewis argues that the second kind of pretending is a powerful force—well beyond the imagination—in human development. Whereas the first type allows for escaping reality, the second form allows us to lean into potential reality by pretending identities and possibilities until they are real.

In this same chapter, Lewis brings up the Lord's Prayer as an example of the second kind of pretending. He reminds the reader how audacious it is to say the first two words of that prayer: "Our Father." His point is that those two words imply that the speaker is a child of God. He finds this presumption preposterous when considered thoughtfully. Lewis argues that if we say these two words and for that moment suspend skepticism, we can experiment with the reality of being a child of God. We can, as it were, try it on as a belief. If we repeatedly speak these words and while doing so experience a real relationship with God growing, our imaginations can move our minds from pretending to taking on this identity. What was at first only a kind of absurdity transforms, through experimentation and building relationship, into a belief that we are, in fact, children of God. These kinds of prayers are not wishful, as Freud or other critics of prayers to a loving God might say. Rather, prayers as the second form of pretending are reach-full. These prayers reach out and drive a stake into the incredible, like a climber who stabs the ice above her head with a peg and then pulls herself to a higher place. Reaching for promised realities in prayer and daily practice can transform our identity.

To Believe or Not to Believe

The Harry Potter books allow the reader to pretend to live in a wildly enticing supernatural world. The Bible offers this imaginative invitation as well, but as we have already explored, there are myriad reasons why this invitation to enter the "whole picture" of living in loving relationship to God has little stickiness with many people in our culture today. Remember all the words of the Atheist Voice about why the Bible does not stick, especially his ideas that "the [Harry Potter] story is much more interesting" and "the moral lessons are much less ambiguous." You do not have to agree with his oversimplifications of Scripture to acknowledge the well-researched reality that more people read Harry Potter in this country than the Bible.

The Harry Potter narrative argues that there are two kinds of people, both kinds living in the same neighborhoods and walking the same streets of London: those who believe in magic and those who do not, either because they don't know about it or because they deny its existence. As the narrative unfolds, the reader is offered the same choice as any Muggle: do you notice the magical realities around you, and if and when you do, do you choose to believe? Similarly to the Bible, the wizarding world is just that: a world. There are nonbelievers in the biblical texts, but they are cast as wrong in light of the biblical authors' point of view. The nonbelievers exist under the reality of the existence of God throughout the whole picture of Scripture. The wizarding world is similar. Muggles exist and are part of the narrative, but their nonbelief limits their experience of what is true in the world. Their world sits under the ultimate reality of magic and is subject to it.

The "whole picture" of the Harry Potter stories is that the world is a magical world—created, sustained, and permeated by the supernatural. Readers want desperately to live in this supernatural world. Therefore, if we can teach Harry Potter fans how the supernatural world of Rowling's epic is grounded and guided by her Christian belief in God—if we can show people that the core of the whole picture of the Harry Potter narrative is a retelling of the gospel and its invitation—then we can help generate belief that the Bible is also an epic invitation to transformation through relationship with God.

Hogwarts is an amazing and enviable sacred place in a magically supernatural world. It is a perfectly formed faith community, in that everyone is on board with the whole picture of magic. Every day, magic is seen and taught and practiced in person, creating a constant authoritative experience about truth. The culture *is* the catechism. And the learners—the disciples—are students who ask themselves every day, how do I channel magic in my life? Or, how do I act on what is true? The professor and the student have the same goal: learn what must be learned in order to incarnate the truth. Every day, Dumbledore models lifelong discipleship, pacing for hours in his office while figuring out deeper dimensions of truth. He lets the supernatural power that runs and rules in the world run and rule in him.

Archbishop Rowan Williams discusses Christian discipleship of Christ in a similar way. "A disciple is . . . simply a learner; and this, ultimately, is what the disciple learns: how to be a place in the world where the active God can come alive."[12] Dumbledore and every other witch or wizard in the Harry Potter series exemplifies Christian discipleship: they are all learning throughout life how to have their own lives be a place where the active power of magic functions to the full. This is the dynamic and catalytic relationship to God that disciples of Christ seek to inspire in others. Harry Potter invites readers to pretend all the skills of the disciple. And for that reason, we should share Rowling's work with as many would-be disciples as possible. She knows how to make lifelong discipleship stick.

Dragons

If this connection between Harry Potter and the biblical narrative exists, then why are people all over the world not devouring Christian theological treatises and devotional tracts? That may have to do with what C. S. Lewis calls the "watchful dragons" that guard against anything that smacks of religion. Lewis writes that after he chose the fairy tale as the most appropriate form for his images of *Narnia*, he began to realize other benefits:

> I saw how stories of this kind could steal past a certain inhibition which had paralyzed much of my own religion in childhood. Why did one find it so hard to feel as one was told one ought to feel about God or about the sufferings of Christ? I thought the chief reason was that one was told one ought to. An obligation to feel can freeze feelings. And reverence itself did harm. The whole subject was associated with

lowered voices; almost as if it were something medical. But supposing that by casting all these things into an imaginary world, stripping them of their stained-glass and Sunday school associations, one could make them for the first time appear in their real potency? Could one not thus steal past those watchful dragons? I thought one could.[13]

In our contemporary twenty-first-century culture, where there has been a flight from institutions and a multigenerational rejection of the moralizing, marginalizing, and metanarratives of institutions both political and religious, folks are hungry for epic stories but leery of traditional language and mindsets. Lewis is right: we must sneak past the open wounds and thick calluses of the contemporary imagination aiming always to be no one's fool in order to communicate timeless and transformative gospel truths in a timely fashion that is aware of the ambient skepticism of our age.

Carrie Birmingham has written a phenomenal essay on the need to resuscitate the postmodern imagination in order to teach and preach the gospel to ears at least willing to be open to it. She says:

> The crest of Hogwarts School of Witchcraft and Wizardry includes the school's motto *Draco dormiens numquam titillandus*, or *Never tickle a sleeping dragon*. On the surface, the motto seems to represent nothing more than the humor of randomness, reminiscent of Dumbledore's announcement at the sorting feast in *Sorcerer's Stone*, "I would like to say a few words. And here they are: Nitwit! Blubber! Oddment! Tweak!"
>
> However, perhaps the motto of Hogwarts is not random at all but an allusion to Lewis's notion of stealing past the watchful dragons, instructing in Christian doctrine while delighting. It would be as if the motto of Hogwarts were also Rowling's motto. In writing a work so rooted in Christian symbolism disguised as an attractive adventure set in a fantasy world of magic, Rowling sneaks past the watchful dragons, careful to avoid tickling them into wakefulness. Furthermore, in disguising Harry Potter as a series about witches and wizards, Rowling has lulled the dragons into deeper slumber, for a story that raises so many Christian hackles would appear to be a most unlikely venue for Christian teaching.[14]

We are called in Scripture to do all we can to be faithful, credible, and nonjudgmental storytellers of God's love in creation. Jesus invites our creativity, not just our compassion, into the work of sharing the gospel in the world. "Be innocent as doves" is a popular phrase of Jesus that you see on bumper stickers and T-shirts; it feeds the notion that Jesus is mostly or only a balm, a peacemaker, or a reassuring presence in an unstable world. But also heed the earlier part of that very verse: "be wise as serpents."[15] Keep in mind that these two directives are among the last words Jesus spoke to his disciples before leaving the earth. These words are not just a farewell of our Lord but also our marching orders in living and sharing our faith. We are to be as crafty as we are to be compassionate in sharing the words of abundant life. So to a culture asleep or against the traditional words, images, or rituals of the Christian story, we must be serpents in our storytelling. In the words of Paul:

> For though I am free with respect to all, I have made myself a slave to all, so that I might win more of them. To the Jews I became as a Jew, in order to win Jews. To those under the law I became as one under the law (though I myself am not under the law) so that I might win those under the law. To those outside the law I became as one outside the law (though I am not free from God's law but am under Christ's law) so that I might win those outside the law. To the weak I became weak, so that I might win the weak. I have become all things to all people, that I might by all means save some. I do it all for the sake of the gospel, so that I may share in its blessings.[16]

NOTES

1. Acts 2:2–11.

2. Malcolm Gladwell. *The Tipping Point: How Little Things Can Make a Big Difference* (New York: Little, Brown and Company, 2000), 92.

3. Hemant Mehta, "16 Reasons Harry Potter Is Better Than the Bible," Atheist Voice, YouTube, October 7, 2014, https://www.youtube.com/channel/UCUTBvu9NrpVQFiICTu3-dvw.

4. Sarah Pulliam Bailey, "How Christians Warmed to Harry Potter," *Wall Street Journal*, July 15, 2011, http://www.wsj.com/articles/SB10001424052702303812104576441641674217076.

5. Jonathan Petersen, "On the Bible and Being Christian: An Interview with Dr. Rowan Williams," Bible Gateway Blog, February 9, 2015, https://www.biblegateway.com/blog/2015/02/on-the-bible-and-being-christian-an-interview-with-dr-rowan-williams/.

6. C. S. Lewis, "The Weight of Glory," in *The Weight of Glory and Other Addresses* (1949; repr., New York: HarperCollins, 2001), 29–31.

7. Augustine, *The Confessions of Saint Augustine*, trans. John K. Ryan (1960; repr. New York: Image Books, 2014), 1:1:1.

8. Lily Tomlin, "Is This the Country to Whom I'm Speaking?" *People* 8, no. 26 (December 1977), 58.

9. J. R. R. Tolkien, "On Fairy Stories," accessed November 9, 2016, http://www.rivendellcommunity.org/Formation/Tolkien_On_Fairy_Stories.pdf; C. S. Lewis, *On Stories, and Other Essays on Literature* (1966; repr., London: C. S. Lewis Pte. Ltd., 1982), 45–48.

10. Benjamin Franklin, *Autobiography of Benjamin Franklin*, ed. Frank Woodworth Pine (New York: Henry Holt and Company, 1916), Project Gutenberg Ebook, https://www.gutenberg.org/files/20203/20203-h/20203-h.htm.

11. Lewis, *Mere Christianity*, 162–64.

12. Rowan Williams, *Being Disciples: Essentials of the Christian Life* (Grand Rapids, MI: Eerdmans, 2014), 8.

13. C. S. Lewis, "Sometimes Fairy Stories May Say Best What's to Be Said," in *Of Other Worlds: Essays & Stories* (New York: Harcourt Brace Jovanovich, 1966), 37.

14. Carrie Birmingham, "Harry Potter and the Baptism of the Imagination," *Stone-Campbell Journal* 8 (Fall 2005), 211–13, 214.

15. Matthew 10:16.

16. 1 Corinthians 9:19–23.

CHAPTER THREE

Learning *Is* Magic
School Is the New Cool

W hen I first saw the power of the Harry Potter epic during that high school Homecoming week a few years ago, I decided I needed a crash course in Harry Potter as soon as possible. I borrowed the DVD set for all eight movies from a friend on the last day of that Homecoming week. I ordered a pizza and began my movie marathon. Not more than thirty minutes into the first film, I paused the film and said out loud, "I can't believe how much of this story is about *school*." I watched whole scenes (and read chapters in the book) devoted to buying textbooks, worrying about and taking tests, doing or copying homework, planning or skipping study sessions, avoiding or getting detention—scene after scene, putting the experience of being an actual student at the center of the metabolism and the meaning of the seven-book series.

I had heard since 2000 that the Harry Potter stories were about magic. What I didn't know was that they are also about teaching and learning. In a word, these stories are largely about *school*. And this is miraculous news for those of us who want to understand, share, and teach our faith to others. There are surely spiritual themes and theological concepts in Harry Potter. But you could say the same about the *Narnia* books, *The Lord of the Rings*, or even *The Hunger Games* trilogy, although having taught faith with all these other works, I can say that often the spiritual or theological ideas are either too obvious (Lewis) or too ambiguous (Tolkien) for many readers to appreciate. The unique gift that Harry Potter has for people who want to teach spiritual themes and theological concepts is that the story itself is about teaching and learning supernatural and theological truths. Teaching and learning about the supernatural is not just an idea or theme embedded in the narrative that hundreds of millions of readers love; teaching and learning about the supernatural is the epic journey in the narrative.

Adolescence

Choosing school as the place to set her epic is brave for Rowling. School is a space often unpleasant for people at any age and a place that can create some of the worst memories we carry in our lives. Even when middle school or high school is mentioned in adult company, it usually unlocks feelings of frustration, isolation, pain, bad decisions, cliques, teasing, or bullying. But Rowling believes in school and in school-aged human beings as potentially active agents of their destiny and the social fabric around them. She also believes in adult mentors who abide the struggles of young people. Rowling's adults are not helicopter parents or taskmaster travel-team coaches. On the whole, her adults know and respect the boundaries of adolescent life and development. Even the overparenting Dursleys and the Malfoys know when to give their children freedom to live and learn.

All the unknown places of Hogwarts stand as a sign that the developmental period from age eleven to adulthood is by no means a known landscape. Rather, like the castle itself, adolescence is a time and place for discovery, failure, identity formation, and friendship. More than classes in Potions or Ancient Runes, the book series proves that Rowling believes the primary role and responsibility of school is to shepherd young people in community toward an awakening to the power of their own decisions. It's the job of the teenager to figure out how and what to learn.

Hogwarts is a particularly effective school in the way it forms joy, skill, friendship, bravery, and love in people of all ages in a supernatural world. Anyone wanting to help form the faith of others should study the ethos and environment of Hogwarts. The fictional Hogwarts School of Witchcraft and Wizardry is a powerful example of effective teaching and learning to use magic in the world. The Harry Potter fandom, like the students of Hogwarts, loves learning, experimenting, and changing the world with other people. (Later we will consider organizations and social justice causes that have been spearheaded by Harry Potter readers in explicit public performance of values they attest to learning from Hogwarts and Albus Dumbledore.) Rowling presents the educational process not primarily as a means to acquire knowledge, but instead as a journey aimed at changing the world, at fighting for who and what is right, at learning who your friends are, at finding the wisdom that other people have shared with you and putting it to work. In the words of Dumbledore, "It is our choices, Harry, that show us who we really are, far more than our abilities."[1]

When you consider J. K. Rowling's early life, it is clear that reading and writing stories was a source of safety, joy, and freedom while surrounded by a complicated and stressful home environment. In her early adult life, writing the Harry Potter books continued to be a source of agency and liberation from her own broken relationships, financial insecurity, and vocational frustration. Rowling's magic in life has always been learning.

The Lever of Learning in the Narrative

You cannot read any of these books, or even a chapter of any of these books, and not notice immediately that Ron, Harry, and Hermione love going to school. They certainly complain about homework, detention, and exams (Hermione only complains about exams when they're canceled). But what I find most refreshing is that this is a story about young people actually being in school, and not just a story of youth socializing and drama with school as a mere backdrop. Whereas in blockbuster teen television shows over the past few decades, such as *Beverly Hills 90210*, *One Tree Hill*, *Gilmore Girls*, *Buffy the Vampire Slayer*, *Gossip Girl*, *Saved by the Bell*, and *Glee*, there is little or no actual homework, test taking, studying, or teaching, Harry Potter and his best friends stay up or sneak around at night not to drink, smoke, or cheat, but to read books under their bed sheets in order to know and hone their gifts and practice magic. They lurk in the library mostly for books, not boyfriends or girlfriends. They are driven by their longing to learn magic because magic is the means to fully function in the world.

Unlike much of the academic content we force on teenagers in traditional schools, magic is so immediately relevant and powerful that not learning or at least trying to learn magic would be an act blatantly against self-interest. It's not that students at Hogwarts don't try to skirt the rules or use magic to bully at times, but most often our favorite characters in the narrative break rules precisely to use magic to right a wrong, fight against evil, or defend the weak. Even when rules are broken, they are usually broken because someone, somewhere, feels called to engage injustice.

If you had asked any literary agent or television producer in the late 1990s to script a story about the intellectual and social struggles and heroism of doing actual schoolwork—at the height of popularity for high school–themed shows that never really depict schooling because of its boring or negative associations for people of all ages—they would have laughed at you. Keep in mind that Rowling's manuscript about a school, magic or otherwise, was shopped to seventeen publishers before she got one shy acceptance. Yet against all common wisdom, Rowling has proven that telling a story about working hard in school and learning something new every day can be a compelling and blockbuster storyline. But the equation does require one essential element to explain why Rowling succeeded where other school-themed narratives have failed or not even tried to depict school: the learning must be about the supernatural.

How *does* the Hogwarts School of Witchcraft and Wizardry make learning about the supernatural so compelling? I believe it is the fact that there is such a short time between the hard-learned lessons about new charms, spells, or potions and the immediate real-life moments when those lessons can be applied. Children learn a spell in the morning and can use it to delight others or fight evil by the afternoon. Students learn a new potion on Monday and drink it on Tuesday to save the life of a friend, their school, or the world. As a lesson begins, the students can begin to imagine an urgent purpose—in many cases, a moral purpose—for each new piece of information they learn. They can also aim to brew some Liquid Luck for perhaps more playful purposes. But either way, there is an immediate incentive for every new level of skill. Everything they learn enables students (and professors) to do something new as soon as they can learn it.

Both Dumbledore and Voldemort, despite their vastly differing missions in life, continue to seek higher levels of knowledge and magic mastery with unyielding effort. Witches and wizards are incentivized to learn something from every lesson because every lesson in magic offers them more power, more opportunity, and more freedom to accomplish their goals, good or evil. The students know that the ones who learn the most at Hogwarts are the ones who can then do the most after Hogwarts. They know that good wizards and bad wizards who are famous all have one thing in common: they were good learners. This is what Ollivander meant when he first looked at Harry and said, "I think it is clear that we can expect great things from you. After all, He-Who-Must-Not-Be-Named did great things. Terrible! Yes. But great."[2] Not learning at Hogwarts means missing out on the meaningful, epic challenges that everyone else who is learning can share and celebrate. It is not just cool to learn; it is abundant life.

Cedric Diggory is the kind of student who exemplifies the unique learning culture of Hogwarts. In the normal high school narrative, he might only be known for being popular, attractive, or athletic. But at Hogwarts, it goes without saying that he's also one of the most skilled students at magic because nothing makes a person cooler to both students and professors than magical ability. As Mad-Eye Moody described Cedric to Harry, "Listen to me, Potter. Your pal Diggory? By your age he could turn a whistle into a watch and have it sing you the time."[3]

Rowling is not naive about the cliques that are part of high school life; they are in operation at Hogwarts, though mostly as part of the House subcultures. Joanne went to high school only a little over a decade before writing the Harry Potter epic, and her precise depictions of rivalries and tribes demonstrates her learned wisdom concerning the herds of high school. But in her Hogwarts, learning trumps all tribes. And this is one of the reasons readers love Hogwarts: it holds out the hope that learning is agency enough to overcome tribalism, clique culture, and bullying. Learning is the coin of the realm at Hogwarts because it is the great equalizer against any social caste system. At what other school could a student who began the first day looking for his lost frog amid the laughter of peers be the man who destroys the last Horcrux? Neville Longbottom is the face of the pace and power of becoming a person at Hogwarts.

Purpose and Agency

Harry Potter reminds me that children (all people, really) are open to the hard practice of learning if they can identify usefulness for that learning. Think of how urgently we read the manuals for a new toy we've longed to have. Think how much focus we employ when reading medical information for our own health issues or health issues of those we love. Think how dutifully we study a map when we are trying to arrive at a desired destination. Purpose is a magnet for our mental muscle, and Rowling has created a school that offers agency in reward for learning. This is the magic of magic: not that magic entertains or enthralls, but that it empowers.

When speaking to teachers, I encourage them to consider the subjects they teach in traditional high schools and think about how they might present immediate applications for their lessons in the daily lives of their students, no matter what they teach, languages, economics, history, or science. I challenge them to find the ways that math, drama, or Latin can address an immediate and pressing social or moral issue in their students' lived experience or in the lived experience of "other" communities. Social justice work shows all of us that there are real issues that need real workers and real creativity and real solutions right now. The brokenness of the world, when it is not sidelined from our students as a distraction from traditional content, is enough to inspire them to do their homework. This has been my experience when taking students on trips to Haiti or Habitat for Humanity to spend days or weeks trying to build schools or houses. It is incredible to watch first-world students meet the people who will one day live in the house or study in the classroom being built. For many upper-middle-class adolescents, the first time they've met people that society calls "the poor" has been on these community service trips, even the most shallow "voluntourism" versions.

It is amazing to see how hard students are willing to work in those immersion experiences with people in need, how much math they're willing to figure out to measure the size of siding, how much physics they will cram to calculate angles and levers, how much patience they will find to fill attics with insulation or hang doors in closets. I watch habitually unfocused or undisciplined students dive into complex academic disciplines out of a deep and immediate longing to help one family of real faces move into their first house or one child sit down in a classroom with a new roof. This is why community colleges and later-in-life educational programs have some of the best students in the country. Many of these students arrive to learn, keenly and courageously aware of what they need to learn and for whom.

The magical marriage of agency and productivity, ever the challenge in working with students of any age, happens when there is a palpable need for knowledge—when the need for learning has skin and eyes and hearts. I have witnessed students with even the most calloused and catatonic curiosity, put to sleep by traditional education, religious or secular, become busy and brave when the need for learning is immediate and incarnate. If you want your students to be skilled, brave, and bonded with others to take on every Death Eater and dementor in life, then you had better offer them a teaching and learning environment that is keenly aware and immediately aimed at the needs of the world. If you want Hogwarts heroes, you need Hogwarts habits.

House Points at Hogwarts

This book is about more than how to use content from the Harry Potter stories to teach the Christian faith. It is also about using the Harry Potter series to form your own methods of teaching faith, whether you are explicitly using Harry Potter or not. In the second part of this book, you will read how to use content from Harry Potter in many different teaching opportunities, from parenting to preaching to marriage preparation. But this part of the book explores what the Harry Potter phenomenon tells us about human longing and human learning. Rowling's story is too popular and has too strong a stickiness factor for us to ignore its architecture and its convictions. There are truths in this narrative that speak across vast cultural differences, evidenced in the translations of Harry Potter into nearly seventy different languages. If Harry Potter readers were a religion, they would be the third-largest religion in the world. The sheer numbers of people touched by this epic beg the question, what is Rowling's systematic understanding of human beings and how they develop, as seen in this story? Something about her theology has touched and connected more of the world than any other fiction writer in recorded history. She has created a community approaching one billion members. Put simply, why does everyone who reads Harry Potter want to go to Hogwarts School? Rowling's genius is that she has not only created a compelling story but also embedded in that epic a whispering wisdom woven into every chapter about how to teach faith in things unseen.

Transformative Learning

Jane McGonigal's 2010 TED Talk on gaming is ranked in the top fifteen TED Talks of all time. In achieving this rank, she beats out Bill Gates, who is number sixteen. This game designer's lecture shares wit and wisdom from her twenty years studying and creating in the game industry, both in the academy (she did her PhD at Berkeley in the efficacy of gaming) and in the private sector (as a research affiliate and chief creative officer with the Institute for the Future). But more important, her work explains precisely why Hogwarts is such an effective place of teaching and learning. Allow me to justify why talk of gaming helps us understand the appeal and inspiration of Rowling's Hogwarts School. Because understanding why and how Hogwarts makes school so appealing to all ages can help any teacher or student create a Hogwarts environment for learning. And the fact that the mission of Hogwarts is to teach and train students for a supernatural world in which the realities are both seen and unseen is even more exciting for those who want to teach faith to others.

So what is the magic metabolism of teaching and learning depicted so delectably at Hogwarts? In a word, Hogwarts is gameful. In fact, the whole wizarding world is gameful and, I argue, this is why we love it. According to McGonigal, the world is currently spending three billion hours per week playing online games. Though many people might consider this number unbelievable (or just plain depressing, if you have concerns about gaming), McGonigal argues boldly that three billion hours a week globally is "not nearly enough gameplay to solve the world's most urgent problems." In this one utterance, you catch a glimpse of McGonigal's radical thesis and equally radical life mission. She believes games engage and empower people in unique ways, thereby potentially training them in skills that can be applied outside of gaming. Game skills are life skills, she says, so the more (well-designed) games we play, the better at bettering the world we become.

McGonigal maintains that games can create an environment with four empowering components: blissful productivity, a social fabric, urgent optimism, and epic meaning. I will delve deeper into all four of these dimensions of gaming, but for now, suffice it to say that McGonigal thinks the right games make us more intelligent, resilient, connected, imaginative, brave, patient, and empathetic toward other human beings. Hence, she argues, "if we want to solve problems like hunger, poverty, climate change, global conflict, or obesity, I believe we need to aspire to play games online for at least twenty-eight billion hours a week."[4] Her TED Talk on gaming is full of such fantastical claims. But as you watch and listen to her lay out both the methods and metrics to bolster every one of her claims, it becomes clear why she beat Bill Gates.

McGonigal invites people to look at the face of someone who is playing a game. (As you read her description, ask yourself if this isn't also a great description of the face of someone watching a Harry Potter film or reading one of the Harry Potter books.) "There's a sense of urgency, a little bit of fear, but intense concentration, deep focus on tackling a really difficult problem." She adds, "There's a sense of optimism and surprise." Gamers feed on the possibility of what she calls an "epic win." Those of you already familiar with gaming know this term well. She defines it this way:

> An epic win is an outcome that is so extraordinarily positive, that you had no idea it was even possible until you achieved it. It was almost beyond the threshold of the imagination, and when you get there you are shocked to discover what you are truly capable of.

Is this not also a precise description of nearly every hurdle faced by Harry and his fellow members of Dumbledore's Army? Following the story of Harry and his friends, from their first boat ride toward Hogwarts across the Black Lake to the sunrise after the Battle of Hogwarts, is to follow a group of souls seeking an epic win. The experience of seeking and achieving an epic win, promised and ritualized in gaming, is the reason games are so engaging and inspire people to spend so much of their time, energy, and passion.

Wired for Seeking

McGonigal, though not religious, nonetheless promotes a philosophical anthropology very similar to Christian theological anthropology in arguing that human beings are wired for seeking and sacrificing for an epic win. In the Bible, this view of human nature is described best in the book of Ecclesiastes. "[God] has made everything suitable for its time; moreover he has put a sense of past and future into their minds, yet they cannot find out what God has done from the beginning to the end" (Eccles. 3:11).

Another common translation renders the Hebrew this way: "we have eternity written on our hearts."

We have "a sense of past and future"—our epic story as creatures seeking to know, love, serve, and live with our Creator in peace forever—knit into our being. Distinct from rationality, intellect, conscience, or memory, our imagination is the human faculty that whispers this epic story and calls us to *play*. Games tap and tempt this longing for joining an epic quest. The story written in us is a magnet that tugs us to enter it and create its plot as we endure struggles, encounter loss, gain knowledge, build community, and work tirelessly for the chance of an epic win.

When we seek an epic win, it is not just something humans do. Seeking epic wins is who we are. This is why the term "Seeker" for the Quidditch player with the most power to win the match is a truly inspired creation of Rowling's and perhaps her clearest statement throughout the series on the true identity of any human person. Numerous biblical texts and the words of many Christian liturgies describe and declare that we are seekers by nature and not by choice or action. Whether one scores or not, one *is* the Seeker. In the words of Augustine, "God, you have made us for your own and we are restless until we rest in you."[5] Our identity as children of God, envisioned and earned by God alone, plants in us the seed of longing for God. We are seekers because we are "wonderfully and fearfully made" (Ps. 139:14). Our imagination is the lure and lever within us that leans into our freedom and hints at a home outside ourselves. The journey home makes meaning of the landscape of our lives.

Consider the precise language in the Baptismal Covenant from the Book of Common Prayer. As in many other Christian denominations, after the confession of the Trinity, the vows that follow do not outline dogma or doctrine, but instead invite the person into the epic journey of a new life in Christ. Every vowed verb points toward an epic journey.

Celebrant: Will you continue in the apostles' teaching and fellowship, in the breaking of the bread, and in the prayers?

People: I will, with God's help.

Celebrant: Will you persevere in resisting evil, and, whenever you fall into sin, repent and return to the Lord?

People: I will, with God's help.

Celebrant: Will you proclaim by word and example the Good News of God in Christ?

People: I will, with God's help.

Celebrant: Will you see and serve Christ in all persons, loving your
neighbor as yourself?
People: I will, with God's help.
Celebrant: Will you strive for justice and peace among all people,
and respect the dignity of every human being?
People: I will, with God's help.[6]

A God who respects our freedom but who also longs for a relationship
with us can do nothing to coerce or force us into a relationship based in
love. But we can in fact be wired from the beginning to participate in an
epic story of reunion and relationship between creature and Creator. This
longing for relationship is a homing device that does not trample our freedom, but instead tempts it. We are free to follow this longing or not, but
a loving God has not left us free from longing for truth.

Because we are wired for an epic journey home, we are joyfully vulnerable to games that offer adventures. Much of the social commentary
on gaming argues that it is the animal part of our nature that drives us to
play.[7] These voices argue that gaming channels the fight-or-flight forces in
us or relies on some notion of a Darwinian defensiveness in our species
to find lunch and not be lunch for others. But McGonigal's more holistic
view of gaming goes well beyond any argument that games are powerful
because it is our nature to compete against others or to conquer. Though a
part of gaming is competition, the deeper longing in us is not to compete
against others, but rather to seek an epic win with others. This is a more
precise diagnosis of gamer longing, and it is crucial to understanding how
Harry Potter touches and talks to the gamer in all of us. McGonigal's deep
conviction is that we are wired for seeking and sacrificing for epic meaning
in fellowship with others. This innate drive to game breeds urgency and
energy for the countless hours of attention and hard work that massively
multiplayer games (MMGs) require. The informational wiki about the
MMG "World of Warcraft" is the third-largest wiki in the world. Take in
that fact: the third-largest online collection of information about anything
in the world is a collection of information about an online game. McGonigal explains some of the motivation of the global community of gamers,
observing that in gaming there are "tons of collaborators, hundreds of
thousands of people ready to work with you to achieve your epic mission.
That's not something we have in real life easily, and also there's this epic
story to explain why we are there and what we're doing."

It is hard to read this description of what works in gaming and not
see how brilliantly it explains what works in the Room of Requirement

or how it explains why everyone I've ever met who reads the Harry Potter stories says they would not mind going back to school if they could go to Hogwarts. Think of Harry's words to his fellow students while they are training themselves to fight Voldemort: "Every great wizard in history," he declared, "has started out as nothing more than what we are now. If they can do it, why not us?"[8] According to McGonigal, there are half a billion gamers in the world right now. Research shows that over the next ten years, another billion gamers will be added, as new consoles are being developed that run on low energy or hand cranks. The emerging middle class in markets such as China and India are opening up so much that it is predicted that by the end of 2020, the world will have over 1.5 billion gamers. This is joyful news if the skills of a gamer do indeed involve being able to handle failure, build social fabric, sacrifice for epic meaning, or be blissfully productive. I think of this as a potentially huge and well-trained Dumbledore's Army. What if we could inspire even a fraction of people with game skills to engage and enter the gospel as an epic adventure with a life in Christ and his body (the church) as their epic win? Games have already trained them how to be industrious, faithful, sacrificial, mission-driven, and communal. Games draw us in because the invitation to be a Seeker is written on our hearts. Games are not popular because they teach us to play; they are popular because it is our nature to play and they offer a way and a world for our wonder.

Harry Potter, both in the narrative and among the community of readers, operates like gaming in bringing together focused, curious, and driven individuals with a desire to learn the necessary skills to affect real-time change in the world. The narrative invites readers—who are gameful by God's design—into a world in which they can dare to seek and share an epic win.

Mentoring as Formation

My favorite example of teaching faith in the Harry Potter series is Dumbledore's slow, multiyear discipleship of Harry. From the moment Dumbledore leaves Harry on the step of 4 Privet Drive, he senses that Harry's fate is already fused with Voldemort's and that his life will need protection, direction, and love. As each year passes for Harry at Hogwarts, and Dumbledore's awareness of and wisdom about Harry's fate comes into view, Dumbledore commits his own life to teaching and training Harry to be ready to sacrifice himself for others or for the greater good. Snape brushes off Dumbledore's goal, saying, "You've kept him like a pig for slaughter."[9]

But Dumbledore knows that no one but Harry can offer himself as a willing sacrifice in the fight against evil, and therefore Harry will have to be taught the value of living and giving one's life for others. Dumbledore is not mechanistic about Harry's life, preparing Harry only for sacrificing himself to Voldemort, as Snape accused. Dumbledore instead takes on the challenge that faces all of us, charged and commissioned in our own baptism and in witness to the baptism of others, to share and teach our faith to others. Dumbledore seeks to disciple Harry in the power of magic (the supernatural) and the power of love. Harry is not just discipled to die, but rather he is formed in courage, community, and commitment to love the good and the world with reckless abandon. Dumbledore weeps with Harry in the purgation space of the cloudy and mystical King's Cross Station at the end of the last novel, admitting to Harry that he did not always love others as himself or seek the liberation of others over his own power.

In his mentoring of Harry, Dumbledore seeks to form a soul into something stronger and purer than his own. And Dumbledore's own willingness to die for Harry and others shows he had learned from his own life how better to love the good and the world unto death. Dying is not an end in itself, either in these books or in the Christian life. The death Dumbledore prepares Harry to face is only a means through which freedom and peace come to both the dying and the living that are blessed and protected by sacrificial love. As Neville says to Voldemort in the last battle, "Harry didn't die in vain. He's still with us." Similarly, Sirius echoes Rowling's view of death leading to life when he reaches out to point at Harry's heart in the Forbidden Forest, saying of the dead, "We're in here, you see." Lupin also defines and defends his own sacrificial death and that of his wife Tonks, saying, "Someday someone will tell Teddy what his parents died for."

The real question is not whether Dumbledore is preparing Harry to die. Nor is it simply whether Harry has the skills and tools that he needs to defeat Voldemort. Rather, the key question is whether he has been adequately trained in a way of life that will allow him to lay down his life for his friends. Dumbledore tries to form Harry in precisely this way. He tells and retells the story of Harry's mother's sacrifice, helps Harry nurture friendships, and even spends time helping him love his enemy (as seen in book six, in which we are given a glimpse of Voldemort as the human, vulnerable Tom Riddle in need of compassion more than hatred). Dumbledore also tells Harry so many times that the most powerful thing that he has—that Voldemort does not—is love. Dumbledore is forming Harry in a way of living that will embrace a sacrificial way of dying.

Becoming a Better Person

Having Dumbledore as a loving mentor makes Harry into a better person. But an interesting question for anyone witnessing the global popularity of the Harry Potter stories is this: does reading the story of Harry Potter becoming a more whole, brave, and loving person tempt or cause the reader to become a more whole, brave, and loving person? Not surprisingly, many academic researchers have asked whether reading Harry Potter makes one a better person, and so far, all who have analyzed the data have come to the same conclusion: yes.

Just one of these studies, published in the *Journal of Applied Social Psychology*, found that reading the Harry Potter books has the effect of creating a stronger sense of empathy.[10] The research group led by professor at Loris Vezzali of the University of Modena and Reggio Emilia, in Italy, conducted three related studies. In the first study, thirty-four elementary school children were given a questionnaire assessing their attitudes toward immigrants, a group frequently stigmatized in Italy. The children were then divided into groups that met once a week for six weeks to read Harry Potter passages and discuss them with a research assistant. One group read passages related to prejudice, such as the time Draco Malfoy, a shockingly blond pure-blood wizard, calls Harry's friend Hermione a filthy little Mudblood. The control group read excerpts unrelated to prejudice, including the scene where Harry buys his first magic wand. A week after the last session, the children's attitudes toward out-groups (the "other") were assessed again. Among those who identified with the Harry Potter character, attitudes toward immigrants significantly improved in children who had read passages dealing with prejudice, while the attitudes of those who had read neutral passages hadn't changed.

Vezzali and colleagues conducted two follow-up studies with similar results. One found that reading Harry Potter improved attitudes toward homosexuals in Italian high school students. The other linked the books with more compassion toward refugees among English university students.

Another study published the same year in *Science* magazine found that reading literary fiction rather than popular fiction or nonfiction results in keener social perception and increased empathy, empathy being defined, more or less, as the ability to alternate between different perspectives on a particular person or situation. Literature with complex, developed themes and characters appeared to let readers adopt or see things from perspectives that they might not otherwise have considered, and it seems that Rowling might get at the beautiful, sobering mess of life in a way that could have a meaningful impact on our children's collective character.

So the research is in: games can make us better people if they are designed to do so. Reading fiction, written well, can make us more empathetic. And perhaps most important for those reading this book, apparently reading Harry Potter in particular could help make you a better person.

Social Justice and Community Service

For those of you who don't make a habit of reading scholarly journals, there's an easier way to witness for yourself the proof of the power of Harry Potter to make people into better people. Look no further than the Harry Potter Alliance (HPA).

The HPA was founded in 2005 by comedian Andrew Slack along with the wizard rock band Harry and the Potters. Their idea for an international Harry Potter social justice network of fans was initially funded with donations for Amnesty International at their public performances. The group believes strongly in the conviction J. K. Rowling stated in her Harvard Commencement Address of 2008: "We do not need magic."[11] The HPA currently has over five million members, making it the largest social activist literary fandom in the world. If you go to the HPA website, you will see in its "Values" a codification of lessons learned from Harry Potter by the founders and members of the organization. You can also hear resonance of gamer culture—a group passionate about seeking and sharing the epic win of a more just and loving world.

> We believe in magic.
> We believe that unironic enthusiasm is a renewable resource.
> We know fantasy is not only an escape from our world, but an
>   invitation to go deeper into it.
> We celebrate the power of community—both online and off.
> We believe that the weapon we have is love.[12]

The organization has chapters all over the world that stay linked through the internet but take on local projects (as well as participate in nationally or internationally coordinated projects) in response to needs assessed by HPA members. HPA chapters meet in schools, libraries, synagogues, retirement homes, VFW halls, Masonic temples, churches, community centers, basements, and public parks. I led a chapter in a high school and can attest to the uniquely fun, inspiring, and passionate culture of local social activist fandoms that are woven together by small and intimate local groups. Think of the Girl Scouts or Boy Scouts—organizations with undeniable national recognition, identity and structure, but held together by the innumerable souls of small troops with their own leaders, plans, traditions, and creative power. In the HPA chapter I ran, we envisioned and implemented a number of social justice events and programs, similarly to any other community service group. But our HPA chapter, like many others, held meetings and did work in the community wearing Hogwarts robes and House ties, as well as carrying wands to remind us of the story that inspired our work together. The confused but delighted looks on the faces of food pantry workers or homeless shelter employees was priceless when my students and I arrived with donations or showed up to volunteer in Hogwarts robes worn over our HPA T-shirts that declared the international motto: "The Weapon We Have Is Love."

Andrew Slack, the original executive director of the HPA, said it best: "Dumbledore had a vision that could truly make a difference in our world if acted on and believed in."[13] And Harry Potter readers have acted on it. Now the world can see the power of the unseen force of love soaked into every page of Rowling's call to action.

NOTES

1. J. K. Rowling, *Harry Potter and the Chamber of Secrets* (New York: Scholastic, 1998), 333.

2. J. K. Rowling, *Harry Potter and the Philosopher's Stone* (New York: Arthur Levine Books, 1997), 85.

3. Mike Newell, "Harry Potter and the Goblet of Fire" (Warner Bros. Pictures, 2005), film, 00:53:17.

4. Jane McGonigal, "Gaming Can Make a Better World," TED Talks, February 2010, http://www.ted.com/talks/jane_mcgonigal_gaming_can_make_a_better_world.

5. Augustine, *Confessions*, 1:1:1.

6. Service of Holy Baptism, Book of Common Prayer, 304–5.

7. McGonigal, "Gaming Can Make a Better World."

8. "Order of the Phoenix," film, 01:32:57.

9. *Deathly Hallows*, 182–85.

10. Loris Vezzali, Sofia Stathi, Dino Giovannini, Dora Capozza, and Elena Trifiletti, "The Greatest Magic of Harry Potter: Reducing Prejudice," *Journal of Applied Social Psychology* 45, no. 2 (July 2014): 105–21.

11. Rowling, "Fringe Benefits of Failure."

12. "What We Do," Harry Potter Alliance, http://www.thehpalliance.org/what_we_do.

13. http://www.thehpalliance.org/who_we_are.

CHAPTER FOUR

Do This in Remembrance of Me

The Patronus Charm Works

The only time I ever went to the principal's office in high school was when I demanded to go. It was my senior year and there was a lot of stress in my life. Much of it was shared stress felt by any other girl or boy in the twelfth grade trying to finish high school, apply to college, and prepare to leave home. Some of high school stress stems from looking around you and realizing that you will walk away from everyone and everything you know—the teachers, coaches, and peers you enjoyed or hated in your teenage life—once high school is over. Some of us would go off to college, others to the military, but most of my friends and I could feel the clock running out on the familiarity and stability of adolescent life, at school and at home. That was the year we all tried to get a great yearbook photo of ourselves and pick equally epic words to go along with it that might show how deep or funny we could be. There are so many dimensions of high school anxiety for young people that are universal experiences in our culture. But what brought me into the principal's office was something rare for high school students, I hope.

It was a book assigned in my senior year English class that sent me to the principal that day. I have never been the type of student that looks ahead at the syllabus to see what books are listed for the semester. So I arrived at class one day to find out that the next book we were reading was by William Faulkner, an author about whom I knew nothing at that point in my life. *As I Lay Dying* was what we would be reading, discussing, and writing about for three weeks. Breaking a cosmic rule, I judged the book by its cover and determined it to be a real downer.

I'll never forget seeing the old and tattered book land on my desk, passed to me by the teacher. In public schools, you are given books owned by the school, recycled and reused by students, sometimes year after year. There was always a ritual to open those tattered schoolbooks quickly and see which names from prior years you might know. A competitive classmate next to me had already read this particular book over the summer to get ahead of everyone else in English 12. She leaned over to me and whispered, "This book is totally depressing. Saddest thing I've read in a long time." My spirits dropped quickly. I had a lot of sadness in my life already, and this prophecy that I would spend the next three weeks reading a "depressing" story was discouraging. "What happens in the story?" I whispered back to her, proving that I would rather hear the summary of the sad story quickly than wait and watch it play out over time. I can remember clearly her know-it-all tone and sassy summary. She even looked like Hermione. Proud of her summer sprint through the syllabus, she said matter-of-factly, "There's this family and the parent dies and they, like, drag the body around in a coffin in their old car. That's, like, the whole story." She then opened her notebook to a clean sheet of paper and looked toward the teacher, ready to take notes.

I think the teacher started talking at that point. My heart was pounding so loudly in my chest that all other sounds were a blur to me, then and now. All I remember is standing up and walking out of the class. Did the teacher ask me where I was going? If she did, I didn't hear. All I remember is walking swiftly through the silent halls of my public high school, passing the endless rows of lockers of all the other students who were, at that moment, sitting in classrooms as students should. I was determined not to cry. I got to the principal's office and stood in front of his secretary's desk. I asked to see the principal. "Now?" she said incredulously. "Yes. Now. Please."

She got up and walked to the principal's office door, opened it, and said sarcastically, "There's a student here asking to see you. Right now." Mr. Saltzman was at his desk. He looked puzzled. I walked into his view. He smiled at my face. "Come in. Sit down. What's up?" I was friendly with my high school principal. I was president of the youth council and president of the school athletic council and also held other such leadership roles that kept me in conversation with administrators at school frequently. I had been a student in that school building since kindergarten. I was one of the few students who had spent summer days with the administration, always playing the role of the student volunteering to show up, set up, or sit down to talk to adults about school life. So I knew this man as well as any teenager in the community could. I walked over to a comfortable chair as he sat back down at his desk. He put his feet up on the desk and spoke to me like an old friend. "Seriously," he said, "what's up?" He was cheerful. I was screaming inside: "Don't cry. No matter what, don't cry."

After a deep breath, I declared, "I either have to get out of English class or I have to get out of reading this book we've been assigned, but I'm not going to sit in that class for the next three weeks. In fact, I'm cutting English class now to talk to you." His face froze. He was not angry. His blinking was so rapid and obvious I could almost hear it happening. In a voice I had never heard from him, he said anxiously, "So you're telling me that you intend to cut this class for the next three weeks? Over a book?" He put his feet back on the floor and leaned heavily on his folded arms, coming as close to me as possible across his desk. The mantra in my head continued: "Don't cry." I took another breath. "Yes. Just for one book. And just for three weeks. I thought you should know." We sat in silence. He ran his hand over his bald head more than once. I was sure he could hear my heart pounding.

I was immature enough to think my brief declarative statement was enough and that somehow my good reputation with grown-ups meant I didn't have to say anything more. Although at the time I felt very humble and vulnerable, looking back now, I realize there was no small amount of arrogance in thinking that I didn't need to ask for permission. I had never discussed my home life with any adult or peer in thirteen years at that school, and I had no intention of breaking that silence in my senior year. He finally found some words: "Can you say more about this book you don't like?" I was frustrated that the meeting wasn't over already. "No, I can't. I haven't read it." Now he started to look frustrated, and for the first time since meeting him years before, I felt like a child in his presence. He put both hands flat on his desk. "You have to say more." Having been a high school administrator myself for almost twenty years now, I can imagine the frustration in the principal's head. And in his heart. As teachers and coaches, we think we know all the essential facts about our students. And once we become administrators with access to files and experts, we often think we know more about families and their children than they do.

Since kindergarten, I had been one of those students that teachers and administrators don't spend much time thinking about, a kid adults enjoy because I was compliant, loved school, was appropriately curious about their lives outside of school, and was articulate about current events or town-school political news. I actually went to school board meetings just to learn about how schools worked on public funding. I knew which adults were the union reps, and I periodically brought coffee or tea to my first-period teachers. I knew their birthdays. I helped teachers set up their classrooms in August because I lived a block from school and would wander the campus looking for adults that I could talk to when school was not in session. I was not a brownnoser at all. Looking back, I think the adults at school sensed that I needed them in my life, though it was never clear exactly why. But what teacher doesn't like an unexpected cup of coffee or a doughnut from the nearby town bakery on their birthday? Understandably, though inappropriately, I had come to believe that I was a peer to the adults around me. But when the principal stood up and walked over to my chair to talk down to me in my seat, I woke up to the reality that the photos all over his desk were of his grandchildren, who were all older than me.

He began: "You cannot cut class. You cannot skip three weeks of the course, and you have to read this book like anyone else, unless you give me some kind of reason you can't. Otherwise, go back to class." I took what felt like an hour, but was probably more like thirty seconds, to gather my thoughts. The room was so quiet. To this day, I can still hear the muffled sound of the secretary's ever-ringing phone. I made the decision. After all the years of the school being my own kingdom with little or nothing to do with my family, I felt short of breath at the thought of finally speaking the words. I had worked so hard to have a wall of separation between my home life and my orbit of school. But I thought about that sad book by the guy named Faulkner, and I knew I needed to say whatever I needed to say to get away from wading into such a despairing narrative at that time in my life.

Though known by others as joyful and steady, I had always known inside that my sanity felt like a fragile thing, needing not constant but no less committed attention to possible triggers. I made excuses for not going to sad movies with friends. I avoided intense dramas on network television. I never voluntarily read stories that were sad. I had made a decision early in life that real life is too sad and too uncertain in reality for me to seek forms of darkness in entertainment. My goal as a teenager was to be successful enough in school to go to a good college and begin to build my own adult life—one that I hoped and prayed would be less sad, less turbulent, and less anxious than my family's home. Don't get me wrong: my parents loved me more than anything in life. Their care was endless, and their sacrifices for their children remain an inspiration to me. They too seemed overwhelmed with their own fears, grief, and sadness. In so many ways, we were as common and as tragic as any struggling working-class and alcoholic family system. School was the island away from that, for me and for so many young people across so many generations. I am sure that one of the reasons I sought teaching and ministry in high school as a vocation is that I knew in my bones the power of safe, healthy, nonparent adults in my own development. Those walking wells of love and support in schools showed me that listening ears and appropriate hugs can literally preserve and even save lives.

I have no doubt that Hogwarts touches and soothes millions of vulnerable readers the way it does me. Rowling created the school we always wanted. She built the castle away from our family chaos. And this safe and sacred supernatural home is just a train ride away. There will always be help at Hogwarts for those who ask for it, whether you come from the stability of parents who were both boring dentists or from the hellish home of a closet under the stairs.

I looked back at the principal. He had stopped blinking. I noticed for the first time that he had deep blue eyes. In a cold voice over the screams of "Don't cry" in my head, I began to speak words I remember to this day. "Sir, you know I've been here since kindergarten. I have done my best to give the school as much as it has given me. I've never really asked this school for anything, but I'm asking you for this. Please let me miss this book." His mouth opened a little, but no words came out. This thirty-year veteran in public schools seemed unable to find the next thing to say. I tried to end the conversation. "Please?"

He walked back to his chair and spoke in an authoritative voice. "Do you think you're smarter than your AP English teacher? That you know what books should be read or not?" I shocked him by interrupting, "I don't know what books should be read. But I'm not reading this one."

He said with a sigh, "One last time: you must give me a reason."

Something in me decided to give up and give in. Holding back the real answers to so many questions I had been asked by teachers and coaches about my life outside of school had taken enormous amounts of energy since the second grade. I scanned the office, not wanting to see his blue eyes for fear mine would well up with tears. I noticed how tired that office was and that I too felt suddenly tired—too tired to manage multiple lives anymore. I uncrossed my legs and put both feet on the floor, ready to walk a new path of authenticity with the school that had been my safe place since childhood. "Sir, the deadline for seniors to request graduation tickets for our immediate family was yesterday." He looked lost. I could see him asking himself what graduation tickets had to do with Faulkner. "Yes, I think so," he answered. I continued, "The letter from school said that only parents and siblings are guaranteed seats." He didn't move. "Sir, I don't know how many tickets I will need by June."

★　　★　　★

Not being a football fan, I decided long ago that I would watch the Super Bowl every year simply to cheer for entertaining commercials. Do you know what commercial holds the all-time record in online polls for being the most watched, posted, and shared? The 2011 Volkswagen commercial with that sweet little boy dressed up as Darth Vader. We never even see his face. His huge costume helmet appears nearly half his height. As millions have seen, the little boy runs around his house with his Darth Vader cape flowing behind him. He boldly waves his hands all around the house to use the Force on things like books, his sandwich, and the family dog. Of course, nothing moves, but he is undaunted by failure. In the last scene of the commercial, he is standing outside in the driveway, aiming his little hands at the new Volkswagen. You can tell by his trembling arms that he is trying as hard as possible to conjure the Force and move the car. Unseen by viewers or the little boy, the father pushes the remote ignition button to start up the lights and engine of the car. The boy jumps back from the humming engine and looks proudly at his hands. Viewers then see his father's hand holding the remote. As his parents watch the little boy from the kitchen window, the father winks at his wife. The little boy turns toward the house to see if anyone had witnessed his supernatural power. For the last few seconds of the commercial, we witness his delight. He knew the Force was real.

The first *Star Wars* movie came out in 1977. That's forty years ago. One of the most popular contemporary commercials of all time is based on a story that is forty years old. And for the record, there is no talking in the commercial. No one tells you who the child is trying to be. No one tells you why he raises his hands and waves them at a sandwich or the dog. No one has to tell you. We all know who he is trying to be, and we all know he is trying to use the Force. Though it has been decades since the film was released, can you honestly imagine anyone in America asking you, "Who is Darth Vader?"

The fact is that Americans are still completely culturally fluent in *Star Wars* messages and meanings forty years after its release. Even the sight of a supporting character from the original narrative needs no explanation at all. And how could we not be so familiar with this story? Since 1977, the masterful marketing and liberal licensing of the *Star Wars* brand has given the world enough *Star Wars* Legos, toys, Happy Meals, and countless other movie-themed products to gross over $5 billion for the franchise. The narrative kingdom created by George Lucas continues to be a vernacular for all ages in this country.

By comparison, in just the first few years since the last movie was released, Harry Potter has already grossed nearly $20 billion. And what's stunning about that fact is that unlike many other movie franchises, J. K. Rowling has licensed only two or three manufacturers to make products or promote her epic story. Despite one of the most limited licensing habits of any brand in modern times, over eight hundred thousand copies of the books have been sold so far. The last installment of the series, *The Deathly Hallows,* sold over fifteen million copies within the first twenty-four hours of its release, making it the fastest-selling book of all time. After forty years, the *Star Wars* saga is still a near universal grammar of characters and ideas for appropriation and new adaptations in our time. This is strong evidence for the thesis that forty years from now, Super Bowl commercials will still have a cute kid, but he'll have a wand, not a mask. And thanks to J. K. Rowling, it will probably be a girl.

The metrics of *Star Wars* argue, but also help us understand, that we are only at the beginning of the coming decades of cultural impact of the Harry Potter stories. But is Rowling's series relevant only to those who want to share and teach their faith because the stories are so popular, enjoyable, or inspiring? Are they meaningful to people of faith only because they carry theological meaning in the symbols and plot lines? Perhaps to this point, you feel that my agenda is simply to help you understand the Christian themes or use passages of the book to share your faith. Those goals are certainly part of my project. But in this chapter, I want to explore another dimension of Harry Potter. I want to suggest something more specific that can happen to you when you read Harry Potter. These stories are not just useful; they are also potentially transformative for your own faith.

In my personal experience, something Rowling wrote about in the series actually and precisely explained something that happened to me in a way I had never (and would never have) thought. A spell she invented actually functioned in my life in more or less the same way as it functioned in the novels. I found words and meaning in Harry Potter that brought new and life-changing levels of faith, maturity, and understanding of God into my life. I believe in my heart that certain convictions and practices in these stories can explain some of our own lived experiences in new and exciting ways. Said simply, some of Rowling's suggestions for life, love, and faith found in her theological fiction actually *work.*

A spell taught and practiced in Harry Potter helped explain to me how I experienced and survived one of the most mysterious, terrifying, and impactful moments in my life. I remember exactly where I was when I first read the passages about a certain spell in the *Prisoner of Azkaban*. Instantly, an intense memory from when I was eighteen flooded into my mind. It was an incident I had not thought much about since it happened. I put down my copy of *Prisoner* for a few moments and moved slowly and studiously through the memory as if it were a one-scene museum. I whispered out loud to myself, "So that's what happened in that hospital room."

★   ★   ★

My older sister had always struck me as a normal teenager: smart, funny, very social, and passionate about boys, her looks, and the rock band posters hanging in her room. As far as we know, she did a little bit of drinking and smoking in middle school and even more in high school, eventually adding drugs and tattooed boyfriends on motorcycles to the mix. She fought with my parents often. As she approached the end of high school, her relationship with the family was strained. Often we all seemed to be in her way. She never lost her witty intelligence or her deep love for my brother and me. She was twelve years old when my brother was born, fourteen at my birth. In our presence, she was often distracted by her own identity development but never so much as to forget our birthdays, our wonder at Christmas, and our endless childlike questions about her school and social life. Though constantly at war with my parents for freedom to discover (they would say, endanger) her life, she was a loving older sister.

Though she finished high school and held out hope for a more stable young adult life, her drinking problems persisted. One night she drank and drove and was killed in a car accident a few miles from our home. I was eight years old. My young parents were in their forties. We lived in a small town with one school and one Catholic church. More than a thousand people signed the guestbook. Who knows how many more came to the wake and funeral. Her death broke something foundational in each of us. And each member of our family navigated that permanent fault line differently as the years of grief unfolded for the four of us remaining at the dinner table.

I related immediately to Harry Potter as he first walked the streets of Diagon Alley with Hagrid. Similarly to his experience, the death of my young adult sister in a small town marked me as the kid people knew things about before I knew their names. As I grew up, I was reminded year after year that everyone around me seemed to know that my sister had died in a car accident. Every town has its stories of lives lost too young from drinking and driving. My sister was my town's tragic local lore.

When you lose a child, you feel as though you won't ever heal. And some people don't. It took my mother years to put her life back together, but she did. My father never recovered. By the time I started middle school, the combination of his alcoholism and unspeakable grief started to take a noticeable toll on his health. He was sicker and sicker every year. The man who had been a heroic and herculean sergeant in the Marine Corps during the Korean War started to waste away in front of our eyes. By the time I started high school, doctors were already speaking of his compounding health problems as terminal. I never paid much attention to the particular diagnosis of the day. It was clear to me even as a child that my sister's death was just too sad for him. Drinking was his only means to get through the emotions of each day. He slowly stopped working and spent more time in and out of the hospital. We did not have any medical insurance, so he spent his hospital time in a crowded Veterans Administration hospital in New York City. I would drive there before or after school, always showing up to tell him stories about my high school life. Whether he was at home or in the hospital, I brought him every medal won, every test with a high grade written on it, every photo of a moment of triumph. Whatever his known and mysterious infirmities were, they eventually struck his brain, and more than once I sat with him in his hospital bed while he did not know who I was or who he was. He would grab the edge of the bed tightly, thinking he was on a roof or bridge. I would laugh to try to reorient him. I made a habit of doing my homework in the hallways at school at sunrise, because evenings at home or the hospital were never a good time to think about high school.

After pouring out that exact story to the principal, I ended by saying to his pale white face strewn with more than one tear, "I don't know how many tickets to order for graduation, Sir, because I do not think my father will live to graduation. I have been living with his dying from my sister's death for years. I don't even know how this will turn out, but I know this: I cannot sit in a class right now and read a book about a family dragging their dead father around in a truck. I don't want anything else from you or anyone else at school, and I am not going to talk about any of this again. I can handle my family. I cannot handle reading about it with my friends."

The principal did not move. We had known each other since I was twelve years old. We had driven to local and regional conferences and panel discussions to represent the school. I knew his favorite flavor of ice cream. He knew my birthday was in January. He wiped his face, cleared his throat, and said something like "You may skip this book. I will tell your English teacher. Don't think about it anymore. We have a school counselor if you want to talk more." I can't remember his mouth moving for those words. He appeared frozen. Finally he stood up and walked toward me, but I jumped up first and walked away from him toward the door. I had somehow managed to get through this meeting, and get through middle and high school, without crying, and there was no way I was going to let the hug I longed for crush my control. I opened the door myself and threw the words "Thank you" over my shoulder.

★   ★   ★

Dementors are perhaps one of the great character creations in recent literary fiction, or so say countless book reviewers of Rowling's series. These deathly creatures were born in Rowling's imagination and embody for her the depression that nearly took her life more than once. Rowling has been open about her bouts with depression, sharing with the world that she seriously contemplated suicide more than once as a teenager and young adult. Dementors are not essential to the plot line of the story. I believe Harry Potter would be just as popular today without the role of dementors in the narrative. But for Rowling, these hideous creatures were essential to Harry Potter because she believes that there are dementors in real life. The definition of a dementor given in the books is chilling, as is the reality of depression in human life:

> Dementors are among the foulest creatures that walk this earth. They infest the darkest, filthiest places, they glory in decay and despair, they drain peace, hope, and happiness out of the air around them. . . . Get too near a dementor and every good feeling, every happy memory will be sucked out of you. If it can, the dementor will feed on you long enough to reduce you to something like itself . . . soulless and evil. You will be left with nothing but the worst experiences of your life.[1]

Dementors reek with the presence and the stench of death. Even from a young age, we all know what it feels like to stand in the presence of death—death in all its forms of disease, divorce, betrayal, loss, injury, or abandonment. We all have our own dementors that "drain peace, hope, and happiness" out of your soul. I met my first gang of darting and swooping dementors the day I watched two state troopers reverently remove their stiff patrol hats and speak the brief rehearsed words to my parents that their daughter had died driving her car the night before. On and off in the years that followed, I would feel the chilling and moaning winds of death, whispering or at times howling through my heart and soul. Part of the genius of Rowling's characterization of death is that dementors represent more than physical death. They are beacons of death that haunt and hunt human happiness. The question is not whether a person has dementors in their life. The only question is how often.

Once we admit that there are real and ravaging dementors in our lives and we are unable to dodge or defeat them, the promise and power of the Patronus Charm comes as a means and miracle of grace. We learn from Professor Lupin that there is a spell to repel these faceless figures of death. I was mesmerized to the point of holding my breath the first time I watched the scene in the film where Lupin leads Harry in a private lesson in the Patronus Charm. For any reader with real dementors in their life, this sacred scene about how to conjure a Patronus Charm feels like a hand from heaven is reaching down to pull you out of a deep and dark hole. Dementors are too real in lived experience for readers not to be deeply moved at the possibility of a defense against them, no matter that the method of defense is something like a spell found in a fictional narrative. You have dementors, we all do, and the stakes couldn't be higher in the scene with Lupin: can Harry (or you) learn a way to resist and restrain dementors?

For all of us, the Patronus Charm is the spell to fight death, and learning it might be one of the most important real-life skills we can muster and master. I believe in the Patronus Charm in real life because I used it and it worked. And I believe that the Christian faith trains the church in the Patronus Charm at every Eucharist, though we do not use explicit Harry Potter language.

My father did live to see my high school graduation. He even lived a few months past it, all the way to my first month at college. That October, I traveled home to visit him for a day and talked all about my freshman year. He was going deaf, among other signs of impending death. I had the last conversation I ever had with him, telling him about my roommates, a History of Jazz class I was taking, and how college was expensive but worth every student loan. I drove the fifteen minutes back to my house from the hospital, only to see my mother waiting for me on the porch. I knew when I saw her standing silently in vigil for my return that he had died. The nurses said he had passed away minutes after I left. He was buried in the same grave as my sister. Interestingly, they shared the same birthday. There is such truth hidden in the dates carved on that grave. The stone lists the same day for their births. Then it states the day she died. I ignore the date listed for his death because I will always think of her death date as a shared day for their deaths, for her death was definitely the same day something died in my father. That real death in his heart took a decade to take life slowly from the rest of his body.

My mother got into my car because we had to go back to the hospital to fill out forms and begin the bureaucracy of death. She found a stoic calm in those first minutes and hours; she was a machine of manners, making sense of what people were saying. I was in a trance, trying to make sense of the experience of talking to my father thirty minutes prior to being told he was dead. I felt dizzy and wobbly as we walked the noisy hospital halls. My mother stood at the nurses' station filling out forms, and I walked back toward the room where my father had been. I just had to go back to that place and see the empty bed to help me accept what had happened. I walked in unprepared for the reality of the room. He was still there. As is often the case in VA hospitals, necessary processes are not always accomplished as quickly or cleanly as in private hospitals. So there he was, mouth open, eyes open, hands hanging off the bed. The television was still on, his uneaten dinner still on the tray up to his face. The only thing different from an hour before was that he was dead. Nothing in the room helped me comprehend the change. I couldn't move. Breathing was hard. My head started to pound. My arms felt pulled downward. My fingers wouldn't bend. My feet felt stuck to the ground. I wanted to scream something but didn't know what word to choose.

That moment in the presence of my dead father—at first the most terrifying and sad moment of my life—bloomed almost immediately into the most graceful and spiritual moment of my life to this day. I remember clearly that I put my head down and started to speak. I felt oddly like a passive witness to my own actions, as if the words were coming without my choosing them. In that moment and presence of death, with every dementor I had ever fought and a dozen more filling that tired hospital room so tight with despair that I couldn't breathe, I closed my eyes as if to die from the darkness. But then I recognized the familiar words coming out of my mouth. The words that came have come to billions of people before me. I heard myself say, "I believe in one God, the Father Almighty, Maker of Heaven and Earth, of all that is seen and unseen."

As I spoke, I opened my eyes and finished the creed. I walked toward my father and began to put his body at peace. While repeating the creed again and again, I felt steady and sure of my role. When I had entered the room, it felt haunted. In speaking the creed, it felt holy. I closed his mouth and eyes and held his cold hands until they felt warm in mine. I thanked God for that body that carried the soul of a man who loved his family with all his broken heart. At some point, I felt he was at peace. And so was I. I scanned the room as I left, feeling that it had somehow gotten bigger and lighter, and even seemed cleaner and more loved. Yes, even the walls and old windows seemed less worn and more warm. Something had radiated from the words, and the peace and power of them grew to fill the room so completely that I was able to leave only because the light and life spreading pushed me out. I walked past the heavy door to the room, which at that moment looked like a stone rolled away.

Professor Lupin said the Patronus Charm is conjured only when a person recalls a memory of profound power and love. Unlike other spells, the Patronus power comes not from the wand or words, but from the memory of the wizard. The memory must be strong and must be held with focus and discipline. Then and only then will the Patronus radiate from the wand and repel the dementor. We are as powerful as our ability to recall realities of love. And the most powerful form of love in the Harry Potter series, and in the epic stories of our own lives, is the power of sacrificial love. Once Harry grasps a vision of the love of Lily and James, who gave their lives for him, he is able to push back against the invading forces of death. You cannot kill dementors because there is no life in them. They are, in this way, a perfect example of death to the Christian. Death has been defeated in Christ's resurrection. Death has lost its sting. And yet, on earth we live in the reality of the "already and not yet" power of resurrection. Death may have lost its sting, but it has not lost its stench and clench on our lives.

What is the Patronus Charm to me? In that hospital room, it was the creed. In my daily life, it is the Eucharistic Prayer. Millions of altars in the world have the same words carved into them in hundreds of languages over centuries: "Do this in remembrance of Me." Our tradition is one of remembering an act of sacrificial love and focusing on that memory to push back the haunting and hunting forces of death in our lives. The Eucharistic Prayers of many different denominations begin as a memory: "On the night he was betrayed . . ."

I did not learn the Patronus Charm from reading Harry Potter. I recognized the Patronus Charm in Harry Potter because the Christian faith works very much like the Patronus Charm. In liturgy, we gather together and recite our shared memory of sacrificial love on our behalf. And in that moment, grace and power radiate from the altar and into the world, pushing back all that would suck the "peace, hope, and happiness out of the air."

When I first read the words of Remus Lupin about what the Patronus Charm is and what it does, my soul sang the words, "That's what happened in that hospital room." The memory of the love of God in the creed came to my rescue when I focused on it. And the love I remembered arrived in me and filled me with strength. The forces and faces of death I was battling lost their grip. I now wouldn't dare to teach the creed or the Eucharistic Prayers without calling them my faith's Patronus Charm. And if critics attack me for calling our deepest liturgical language by the name of a charm from Harry Potter, I will offer the only defense I've experienced: the Patronus Charm works.

NOTES

1. J. K. Rowling, *Harry Potter and the Prisoner of Azkaban* (New York: Scholastic, 1999), 187.

CHAPTER FIVE

Peace by Piece

Wholeness and Holiness in Harry Potter

The first time I read through all seven books of the series, I did not notice how many things get broken in the 1,084,170 words of the Harry Potter narrative. In your next reread of the books, take note of the remarkable number of times you read about something that is or was once broken. Once you start looking for broken things, you'll notice that every book presents the reader with something broken as early as the first or second chapter, as well as throughout each book. Even if your category is as narrow as "broken wands," you have a long list including Hagrid, Ron, Draco, Lucius, Umbridge, Neville, Voldemort, and, among others, Harry. Voldemort's wand breaks early in the first book (and this is only the first time he breaks a wand) in the killing curse that scars Harry in *The Philosopher's Stone*.

At the very beginning of the series, one of the first facts we learn about Harry is that he has frequently broken glasses, a sign of his rejection and being bullied at home. The first successful spell cast in the four-thousand-plus-page spell-casting saga is "*Reparo*," spoken by Hermione as she heals Harry's glasses in their first meeting. Another foundational friendship sealed with an act of repair is when Harry's nose is broken at the beginning of *The Order of the Phoenix* and Luna Lovegood's spell heals the broken bone. The second year at Hogwarts begins in *The Chamber of Secrets* with Ron and Harry unlawfully arriving at school by soaring out of the sky in a Ford Anglia that crashes into a tree. Unbelievably, the weaponized vehicle doesn't break the tree, but instead, the Whomping Willow proves itself as the sturdiest but crankiest of characters at Hogwarts for breaking Ron's wand. Despite the immediate sense of tragedy for Ron, whose family can barely afford his textbooks in any given year, much less a second wand for their sixth child, we learn later that if Ron's wand had not been broken,

Lockhart would have been able to destroy Ron's and Harry's memories forever. In this fact, we learn early in the series that fixing something broken as quickly as possible, though it is our nature to seek such quick fixes, does not always bring about the best outcome.

Some Harry Potter friends and I have an ever-growing list of things that break in the series, and we have over a hundred things so far. Our list is so long we have separated it into categories, such as material things that break, material things that were broken before or after the seven books, immaterial things broken (such as family bonds, promises, vows, hearts, or trust), and flesh that is broken (injuries). This informal group project to track the brokenness in Harry Potter reveals that there are too many things that break in this narrative not to think that Rowling is writing some of her convictions about brokenness and wholeness in human life into the story. And in the unlikely case that Rowling did not intend to focus on brokenness, we readers are nonetheless free to make our own meaning out of the undeniable ubiquity of things coming apart and (some) being repaired in the story. We are left with profound questions. In Harry Potter, is brokenness the opposite of wholeness or the means to become whole? Is brokenness or wholeness the path to holiness? Are wands or human lives ultimately weaker or stronger if they are broken? In the end, is it magic that repairs brokenness, or is it human hope in healing that repairs and restores material or spiritual breaks?

The Fraction

For the follower of Jesus, finding our own answers to questions about the relationship among brokenness, wholeness, and holiness is central to understanding and experiencing what happens to the world and to us in every Eucharist. At the core of this ancient sacrament, we celebrate a moment called the Fraction—that moment and action in the Eucharist when the bread is willfully broken at the altar to represent the willful sacrifice of Christ's own body, broken in solidarity with human brokenness and in sacrifice for the redemption of creation. The questions about the meaning of brokenness and wholeness stirred by the Fraction are similar to the questions in Harry Potter concerning things that break. Is the breaking of bread on the altar a symbol of the brokenness of humanity, or is it instead a symbol of how humanity is healed? Is the bread broken to symbolize its frailty or its strength? Can bread or a person be both broken and holy?

I don't know exactly what is happening at the Fraction, but considering some of the possible meanings of brokenness and wholeness found in

Harry Potter helps me consider new dimensions of what it means when I offer communion bread to someone and say, "The body of Christ, the bread of heaven." What I do know is that Mark's Gospel, arguably the earliest, puts the words of the Eucharistic Prayer this way: "While they were eating, he took a loaf of bread, and after blessing it, he broke it, gave it to them, and said, 'Take; this is my body'" (Mark 14:22). Notions of breaking in Harry Potter may not explain what the breaking of the bread at the altar means, but its deep and diverse characterization and conceptualization of brokenness and wholeness can lead you to deeper curiosity and conversion in your experience of the Eucharist.

The truth is that there are varied and even competing notions in the series about what breaks, why, and what can or should be repaired. At times, spells can fix what's broken. In the case of certain kinds of dark magic, such as the curse on Dumbledore's hand or the curse that strikes George's ear, magic cannot mend. Harry's broom cannot be mended, but his wand eventually is repaired. Is there a unified message about what it means to be broken or whole in Harry Potter? Despite apparently different destinies of things broken and fixed, I argue that there is a unified message about what is holy about breaking and mending. Is there a unified message in Christianity about what it means to be broken or whole? I believe there is and that we witness these convictions about brokenness and holiness in the breaking of the bread at the altar. For this reason, folks who want to share and form faith ought to pay attention to what breaks and what mends in Harry Potter. Because the series offers priceless images and characters to help readers understand the symbols in the Eucharist that are vessels and vehicles for the transformative power of the sacrament. Thinking about brokenness and wholeness in Harry Potter can make you better at understanding and experiencing the Eucharist.

Rowling's lived experience and convictions about brokenness and wholeness are buried at the core of the Harry Potter series. My metaphor for how deeply her Christian faith is buried at the core of the stories comes from Rowling herself. She intentionally names the nature of the core of every wand. A wand is not broken beyond repair until its core is broken, an unseen string or feather running through every wooden wand. Only in breaking a wand does one learn the identity of its core. Likewise, theology runs through every chapter of Rowling's seven-book meditation on death and resurrection. When we peel back the prose, inside the wisely whittled words we see her faith convictions holding all things together.

Many things that break in the series remain broken. But just when you think that general rule is law—that some forms of destruction are permanent—*The Deathly Hallows* closes with the complete restoration of Harry's original and completely broken wand. It is too simplistic a reading to say that the Elder Wand fixed Harry's wand and therefore things broken in this narrative are meant to be fixed, that brokenness is a problem to be solved, or that wholeness means undoing brokenness. I do not believe this is the message of Harry's wand or Rowling's message about the universal plight and destiny of things broken. Instead, I believe Harry's wand is healed not by another wand's power, but because Harry himself is made whole by his hope in healing and welcoming of death. We know the Elder Wand obeyed Harry. And we know Harry carried his broken wand pieces on his chest, never giving up hope that somehow the pieces could be made whole.

In Rowling's theology, wands, like people, are never beyond restoration. Harry verbalizes her boundless belief in redemption when, in his last battle with Voldemort, he pauses in the duel to ask, one more time, if Voldemort wants to show remorse. To the last minute, Harry believes that nothing broken at the core of Voldemort's soul is broken beyond redemption. His hope for Voldemort is as bold and audacious as his hope for his wand. Against experience, Harry practices the love described by Paul in 1 Corinthians 13:7. Harry "bears all things, believes all things, hopes all things, endures all things" for redemption. The message is that hope is stronger than magic and can command magic to do its will. (This notion of the human will as more powerful than magic in Harry Potter is most obviously depicted in the ability of students to choose against the Sorting Hat's discernment of House placement.) So the first message about brokenness in Harry Potter that is consistent and hopeful throughout the narrative is that nothing broken is beyond restoration. But is it necessary to be broken to experience wholeness?

To answer this question for the Harry Potter stories, it is helpful to consider the Eucharist. Why do we break the bread at the altar? Two dimensions of meaning symbolized in the Fraction are (1) the bread is broken as an act of remembrance for the way Jesus took bread and broke it at the Last Supper; and (2) the bread is broken as a sign that God enters our brokenness and then God's life goes out in pieces into the people and to the world. Breaking the bread allows it to be shared and build one body among the many who partake. Without the bread breaking, there would be no possibility for sharing and incorporating others into the bread that is the body of Christ. Broken bread is a sign not of frailty, but of incarnation: God breaking into the human condition and bringing into it resurrected life. Broken bread is not a problem to be solved by grace, but a doorway through which the grace of God enters the bread and the lives of those who share that bread. We are not far from God when our lives break. Rather, in our brokenness, we experience God's grace in more penetrating and transformative ways.

The Bread of Life

Christians believe that it is part of human life to experience brokenness. As we watch the bread breaking in the sacred ritual of the Eucharist, we are watching the truth of our lives happen in a sacrament: that we bend, crack, and break apart. But this is precisely the moment when Christians believe that the presence of Christ breaks through the bread that is broken and begins to radiate into the world. Though there has been a turn in modern liturgical practice to separate the Fraction from the sanctification of the bread and wine, in the ancient church the bread was broken immediately following the consecration, symbolizing the notion that the sound of the crack itself heralds the incarnation into bread and life. This Bread of Life then proceeds in pieces from the altar to the assembly. The pieces plant the presence of God in the people. If a seed does not break, it bears no fruit. If the bread does not break, it forms no body. The bread whole on the altar goes nowhere. The bread broken can go forth into the people, who go forth into the world. But this is not just a meal. In sharing the Bread of Life, the assembly becomes, again and again, the body of Christ on earth. The gathered leave changed. In the words of Paul to the Galatians, "It is no longer I who live but Christ who lives in me. The life I live in the body I live by faith in the Son of God, who loved me and gave Himself for me" (Gal. 2:20). In time, all things will be part of the whole body that incarnates and radiates from the altar.

Harry's declaration in the Forbidden Forest toward the end of the story that he "is ready to die" demonstrates his choice and willingness to be broken for others. He gives up trying to stay alive in the fight against Voldemort and realizes that there is a greater good in ceasing to protect the wholeness of his own life. In breaking, he makes others whole. In embracing death, he defeats it. The same is true for the bread on the altar and for anyone who eats of it. The prayers said by the people declare the promise and power of ceasing to fight death and instead embracing it with Christ to share in his resurrection.

> Dying you destroyed our death.
> Rising you restored our life.
> Lord Jesus, come in glory.[1]

Think of Voldemort as the bread on the altar unbroken. He does not want his life broken by death. He wants to preserve it without mark or decay. His pure blood mania is just another symbol of Voldemort's idolatry for the unbroken and the unaltered (the opposite of sacraments that break in and alter human life). The tragedy of Voldemort's choices is that he is willing to break his soul to save his life from being broken. Harry is willing to break his life to save others from being broken. At the Fraction, we commemorate and celebrate that Christ allowed his body to be broken in solidarity with human brokenness, bringing his resurrection into our bodies through him. We break the bread as a symbol that in brokenness, weakness, and imperfection, God breaks through. The radical claim of Rowling's own Christianity present and persistent in Harry Potter is that brokenness is not a problem to be solved, but a means by which transformation enters the human experience. If Voldemort is the bread unbroken, petrified by fear of death, then Harry is the bread after the Fraction: the person embracing the break of death and, in so doing, finding life after death in Christ and sharing that life in the communion of others. If we stood at the altar and held the bread perpetually unbroken, it would be a mere veneration of perfection or act of idolatry. But as the bread breaks, its power is released to go forth from the altar. Christ's abundant life is made manifest and multiplied.

There is a clear and beautiful depiction of what happens in the breaking of bread found in the biblical story of what took place on the road to Emmaus. In this story, two men flee from Jerusalem only hours after the death and resurrection of Jesus. They are scared and confused at the death and disappearance of the slaughtered leader and Lord. They come upon Jesus on the road but do not recognize him. Jesus begins to teach them how to interpret and reconcile the recent events and the prophesies of their faith. They are amazed at his wisdom and moved by his presence. They ask him to eat dinner with them. Jesus agrees to sit with them for the meal.

> When he was at the table with them, he took bread, blessed and broke it, and gave it to them. Then their eyes were opened, and they recognized him; and he vanished from their sight. They said to each other, "Were not our hearts burning within us while he was talking to us on the road, while he was opening the scriptures to us?"[2]

One interpretation of the story is a literal one: Jesus "vanished from their sight." He was there and then was gone. But in truth, this is a story about Christ's presence continuing because the bread is broken, not his absence once the bread breaks. He may have "vanished from their sight," but his presence enters and abides in the bread broken. The physical body they saw can leave their presence (and in coming days of the gospel narrative will leave the world) because the body of Christ enters and remains in the bread broken. Before the bread was broken, they did not recognize him. It was not *until* the bread was broken that the men and the world could recognize and commune with Christ. The talking before the meal was the invitation. Sharing the bread broken was the transformation.

It is through breaking the bread—indeed, it is through being broken in life—that we recognize Christ and can follow him through brokenness into wholeness, through death into life. The reason it is significant that Harry carries a broken wand, a broken mirror, a pregnant Snitch, half a letter, and a ripped picture is that these are all symbols of the fragility of goodness, the hidden grace in discarded things, and the brokenness in the human condition. All those objects are surrounded in love, but human love is ultimately not a protection against fracture or death. But Harry carries the pieces in the hope that one day, he and those objects might experience transformation. He does not give up on what is broken. Nor, in the end, does he refuse to become broken himself. By the end of the saga, he has learned to trust Dumbledore and "choose what is right over what is easy."[3]

Snape never fully accepts the truth, freedom, and good news we ritualize in the Fraction. He asks Dumbledore, "So the boy . . . the boy must die?" Dumbledore answers, "And Voldemort himself must do it, Severus."[4] Dumbledore has discerned and decided that only Voldemort can strike Harry with the death curse and perhaps destroy the Horcrux but not kill him. Dumbledore comes to believe that those two souls share Lily's sacrificial blood. Therefore, Harry and Voldemort both share, though to differing degrees, in its protection. Harry's only hope to live through the killing curse is if that curse is cast by the one who, through the power of shared bloodshed in sacrificial love, cannot ever kill him. In many ways, Snape has never accepted his childhood break with Lily. He carries that break like an albatross of loss, unlike Harry's moleskin pouch of hope. Snape's inability to accept the death of that relationship, and eventually the physical death of Lily, locked him into a prison of mourning, walled off from the transformation that comes when we seek resurrection in our suffering and grief.

The theologian Richard Rohr once wrote, "If we do not transform our pain, we will most assuredly transmit it."[5] Snape menaced children for years as he transferred his grief to others. Snape's heart was broken, which was a moment of potential transformation, incarnation, and path for wholeness through brokenness. But instead, he chose to idolize the broken pieces of his love and cling to the past instead of realize the potential to spread his love to others. Snape could have shared his love for Lily with the world after her death; he could have chosen to die to the notion that his love had only one subject. He loved the dead more than the living. This love for Lily was enough to stir loyalty and even acts of heroic bravery in Snape. But ultimately his unredeemed love for Lily was not enough to start or stir joy and liberation. The angel at the empty tomb whispers throughout Snape's tragic life, "Why do you look for the living among the dead? He is not here, He is risen" (Luke 24:5). Snape chose to stay and to live at the grave. Harry followed the invitation to resurrection found in a Bible verse, and it led him out of the Godric's Hollow graveyard.

One of the reasons reading Harry Potter is good for faith formation is precisely that Rowling is wrestling directly with questions of faith throughout the narrative. According to Rowling, "To me [the religious parallels in the books have] always been obvious. But I never wanted to talk too openly about it because I thought it might show people who just wanted the story where we were going." She described her own faith by saying, "The truth is that, like Graham Greene, my faith is sometimes that my faith will return. It's something I struggle with a lot."[6] Page after page, the plot is peppered with her own doubts and convictions. But in the final book, Rowling's Christian convictions come out of the shadows.

Toward the end of *The Deathly Hallows*, Harry and Hermione investigate the church in Godric's Hollow, hoping to find the gravestone of his parents. They first encounter Dumbledore's family gravestone. On it they find a Bible verse from the Gospel of Matthew: "Where your treasure is, there will your heart be also" (6:21). Moments later, Harry sees the grave of his parents. Carved into the stone below the names of Lily and James Potter, Harry finds a quotation from the New Testament: "The last enemy that shall be destroyed is death" (1 Cor. 15:26). At first Harry is alarmed, thinking that the desire to defeat death is the driving force of Death Eaters, not members of the Order of the Phoenix like his brave parents. We cannot underestimate the importance of this conversation in general and Harry's alarm at the Matthew passage in particular. The fact that Rowling takes the time to describe Harry as upset at the misreading of the Bible verse, and then also takes the time to write a thoughtful answer from Hermione, turns this passage from a scene into a sermon. Hermione answers Harry's confusion and, in so doing, clarifies and codifies Rowling's own convictions about life, death, and resurrection to the reader.

The passage beautifully paints the picture of Harry finding the grave and having to digest the Bible verses in that raw emotional moment. Notice how Rowling brings the climaxing pace of the novel at this Godric's Hollow moment—as Harry and Hermione are trying to close in on the search for the sword and the Horcruxes—to a halt. Clearly, Rowling wants the reader to pause and think about the writing on the gravestone. She writes, "Harry read the words slowly, as though he would only have one chance to take in their meaning, and he read the last of them aloud."[7] The reader should rightly feel tugged to stand next to Harry in the dark, snowy churchyard and engage with the biblical claim. Harry reads aloud:

> "The last enemy to be destroyed is death' . . ." A horrible thought came to him, and with it a kind of panic. "Isn't that a Death Eater idea? Why is that there?"
>
> "It doesn't mean defeating death in the way that the Death Eaters mean it, Harry," said Hermione, her voice gentle. "It means . . . you know . . . living beyond death. Living after death."[8]

Hermione and Rowling's answer to Harry may come in a gentle voice, but the conviction for the resurrection that is the death of death comes across loud and strong.

We don't have to guess how important these biblical ideas are for Rowling. In an interview after the publication of the last book, Rowling declared, "I think those two particular quotations he finds on the tombstones at Godric's Hollow, they sum up—they almost epitomize the whole series."[9] Augustine once wrote of the relationship between the Old Testament and the New Testament, "The new is in the old concealed; the old is in the new revealed."[10] Rowling's foundational faith in resurrection, which was the silent song of the saga from the beginning of the first book, reveals itself in this graveyard scene as Harry reads the verse out loud. At last in the series, Rowling gives words and weight to her belief in death's defeat through resurrection. She waited seven novels to obey the words of 1 Peter 3:15: to "Always be ready to make your defense to anyone who demands from you an accounting for the hope that is in you."

Into the Looking Glass

The Mirror of Erised is the magical object that identifies a person's greatest longing. It shows us not what we are, but what we long to be, thereby forcing the one who gazes to acknowledge a breach between reality and the image. The human condition leaves us all broken, but the mirror shows us images of repair and restoration. Harry sees his lost parents and is forced to face openly in the mirror the grief he holds secretly in his heart. Ron sees himself as an accomplished, celebrated, and significant person in a family whose members have largely ignored his potential. Dumbledore sees the lives lost in his own tragic story. The Mirror of Erised shows more than desire—it forces us to see our brokenness.

If we think about it, the whole Harry Potter series functions like a Mirror of Erised. In this story, hundreds of millions of readers have seen in the plot and characters countless possibilities and hopes for their own lives. We see the maturation of Neville from bullied kid to leader and teacher of others. We see Luna, marginal and isolated, developing friends (as the mural in her room declares) and coming into the center of power in Dumbledore's Army. We see a sense of self grow in Molly, who eventually overcomes her terror for her family's welfare, in the end letting go of her children to enter the battle and fight with them, even killing the skilled witch Bellatrix Lestrange. Because the story shows us the long path these characters took to heroism, we see in these figures glimpses of our own possible glory and ways to get there. These books show us the people we could be and how we can overcome our brokenness to become these people. Just ask any of the five million members of the global Harry Potter Alliance, and they can tell you that reading these stories has given them glimpses of their own paths to wholeness and to a more just and peaceful world.

In a similar way, think of the Gospels as a Mirror of Erised. Like the Harry Potter books, each chapter of the Gospel narratives gives us characters who are broken in some way. We watch them eventually find wholeness in the presence and power of Jesus. Reading the Gospels is an experience of seeing the person we could be and how we might get there from here.

But, some might say, there are so many who are not healed in the stories of Jesus's healing and restoration. Why are there only a few miracles? Why only one sick child or one bleeding woman and not stories of Christ healing an entire city or nation? You cannot teach faith, especially to young people or people of any age who have endured serious suffering, and not hear the question "But where is my miracle?" These are not people who do not believe in miracles; these are people who want to know why there are not more miracles in the Scriptures and in contemporary life. Why does Jesus heal the bleeding woman but no one else among the crowd? Surely there were others with afflictions that day. If we want to say that the Gospels offer the reader or listener images of hope and promises of healing, restoration, and resurrection, then how do we handle the apparent randomness and disparity of Christ's healing ministry in the Scriptures and in daily life?

This is why it is helpful to think and to teach the New Testament like a Mirror of Erised. By using this creation of Rowling's, we can present Scripture as showing truths in images but not offering a literal reflection of the person. The Mirror of Erised shows the cracks and longings of the person looking; its power is to take the person's longing and put that truth into an image of fulfillment. The power of the New Testament, though historical in nature and genre, is that it can function like the Mirror of Erised and make us face our longings. The narratives give us characters and promises that speak to our imagination and invite each of us to take up the path in our own lives that leads to the images of wholeness and holiness we see achieved in the stories.

The Gospel narratives contain signs of all the dimensions of healing and transformation possible for those in the body of Christ. Some are healed in body, others in spirit, and yet others from sin. Each story depicts another image of brokenness turned into wholeness, the passages gathered into the Gospel to show us what can happen in our own experience. Miracles are signs, not mere statements of truth. The Gospels are more like a mirror than a manuscript. A manuscript speaks for itself; a mirror speaks for the viewer. We see images of possibility and can then dare to take the risk and the invitation of Jesus to come and see for ourselves what fruit is born from following Christ. It is tragic to simply gaze into the Gospels or the Harry Potter stories and passively watch possibilities pass by. Even Dumbledore warns against this kind of reading of the Gospels or the Harry Potter series when he says of mirror gazing, "It does not do to dwell on dreams and forget to live."[11]

Talk to a Harry Potter fan or a follower of Jesus and you will find that seeing the possibilities for wholeness through these texts is an experience that can transform you. You cannot unsee visions of yourself whole. This is why the Mirror of Erised is addictive. The Jesuit Volunteer Corps, an organization that supports people taking a year of their lives to serve others in foreign countries, has a priceless unofficial slogan: "ruined for life."[12] In this simple statement, the Jesuits promise that getting out of your comfort zone and experiencing solidarity with the joys and suffering of others is such a powerful experience of the Kingdom of God that you will never recover from that vision of the promised healing and wholeness for all creation in time. In the *Narnia Chronicles*, when Lucy asks the Beavers if the Christ figure Aslan is "safe," the Beavers, who have known and believed in Aslan's power for generations, look Lucy straight in the eye and declare, "Safe? Who said anything about safe? Aslan isn't safe, but He is good."[13] Like the Jesuits, the Beavers know that following Aslan is difficult and will result in feeling more of the suffering of self and others, but in that embrace of the human condition and all its brokenness, one will experience God in new ways, breaking through that which is broken and bringing the resurrection into lived experience.

There is never—in the Mirror of Erised, the Harry Potter stories, or the Gospels—a straightforward path to the image of your wholeness that you see in these stories. There is always uncertainty and risk in choosing to die to your present self and seek the wholeness imagined in Christ. When we gaze into these textual Mirrors of Erised, we catch glimpses of the completion of our baptismal life and experience what Paul describes in 1 Corinthians 13:2: "Now we see in a glass darkly, then we shall see face to face." When Harry is holding the piece of mirror from Sirius, he sees hope and wholeness only in broken and confusing images. Yet he receives enough guidance and care in the broken piece to continue on his journey to wholeness. Though we see through a glass dimly, we can still find and follow the invitation of Christ.

The challenge and the opportunity for those of us who want to share and teach our faith is to recognize that the Harry Potter stories and the Gospels are mirrors that share tantalizing images of possible wholeness to all who are broken. These stories "ruin" people for life. We need to enter into relationship and dialogue with these ruined readers and help them see the invitation in both texts to die to self, to cease to fear death, to "walk calmly into Death's welcoming arms"[14] and experience resurrection. Too often the church reads and preaches the Gospels for comfort or guidance rather than in ways that ruin the listener. Aslan is too good to be safe. We should assume that people see in the Harry Potter stories and the Gospels a potential and radical image of themselves made whole, and we have to respond with equally radical hospitality, invitation, and formation so that they can go further into the promise of their transformation in faith. Remember the game theorist Jane McGonigal's description of the epic win: "an outcome that is so extraordinarily positive, that you had no idea it was even possible until you achieved it."[15] The Harry Potter stories and the Gospels give images of epic wins for potentially anyone who gazes into them. Those who form faith will assume and speak to the shy longing in people who have caught a glimpse of their own lives resurrected. We need to teach as if talking to Seekers on their journey through death toward abundant life.

Harry's Broken Wand and Voldemort's Shattered Soul

Of all the things broken in the pages of the Harry Potter epic, the two most central to understanding Rowling's theology are Harry's broken wand and Voldemort's shattered soul. The movies do not track the story of Harry's broken wand as it is told in the books, though the films do a good job of introducing and investigating the Dark Magic of making Horcruxes with pieces of Voldemort's maimed soul. What we know about Harry's wand is that it is broken while apparating out of Bathilda Bagshot's house in Godric's Hollow. What we know about Voldemort's soul is that he is willing to shatter it with acts of murder. His intention is to separate his being into pieces spread out in the world that would all have to be destroyed in order to kill him.

To understand the intentional destruction Voldemort carries out on his own soul, let us first consider Rowling's description of the nature and relationship of the souls of Voldemort and Harry. In a 2007 documentary, Rowling discusses this pair of souls at length:

> I think we all understand what an act of evil is. And Voldemort qualifies extravagantly for acts of evil. He has killed, not out of self-defense, not to protect, not for any of the reasons that we might all be able to envisage. Most of us could envisage ourselves killing in certain extreme situations, like if people we loved were threatened or in war. He's killed cold-bloodedly, sometimes for enjoyment and for his own personal gain. I call that evil. And yes, at the end of the book you have a clash of two utterly, utterly different . . . souls: one that has been maimed and has become less than human (because to me "human" includes the capacity to love, and Voldemort has deliberately dehumanized himself) and this other, very flawed, vulnerable, damaged, and yet still fighting, still loving, still daring to love, daring to hope soul, which is Harry. And they meet and they clash and it's what happens when they clash that gives us our denouement.[16]

Think of the hearts of Voldemort and Harry as altars, and consider the radically different convictions of wholeness and brokenness practiced at these two altars. Harry carries in the moleskin pouch that hangs over his heart a few precious things of the world that he receives as gifts and holds in gratefulness and hope. More than once in teaching the Christian faith, I have introduced the concept of the soul to Harry Potter readers by saying that their souls are like their moleskin pouches hanging over their hearts.

This metaphor allows folks to playfully consider their own understanding of the soul. What gifts do they carry in it? What truths are held there? Do they experience God in that safe and private space?

What makes this moleskin pouch magical is that it is a small bag used for storing items, but no one except the owner can remove the contents. It appears small on the outside, but an enchantment allows it to have much greater carrying capacity than any Muggle pouch of comparable size. It is hard to imagine a better symbol for carrying your hopes with you as you enter adulthood. Hagrid also spent Harry's entire first year contacting members of the Order to gather photographs so that Hagrid could present a handmade album to Harry when he finished his first year. Again, Hagrid acts as the memory keeper. He does this, aptly, as the Keeper of the Keys. It is worth considering what else is in this pouch:

- the Marauder's Map;
- a shard from Sirius Black's broken two-way mirror;
- the fake Horcrux locket with R. A. B.'s note;
- the Snitch bequeathed to Harry by Dumbledore, containing the Resurrection Stone;
- a letter from his mother to Sirius Black, with part of a photo; and
- his own broken wand.

Harry's altar is full of these treasures, but in the moleskin pouch, he also stores his deepest hope. And what is the content of the hope that he has? Harry's hope is that there is perhaps something in creation that is more powerful than the brokenness that has overtaken his wand, the mirror shard from Sirius, the broken-off letter from his mother, or the ripped picture of his parents. Harry does not know how these things can be made whole, but he has been formed in faith by Dumbledore and others into a person who believes in "all that is seen and unseen," as we say in the Nicene Creed, and that there might be some unseen and undiscovered power stronger than the reality of brokenness. He hopes that somehow there is a way that he will be able to see Sirius or his parents again. The map of Hogwarts is a sign that although his daily relationship with that place has been cut off, he will always carry with him every inch of that sacred safe place. And perhaps there is someone or some spell somewhere in the world that can restore his first wand. Just as the Mirror of Erised shows us what we long for, the moleskin pouch over Harry's heart shows us what he hoped for.

Although the Horcruxes are the most meaningful and powerful objects in Voldemort's life, he does not enjoy or care for them. Voldemort only uses objects, as he uses people, to serve himself. All of Voldemort's Horcruxes were made from objects that had extreme value, in his desire to secure his position as the greatest in history, and only noteworthy items could live up to his standards and have the honor of housing a fragment of his precious soul. His original desire was to collect four items of the four founders of Hogwarts; he found only three and gave up after failing to find another, but he made Horcruxes out of other items that had sentimental value to him, if not as a priceless artifact of the wizarding world. Believing the number seven to be the most powerful, Voldemort intended to split his soul into seven pieces, with six Horcruxes housing one fragment each and his main body the seventh. He hid these Horcruxes in special locations and kept their existence and purposes from absolutely everyone.

Dumbledore explains to Harry that great damage is done to the soul in this process. In fact, according to Dumbledore, the reason Voldemort's body was destroyed when he killed the Potters and tried to kill Harry was that it had become so unstable from the process of shattering multiple times. Voldemort does not hope in any power that can bring his soul's pieces back together, but rather he seeks passionately to keep them apart forever. Oddly, his desire to escape death makes his own body weaker, as the pieces of a soul are never as strong as a soul that remains whole. His mission is for his soul to remain broken. Like Harry's treasures, these objects that are priceless to Voldemort represent ancestors or even family members, but unlike the meaningful treasures in Harry's pouch, Voldemort does not see his cherished objects as a means to know and love those to whom they belonged. All of Harry's items in the pouch were gifts; all of Voldemort's cherished objects were stolen. He does not seek to reconcile with the owners of those objects, as does Harry, nor does Voldemort carry these objects with him with gratefulness or care; rather, he scatters them in dark, hidden places full of protective and destructive dark magic. Whereas Harry believes there are powers and realities that might reunite him with the owners and givers of his gifts, Voldemort does not believe in any power beyond the power needed to avoid death. As Voldemort says to Harry, "There is no good and evil, there is only power, and those too weak to seek it."[17] Harry's heart hopes for healing; Voldemort's heart is driven to escape death.

Many wands break in the seven-book series, but Harry responds to the breaking of his wand in a unique way. He carries the pieces of his broken wand in a pouch around his neck from the moment the wand breaks to the last chapter of the final novel. The pouch was a gift from Hagrid on his seventeenth birthday, another sign that coming of age is the time to gather the lessons and hopes and wisdom of childhood and carry them into the new stage of adulthood. Hagrid said, "Moleskin. Hide anythin' in there an' no one but the owner can get it out. They're rare, them." Harry responded, "Hagrid, thanks!"[18]

When you think about it, Hagrid is the perfect person to give Harry a way to carry his pieces and his hope. Hagrid's life is a study in things broken and things mended. The overt symbol of the message about brokenness in the character of Hagrid is that his wand was broken as a student at Hogwarts in punishment for expulsion. His wand is never fixed, but as a sign of hope and perseverance, Hagrid finds a way to use his wand at crucial moments in the story. It is broken, but not beyond power. Hagrid's life was broken when he was banished from the education of a wizard, but his life was not broken beyond power. Dumbledore brings Hagrid back into the community that expelled him, turning Hagrid's story into one of repair and renewal. Think of the symbolic power of Dumbledore's actions. Do not miss the heavy hand of belief in restoration and resurrection leveraged by Rowling in this fact: Hagrid goes from being expelled from Hogwarts to being its Keeper of the Keys. This is a stunning example of Rowling's commitment to portraying the power of hope and healing for all things and all lives broken.

Peace by Piece

At the risk of my sounding unaware of or ungrateful for the meaning and miracle of my ordination as an Episcopal priest, it was something that happened the night before that glorious gathering of the faithful that profoundly altered my life. It is customary in the Episcopal Church to have a rehearsal with all the participants the night before an ordination. When this walk-through was over, I went out to dinner with my spouse and a dear priest friend of ours. Our plan was to have a fun Mexican dinner together and then go home for a good night's sleep. At some point over chips and salsa, our friend looked me straight in the eye and asked, "Is there anything else you need to do before your ordination tomorrow?" I took a deep breath and thought about putting gas in the car and ironing my vestments. With a mouth full of chips, I muttered out these random chores as my answer. I wasn't even looking at her. She then reached over and touched my hand and said, "No, no, no. I mean is there something you need to do for your soul? Is there anything left undone?" I was immediately embarrassed, because she was exactly right to pause the playful dinner and invite our fellowship to a deeper level that night before ordination.

All three of us fell into silence in the wake of her questions. And in that silence, an image came into my head as quickly as a pebble cracking your car windshield out of nowhere. The image was of a small bag of ceramic glass hidden in a closet. To this day, I do not know why that image came to me at that moment. I knew exactly where the ceramic pieces and the closet were, though I had not thought about them for years. I looked at my friend and said, "Yes. There is something that I need to do."

Recall that when I was eight years old, my eldest sister was killed in a car accident. She had been drinking and driving the family car across town while the rest of my family was a few hours away on a weekend camping trip with our Catholic church. That Sunday morning, we woke up to two state troopers who appeared at our campsite to notify my parents of her death. One of the thousands of effects of that tragedy was the instant sacred status given to any of her possessions that we've kept since her death. As such a young person, she did not leave behind many durable possessions. Eventually we took down the rock band posters in her room and got rid of stuffed animals and clothing. But I have a few rings she wore. And there are a few fading photographs.

One priceless object from her short life was a small ceramic bowl, given as a present from my sister to my mother. At some point after her death, we were moving the bowl around, and it broke into half a dozen small pieces. I remember how crushed my mother was. I gathered up the pieces immediately and promised to find a way to repair the bowl. I put them in a small plastic bag and carried them in my life for years. Every time I moved to a new apartment or house, I would come across the bag of pieces and recommit myself to finding some way to mend the bowl and give it back to my mother as if it had never broken. More than once, I took it to the ceramics teachers at schools in which I taught and consulted with them about how to fix it. But person after person, artist after artist, diagnosed that too many pieces were missing or worn down to ever re-create the same bowl.

In joyful and generous artistic spirit, more than one person suggested new pieces of art that could be made with the pieces, but I always declined the offer. The goal, in my mind, was to remake the bowl my sister had given and my mother had cherished, not to make something new. I wanted—and I believed my mother wanted—the bowl my sister had chosen when she was alive. But as the years passed and the advice of experts piled up, it was becoming clear that the bowl could not ever be restored to its original state. That night in the Mexican restaurant, I was given a gift of inspiration and freedom about what to do with the broken bowl. For the first time since I swept up the broken pieces from the floor, I had a new vision—for the bowl and for my vocation.

It was clear to me what I needed to do the night before the first note on the church organ played for my ordination. I didn't know how to explain all my flooding feelings to my spouse and friend, so I just stood up and told them I needed to drive to the nearby house where my mother had retired to get something, and then I would meet them at home later. After years of carrying the pieces with me through with every move, they had come to live and hide on a high shelf in a closet in my mother's house, where many of my old photographs and old papers slept in unopened moving boxes. As I drove, I planned how I would use my own key to get into the house and try to get my hands on the pieces before my mother found out what I was doing. Someday I would tell her the story, but that night I needed to deal with those pieces alone. The meaning they had taken on in my life was so personal that I needed to finish my story with them before I shared it with others. Once I let myself into the house, I quickly found the bag of ceramic pieces on the highest shelf of the closet where I had hidden them. I had never told my mother that I kept the pieces. I am sure she tried to forget about the sad broken bowl and probably hadn't thought much about the pieces since. It was my own mission to keep them and someday fix the bowl and give it back to her. She never mentioned the bowl after it broke; I never gave up on my quest to undo its breaking.

My insight that night was that my reaction to the shattering of the bowl was emblematic of my patterned reaction to any trauma or tragedy: I want to fix it. Perhaps this reaction pattern began when I was young and surrounded by so many adults who were in deep and prolonged mourning over my sister's tragic death. No doubt I was drawn to teaching, coaching, and ministry as forms of expression for this passion to fix things or fix people. At the very least, this urge is to rescue; at worst, it is a messianic complex. Either way, it is ultimately draining as a way of life and disempowering of others as a way of ministry. A thunderbolt of awareness of the toxicity of this way of living and loving hit me hard at that Mexican restaurant. My friend had asked the perfect question at the perfect moment. On the eve of the ordination event that would solidify and sanctify my shepherding of souls as a priest, her question whether anything was left undone shook me to the core.

I felt a wave of exhaustion from my way of being and my tireless and fruitless fixing. Something in me cried out for help, to be released from a life of rescuing. So much is broken in our lives and in the world. That night, I felt called to stop reacting to that brokenness with manic and ultimately unsuccessful missions to save others or erase pain and suffering. I hadn't yet found a way to undo the breaking of the bowl. That night, I decided to stop trying. The bowl had broken. My sister had died. These events had left so much of our family's life in pieces. That night, I decided to accept the shattering and spend not a single moment more in my life pretending that there was any way to undo that pain. I went to gather those pieces because I wanted to keep them as a sign that my family was broken but is still here and still in relationship with God and ready for grace and healing; that I am broken but still here and longing for grace and healing. I wanted to see in those pieces something new, not an image of something lost. I wanted to play with them, create with them, and learn to live with them in my life, rather than keep them both actually and symbolically locked away. The artists along the way on my journey to fix the bowl were right: The pieces were beautiful in and of themselves. Much could be created with them, if only I would give up imposing a single and impossible vision on their value.

So that night, I brought the pieces back to my own house, and we all opened them up together. For the first time, I looked closely at the pieces. Honestly, there was such sadness at the moment the bowl broke and such focus on fixing it within seconds of the break that I had never really looked at the designs on the ceramic. The pieces were beautiful. You could tell that at one point, it had been a truly beautiful small bowl. I had been carrying that bowl broken in my life for twenty years, and for the first time, I fell in love with the pieces. I didn't feel as if I needed to do anything with them that night. I went to sleep dreaming of what kind of art or mission I might someday make with those beautiful blue shards of ceramic.

The next day, all throughout the ordination, I had tucked in my pocket one of the small pieces of the bowl. Since that day, when I say the Eucharist or act in pastoral settings, I carry a piece with me in my pocket or in my bags. It is a symbol to me that my ministry in the world is not to fix that which is broken, but rather, when I come upon the pieces made by the brokenness in ourselves and in our world, I am to simply sit with them and wait for God's presence to fill them. The Bible tells us that when Jesus was resurrected and came back among his friends, he showed them his wounds. The scars on the hands, feet, and side of Jesus were not erased in resurrection, but rather his body in pieces was made whole and glorified.

On the Monday after my ordination, having been a priest for about forty-eight hours, I presided at the Eucharist at noon at the downtown church where I'd been raised up as a priest. It was my first time saying the

Eucharist in the community where I had first discerned a call to priesthood. My hands were shaking. I was quite nervous and followed every word of the service book on the altar. But in my pocket, I had my broken piece. Already it was bringing me peace, a sign that even if I messed up saying the words that day and broke people's expectations for competent priesthood, I could still embrace the failure and treasure the lessons learned. I was not afraid of breaking the experience, trusting that a broken plan can still be beautiful and glorified.

When it came time to preach the sermon, I pulled the piece out of my pocket and told its story to the group that was gathered for the Eucharist. I held up my piece in silence. I asked each of them to think of something in their life that was broken but that they had been carrying with them in hopes that it might somehow be unbroken. "Where in your lives," I asked, "are you trying to fix rather than sit with and dare to dream with the pieces for a new creation? Is the burden of the false promise of fixing suffocating your imagination of how God can enter your pieces and make a new heaven and a new earth?" I asked them to consider the grief and the frustration that comes with simply longing for the past. I dared them to take the risk of believing in the resurrection, believing that our wounds are real and part of our story forever, but that we can and will experience the abundant life of Christ in every piece of our being if we take our pieces into our relationship with God. I ended the sermon by saying that in the offertory, we don't just put our money in the plate on the altar; we can also pray to lay the broken pieces of our lives on the plate with the pieces of bread, both awaiting the indwelling of Christ's resurrected life. The last line I preached was "Today, let your broken pieces mingle with bread so they can share the transformation into the resurrected life of God, the Bread of Life."

We finished the Eucharist, and most of the congregation of downtown workers shuffled out of church to get back to work. But one man came toward the altar as I was gathering up the holy hardware. I was just about to walk away when the man tapped me on the shoulder. He was shy, and he blinked and bobbed with nervousness as he told me his name. His voice was gentle. He thanked me for the service. Then he pointed to the plate piled high with leftover wafers, still sitting on the edge of the altar. I was about to put them away in the place where the church keeps any leftover consecrated bread. As he pointed the plate, he asked, "Would you mind if I just put something on this plate for a minute?" I didn't immediately know what he meant, but I heard myself say quickly, "Of course." After a deep breath, he pulled his wedding ring off his left hand and set the ring on the very edge of the plate, near but reverently not touching the pieces of bread. He acted as if I knew what he was doing. We stood in silence for a few seconds. He stared at the ring on the plate. I stared at his face and his trembling lip.

I had said at the offertory that people should come forward and think of broken pieces in their life that they are trying unsuccessfully to put back together. This man was listening. I had invited folks to imagine putting their broken pieces on the plate with the pieces of the bread when I said, "Today, let your broken pieces mingle with bread so they can share the transformation into the resurrected life of God, the Bread of Life." After what felt like a long time, he picked up the ring and held it tightly in his hand, and then looked at me and said words I will never forget: "My marriage has been over for two years. There's a part of me that has been holding on to this ring, but she's been saying for a year that there's nothing to save. I've known for a while that it's time to let go. This ring is my broken piece. I can no longer bear the weight of it. I pray for a new marriage in the future. I want this ring to become a symbol of that hope, not just a piece of what was broken. I just needed to put it on the plate. I just needed to see it with the bread."

What did Harry need to see mingling with the bread? What did Neville need to see mingling the bread? The two of them immediately spring to mind because the prophecy could have been about either of them, yet Voldemort marked Harry as "the one." What if we went back to the edge of the forest just before Harry hands himself over to death? He takes the stone from the Snitch and is surrounded by his communion of saints. On his walk toward death, he gave everything else up. He left the bereaved in the Great Hall without a word and shrugged off others who asked where he was going. He told Neville to kill the snake if he had the opportunity. He gave up his friends, his "mission" of hunting Horcruxes, even his chance to say good-bye. He needed to let go of the weight of the souls he blamed himself for being unable to save. He needed to see their souls on the plate next to the bread.

When Jesus goes to the garden of Gethsemane, we see his humanity setting aside similar things. I am not equating Harry with the divinity of Christ, but rather seeing the humanity of Jesus and the similarity between his challenge and choices in the garden and Harry's challenge and choices in the forest. Jesus goes to the garden to walk the path he has been called and chosen to walk, leaving his friends asleep with their own dreams and needs for a messiah to bring about political liberation or religious vindication. Harry, too, walks away from his friends and their immediate needs or crisis to sip, with a kiss, the cup of the Snitch meant for him.

As Christians and Harry Potter fanatics, we have the luxury of knowing the rest of these stories. Easter morning would not be possible if not for Good Friday; the Battle of Hogwarts could not have been won if Harry hadn't emerged from the forest carried by Hagrid in a flood of grief. But among the differences, the Battle of Hogwarts also couldn't have been won if Neville hadn't internalized his mission from Harry to kill Nigini and to believe in hope; if Voldemort's power hadn't been thwarted by the hope of all whom Harry had been willing to die to save; if Snape hadn't stood between Voldemort and Harry; if Sirius hadn't shown up at the Department of Mysteries; if Hermione hadn't stood by Harry when he was insufferable; if each and every character hadn't lived into the possibility intended for them. At some point, we all must put down the weights that are not ours to bear so that we can take up our own cross and our own part in the redemption of ourselves and the world. The piece of our broken body or life can be lifted up toward resurrection by a courageous will when we let go of all the broken pieces around us. In a verse pitch-perfect for Harry's walk with the soul of his saints into the Forbidden Forest, we read in the letter to the Hebrews 12:1–3:

> Therefore, since we are surrounded by so great a cloud of witnesses, let us also lay aside every weight and the sin that clings so closely, and let us run with perseverance the race that is set before us, looking to Jesus the pioneer and perfecter of our faith, who for the sake of the joy that was set before him endured the cross, disregarding its shame, and has taken his seat at the right hand of the throne of God. Consider him who endured such hostility against himself from sinners, so that you may not grow weary or lose heart.

NOTES

1. *Enriching Our Worship 1* (New York: Church Publishing, 1998), 64.

2. Luke 24:30–32.

3. J. K. Rowling, *Harry Potter and the Goblet of Fire* (New York: Scholastic, 2000), 724.

4. *Deathly Hallows*, 686.

5. Richard Rohr, "The Sacred Wound," Richard Rohr's Daily Meditation, August 17, 2013, http://myemail.constantcontact.com/Richard-Rohr-s-Daily-Meditation----August-17--2013.html?soid=1103098668616&aid=VsvGk1wUnuI.

6. Shawn Adler, "'Harry Potter' Author J. K. Rowling Opens Up about Books' Christian Imagery," October 17, 2007, http://www.mtv.com/news/1572107/harry-potter-author-jk-rowling-opens-up-about-books-christian-imagery/.

7. *Deathly Hallows*, 328.

8. Ibid., 328.

9. Adler, "'Harry Potter' Author J. K. Rowling Opens Up."

10. Augustine, *Four Anti-Pelagian Writings,* trans. John A. Mourant and William J. Collinge (Washington, DC: Catholic University of America Press, 1992), 27:15.

11. *Philosopher's Stone*, 214.

12. William Bole, "Jesuit Service Movement Marks 60 Years of Helping Young People Become 'Ruined for Life,'" December 14, 2016, http://www.jesuitvolunteers.org/jesuit-service-movement-marks-60-years-of-helping-young-people-become-ruined-for-life/.

13. C. S. Lewis, *The Lion, the Witch and the Wardrobe* (New York: Collier, 1970), 75–76.

14. *Deathly Hallows*, 691.

15. McGonigal, "Gaming Can Make a Better World."

16. Runcie, "J. K. Rowling."

17. *Philosopher's Stone*, 291.

18. *Deathly Hallows*, 120.

PART TWO

How Does Harry Potter Work for Teaching Faith?

CHAPTER SIX

Spiritual Parenting

Pride and Prejudice at Malfoy Manor

"Love as powerful as your mother's for you leaves its own mark. To have been loved so deeply, even though the person who loved us is gone, will give us some protection forever."[1]

In the Harry Potter stories, two mothers are each willing to die for her only child. These two mothers loved their sons more than anything in the world. Voldemort targeted both of these boys, though to differing degrees. Both mothers were married to skilled wizards from wealthy families. In the modern Muggle and magical worlds, marriages between high school sweethearts often collapse over time; however, both of these women married schoolmates and went on to enjoy stable, lifelong relationships. Both encouraged and supported their sons to strive and thrive at Hogwarts, in the classroom and on the Quidditch field. Both families gave money and time to Hogwarts.

Tragically, only Narcissa Malfoy would live to see her son into adult life. Lily Potter was robbed of that blessing.

If there is one lesson about parenting we learn from the Malfoys, however haunting, it is that in raising children, love is not enough. The Malfoys teach the world that it matters mightily *how* a parent loves a child and what other loves take over the heart of the family. In the end, the patterns of pride and prejudice practiced by Lucius and Narcissa create a family climate of self-absorption and cruelty, even though they love and cherish each other and their son, Draco.

The most accurate term to summarize what has gone so wrong in spiritual formation in their home is *idolatry*. Without ever using the word,

Rowling has written a saga that teaches against, even rails against, idolatry found in multiple forms from the first book to the last. The Malfoy family is just one example of what can happen when a person or a family puts the love of things or class or race over the love for neighbors. The prejudice practiced at Malfoy Manor is a microcosm of the prejudice practiced throughout the wizarding world—a prejudice that predates the Harry Potter years, going back to Hogwarts' founding Heads of School. Rowling writes that even at Hogwarts' founding, ill feeling was arising around pure-blood issues between Salazar Slytherin and the other three founders, Rowena Ravenclaw, Godric Gryffindor, and Helga Hufflepuff. Rowling makes idolatry, and the bitterness leading to cruelty that is ever its fruit, a central force in the narrative. The parenting of the Malfoys is a case study in how one family takes in and practices the prejudices of an idolatrous culture. The Malfoys did not create the values and priorities that rule their bigoted family; like their wealth, they inherited and invested in them.

A Graven Image

As we think about the embedded lesson against idolatry that Rowling is preaching through the Malfoy family and other figures in the novels, it is worth taking a minute to consider specific examples of Rowling's understanding of idolatry. Consider an obvious emblem of idolatry: the soaring statue at the center of the grand concourse of the Ministry of Magic. We are introduced to this Fountain of Magical Brethren in *Harry Potter and the Order of the Phoenix*. Here is the description of that symbolic sculpture:

> A group of golden statues, larger than life-size, stood in the middle of a circular pool. Tallest of them all was a noble-looking wizard with his wand pointing straight up in the air. Grouped around him were a beautiful witch, a centaur, a goblin, and a house-elf. The last three were all looking adoringly up at the witch and wizard. Glittering jets of water were flying from the ends of the two wands, the point of the centaur's arrow, the tip of the goblin's hat, and each of the house-elf's ears, so that the tinkling hiss of falling water was added to the pops and cracks of Apparators and the clatter of footsteps as hundreds of witches and wizards, most of whom were wearing glum, early-morning looks, strode toward a set of golden gates at the far end of the hall.[2]

This statue was meant to depict harmony among all creatures in the magical world, but a harmony based on hierarchy. Keep in mind how important a stance against classism and racism is to Rowling. She had experienced the prejudice of class and gender as a single mother in Great

Britain living on public assistance. She had a small job at a church during that period in her life, and she has since said in multiple interviews that she was judged and at times rejected by the church employees and members for having a child and no husband. She experienced difficulty in getting her first apartment because many landlords were wary of renting to people on public assistance. At the same time, while in her mid-twenties, she was working for Amnesty International, reading and organizing transcripts and testimonies from political prisoners smuggled out of the prisons of dictators across the world. She waded into the letters and literature of those oppressed and tortured based on race, gender, class, sexual orientation, and political convictions. This experience leaks into the countless passages of Harry Potter that draw the attention of the reader to the power and pain that pervade unjust social structures, from Ron having no money for robes or replacement wands to torture being an Unforgivable Curse. Prejudice and pride, which is its fuel, are major drivers and dark forces throughout the seven books.

When the Brethren statue is destroyed in the fight between Dumbledore and Voldemort in *The Order of the Phoenix*, we hear from Dumbledore that such imagery of a wizard-first social hierarchy was problematic from the start. "The fountain we destroyed tonight told a lie. We wizards have mistreated and abused our fellows for too long, and we are now reaping our reward."[3] Dumbledore learned in his youth the folly and foulness of social paradigms that privilege one race, class, or creature over another, even if "for the greater good." The Brethren statue codified and celebrated hierarchies in the magical world. Dumbledore linked the darkest pureblood obsessions of Voldemort and the Death Eaters to the banal forms of symbolism or language, like the Brethren statue, that privileged wizards in any way over other creatures. The Brethren statue had all the beauty of something made morally benign. Even the coins dropped into the water were donated to St. Mungo's Hospital.

The statue continued to be a measure of the soul of the magical world when, during the takeover of the Ministry by Voldemort's supporters, it was rebuilt and renamed Magic Is Might. The prejudice that had only been hinted at in the first Brethren version of the statue took center stage in its replacement:

> A gigantic statue of black stone dominated the scene. It was rather frightening, this vast sculpture of a witch and wizard sitting on ornately carved thrones. . . . Engraved in foot-high letters at the base of the statue were the words MAGIC IS MIGHT. . . . Harry looked more closely

and realized that what he had thought were decoratively carved thrones were actually mounds of carved humans: hundreds and hundreds of naked bodies, men, women, and children, all with rather stupid, ugly faces, twisted and pressed together to support the weight of the handsomely robed wizards.[4]

Itself an actual and physical idol, the statue also depicts the cultural idol of wizard or pure-blood status taking over the wizarding world during the terror of Voldemort. For Dumbledore and Rowling, the notion of wizard superiority and the idolatry of blood status are the core of the evil that animates Voldemort or any dark art. Rowling is just another modern voice echoing Reinhold Niebuhr's famous social and political diagnosis that idolatry is the primal sin from which all other sins are derived.[5]

The very family name Malfoy is formed from old French and translates as "bad faith." Idolatry is not often the sin of the skeptic or the unbeliever. Idolatry is possible only where there is the capacity for and the practice of strong love and devotion. Loving an idol can be as destructive as hate, and it is often more dangerous because disordered love is harder to identify than hate. In "The Weight of Glory," C. S. Lewis made a most significant observation about idolatry. Building on the idea that the beauty and joy we find in created things and experiences are merely containers or reflections of the beauty and joy of God, Lewis explained that mistaking those created vessels for the beauty beyond them is the core and cause of idolatry:

> The books or the music in which we thought the beauty was located will betray us if we trust to them; it was not in them, it only came through them, and what came through them was longing. These things—the beauty, the memory of our own past—are good images of what we really desire; but if they are mistaken for the thing itself they turn into dumb idols, breaking the hearts of their worshippers. For they are not the thing itself; they are only the scent of a flower we have not found, the echo of a tune we have not heard, news from a country we have never yet visited.[6]

The price to the soul of idolatry is a starving and broken heart. Voldemort's soul is literally broken apart by his acts of evil in pursuit of the idol of immortality. Lewis's point is that any object of our love that is not God or part of the common good will eventually break our hearts. Idols devour; they do not feed. It is more legalistic to describe idolatry as sinning but more realistic to describe idolatry as starving. The Malfoy family is an example of how love of economic privilege, social power, or superior position in society comes to starve the family's soul. They participate in torture, murder, and terror just to be seen as loyal to Voldemort and thereby protect their way of life. In the end, their love for each other does not lead to freedom, creativity, or joy. They have worshiped the dumb idols of money and status; the void created caused bitterness and conceit.

Lucius learns that utter loyalty to Voldemort is a one-way street. He is willing to do anything to protect the Dark Lord, but when his acts of loyalty do not work out, he experiences wrath. Lucius is punished for mistakes, and in the wake of Voldemort's two falls from power, the good wizards hunt Lucius, who escapes the first purge of Death Eaters only by claiming to have been under the Imperius Curse during Voldemort's first rise to power. He escapes the second purge of Death Eaters by ratting out his Death Eater peers. All the money in the world does not save Lucius from a life preserved only as a liar and a snitch. His wife lives under a shadow of shame, as does Draco. Their privilege cannot protect them from the price of idolatry.

Voldemort's tragic life is a rarity because it is the story of a total lack of love and abandonment of parents for their son. Draco is a more common case study for American culture: a boy loved by parents who knew only how to idolize that which they loved. For Rowling and the Judeo-Christian tradition, to idolize is to treat any thing or person as god. But how does a parent avoid the understandable temptation to treat one's children—or spouse—with the utter devotion and reverence meant for the Creator and not any other creature? We have to admit that the desire to love one's loved ones with "all our heart, all our mind, and all our soul" is an understandable and perhaps forgivable sin.

Readers of the Harry Potter stories certainly condemn Voldemort's parents for loving too little. It is often the defense of the idolatry of our loved ones that the alternative—not loving enough, as Voldemort's parents were guilty of—seems unspeakably cruel. In this way, the Malfoys are somewhat sympathetic characters. Readers feel easy about condemning their love of wealth, privilege, and pure-blood status. But it is harder to judge their idolatry of their son. But Rowling puts the warning against any idolatry center stage. She shows the reader the ultimate unhappiness, the lack of freedom, and the absence of joy in the Malfoy family, compared with families like the Weasleys, who do not idolize members of the family or the wizard society. But where is the line drawn between loving parents and idolatrous parents? Rowling wants you to find it. She pays too much attention and fills too many pages of her epic with details of the Malfoy family dynamic for us to think that she is not preaching powerfully against idolatry.

The actual dominical command found in Luke 10:27–28 to "Love the Lord your God with all your heart, and with all your soul, and with all your strength, and with all your mind" is not delivered without priceless words that explain how this love is best practiced. Jesus delivers a second command that is connected to the first: "and love your neighbor as yourself." Jesus emphasizes that these two commands go together in the healthy spiritual life. We love God by loving others, and we cannot love others without idolatry if we do not love them out of and as part of our love for God. The teachings of Jesus call us out of idolatry by giving us a way out of idolatry.

Notice that the second commandment of the ten given to Moses, to have "no other gods but God," also commands love in the context of a relationship to other creatures in which to experience and share one's love of God. This is the only commandment of ten that comes with a story, albeit a short one. The commandment says, "I am the Lord your God, who brought you out of the land of Egypt, out of the house of slavery; you shall have no other gods before me" (Exod. 20:1–17). The command to love God alone comes in the context of a relationship in which the Creator God has already chosen, served, and freed creatures. God has already freed the people before God asks for love and obedience from the people. We do not love a God who may or may not respond to our love. Our love is not an invitation to our beloved God to love us back. We have not asked for the first date, sent the first text, or gazed first across the room. It is the love of God, the redemptive and salvific love of God shown and done for us before we are asked to respond, that is the impetus and the animation for our relationship. Paul says it best in Romans 5:1–9:

> For while we were still weak, at the right time Christ died for the ungodly. Indeed, rarely will anyone die for a righteous person—though perhaps for a good person someone might actually dare to die. But God proves his love for us in that while we still were sinners Christ died for us. Much more surely then, now that we have been justified by his blood, will we be saved through him from the wrath of God. For if while we were enemies, we were reconciled to God through the death of his Son, much more surely, having been reconciled, will we be saved by his life. But more than that, we even boast in God through our Lord Jesus Christ, through whom we have now received reconciliation.

The biblical command to love involves loving God and others in a circle of constant movement between loving God and loving others. Love of God without loving our neighbors is a love empty of action and concern for God's other creatures and creation. A love of others, even family members, that lives and serves those people alone is a form of idolatry that will leave empty a part of the heart made whole only by loving God. Again, in the words of Augustine, God "has made us for His own and we are restless until we rest in Him."[7]

In the human condition, and in the hearts of the Malfoys, the restless longing for a lover beyond kin creates a vacuum quickly and culturally filled with lesser loves and obsessions. All the innate power our hearts are given to love our Creator turns destructively toward ideas, material things, or other idols that will never fill the void but will only create darker parts of our heart in those empty, unfilled, and lonely places. I cannot count the times students or adults learning about Harry Potter have described the Malfoys as the saddest family they've read about in a long time. The hunger for God intrinsic and inviting within all children of God will never cease to be a lever of longing in the human heart. The Psalmist cries out this truth: "My soul longs, indeed it faints for the courts of the Lord; my heart and my flesh sing for joy to the living God" (Ps. 84:2). The Malfoys are driven to find a god to fulfill this unique longing. The tragedy is that they identify their pure-blood status, their social status, and even their son as the object of this innate longing to love God.

Rowling lays before the reader the sad truth about idolatry: disordered love breeds disordered lives. Narcissa Malfoy and Lily Potter have devotion in common. But where they differ explains the radically different paths for their lives and the lives of their entire families. Lily loves more than just her husband or her son, which frees and feeds her to love them even more. She loves Snape when others mock him. She loves Lupin when others fear him. She loves James when others give up on him. She follows the teaching of Paul, who prescribes how to love and receive peace and freedom from well-ordered loving in Philippians 4:8:

> Whatever is true, whatever is honorable, whatever is just, whatever is pure, whatever is pleasing, whatever is commendable, if there is any excellence and if there is anything worthy of praise, think about these things. Keep on doing the things that you have learned and received and heard and seen in me, and the God of peace will be with you.

Lily lives, loves, and dies in peace because she loves the good through loving others; in service, she finds perfect freedom. Because its metabolism is idolatry, the edifice of Malfoy Manor stands for all as a prison full of emptiness. Because of its metabolism of sacrificial love, the Potters' mangled home in Godric's Hollow is honored by all as birthplace of freedom.

J. K. Rowling could have easily written this story exclusively about the adventures of children and their professors at Hogwarts. The boarding school backdrop for her story lends itself to telling a student-centered tale with parents having little or no role. Instead, she put the relationships between students and their parents at the center of the students' lives and the plots of the narrative. Even for the most minor characters, the names and occupations of their parents are often mentioned. Clearly, Rowling believes strongly in the power of parents in forming children. There is no more clear evidence of this conviction than the power of Lily's blood to literally bathe Harry in metaphysical protection until he becomes an adult. Her life's hold on Harry was, as Dumbledore said, a more real and efficacious mark than the visible scar from the death curse.[8] Who she was and how she loved was so pure and good and powerful that the corrupted and murderous Professor Qurrill died just from touching Harry's skin.[9] To a lesser extent, we see the making of sweaters by Molly Weasley, the connection of Luna to her father's subversive Quibbler work and beliefs, and the arrival of owls bearing gifts from families to children like Neville or Seamus as constant reminders from Rowling that boarding schools may take the child out of the home but cannot take the parents out of the child. As racist and self-absorbed as Narcissa is, the story tells us that she made and mailed cookies to Draco every day.

Rowling also leaves the definition of parent wide open to include adults who are parenting children that are not their own. The series presents countless examples of adults who are parenting the children of other people. One has only to think of James Potter's parents opening their home to Sirius, or the Weasleys opening theirs to Harry. And there are also negative examples of parenting beyond one's own children. Think of Petunia and Vernon imposing their parenting on Harry, or Tom Riddle's various extended family members affecting his tragic development. In another chapter, I will focus more on the godparenting of figures like McGonagall or Hagrid, but in this section, I want to focus specifically on what the Harry Potter stories can teach us about what spiritual parenting is, good or bad.

Families have many functions, but chief among them is teaching about life and reality. The Dursleys thought it was their job as stand-in parents of Harry to teach him that "there is no such thing as magic."[10] You can disagree with them, but it's still true that they had a parenting message and were faithful to it, even though they knew magic existed. In their hearts, they believed a person was better prepared for adult life without thoughts and practice of magic. The Dursleys and the Malfoys are sad examples of consistent and effective parenting toward all the wrong outcomes. The first lesson in parenting is that love is not enough. The Dursleys remind us of the second lesson: successful and life-giving parenting missions cannot run against reality.

Whenever I have done parenting lectures for schools or PTA meetings, I show two Harry Potter movie clips to start a conversation about what kind of culture parents can create at home. I do not show parenting scenes, such as the countless displays of great and terrible parenting from the Dursleys or the Weasleys. Instead, I show two classroom scenes at Hogwarts. The first is from the first film, and it is the Charms class in which the students learn the Leviosa charm to levitate a feather. After watching the three-minute clip, I ask the parents to talk about what they liked about that classroom style, the verbal and nonverbal teaching of Professor Flitwick, what was risky about the classroom culture, and what was memorable. How would they have felt about learning if they were students in that class? How would they have thought about themselves in this classroom?

I then show a clip from the fifth film, *The Order of the Phoenix*. In this scene, Dolores Umbridge leads her first class in Defence Against the Dark Arts. Her increasing roles at Hogwarts represent the de facto takeover of Hogwarts School by a corrupted Ministry for Magic. She begins the class by making the following speech:

> *Dolores Umbridge*: Your previous instruction in this subject has been
>   disturbingly uneven. But you will be pleased to know from now
>   on you will be following a carefully structured, Ministry-approved
>   course of defensive magic. Yes?
> *Hermione Granger*: There's nothing in here about using defensive
>   spells.
> *Dolores Umbridge*: Using spells? Ha ha! Well I can't imagine why you
>   would need to use spells in my classroom.
> *Ron Weasley*: We're not gonna use magic?
> *Dolores Umbridge*: You will be learning about defensive spells in a
>   secure, risk-free way.
> *Harry Potter*: Well, what use is that? If we're gonna be attacked it
>   won't be risk-free.
> *Dolores Umbridge*: Students will raise their hands when they speak in
>   my class. It is the view of the Ministry that a theoretical knowledge
>   will be sufficient to get you through your examinations, which
>   after all, is what school is all about.

Harry Potter: And how is theory supposed to prepare us for what's out there?

Dolores Umbridge: There is nothing out there, dear! Who do you imagine would want to attack children like yourself?

Harry Potter: I don't know, maybe, Lord Voldemort![11]

We then discuss the same questions we asked about Flitwick's Charms class. How would you describe the teaching style? What is risky about it? How would you feel in this classroom? What impact would it have on your hope for your life and future?

We then consider the hardest question: which classroom atmosphere portrays your parenting style or your family culture? We talk a lot about what we can know about Flitwick and Umbridge as people, just from these classroom scenes. What are their hopes and fears? What inspires them? What role do teenagers have in their understanding of society? What comes out in conversations is that Flitwick's class is definitely less safe. Umbridge tried to create a "risk-free environment" by telling the students to "put wands away" and not use magic in class. Seamus sets his feather on fire in the feather lesson, proving Umbridge's point that experimental learning comes with risks. But freedom to fail is part of Flitwick's pedagogy, unlike with Umbridge, who believes the purpose of school is to prepare for standardized exams.

The freedom created in environments and families where experimentation and risk are allowed becomes a bonding force, where students or siblings can teach each other and solve problems in pairs or groups. In Flitwick's class, students are using magic in the presence of an adult, practice for using it in the real world. Contrast this risky but rewarding experience of teaching and learning with Umbridge's pedagogy. Harry says it best when he complains about a risk-free classroom, arguing that "when out in the world it won't be risk free." Like many modern parents, Umbridge has a fear-driven view of mentoring young people and cares more about control than creativity. She reduces the learning environment to a training ground for standardized tests and their apparent power to ensure financially and professionally stable young adults.

Umbridge also loses the support and investment of the students when she denies that evil visits the lives of children or teenagers. Having visited many different kinds of schools in my research about adolescent faith formation, I have seen many versions of this unfortunate and shallow view of youth capacity. This bias also denies that youth encounter evil or injustice in their daily lives. Young people face the dissolution of marriage, crime, illness, eating disorders, drug addiction, cheating, bullying, and sexual assault, sometimes in their own lives but definitely among their classmates. Adults who deny to students that they are facing dark forces daily lose credibility and influence with youth. When adults deny the reality of evil, they also communicate to youth that there are no heroic acts of youth, since there are no dark forces to fight. So when we ignore their challenges, we also deny their strength. Quite often young people act out simply to fight the view of some adults that youth do not have the capacity for bold choices or consequential decisions.

Parenting: In Command, Out of Control

In my first book on the faith life and faith language of adolescents, I outlined methods for peaceful, fruitful, and joyful spiritual parenting based on my ten years of research on teenagers. I shared the innovative and catalytic reflections on human development by the founding editor of *Wired* magazine, Kevin Kelly. Anyone who reads Kelly's work knows he has never claimed to be a parenting consultant but has been a maverick pioneer and philosopher of technology. From my reading of his work, I would describe him as agnostic, if not atheist. Among many books and publications, Kelly's 1994 seminal work, *Out of Control: The New Biology of Machines, Social Systems, and the Economic World*, broke new ground in the use of human biology and evolution to better explain social sciences and technological trends. He believes that if we study biological evolution, we can glean processes and patterns of adaption, diversification, and innovation that are helpful and transformative when applied to machines or social systems. Kelly looks at the world and sees innumerable species that have faced the same immutable natural laws yet have learned to survive, adapt, and thrive in mind-blowingly diverse ways.

Kelly aims his work at those who seek to structure and sustain machines and communities that are wired for productivity, diversity, innovation, and regeneration. He roots his theories of organizational leadership in the powerful lessons he learned from the study of evolution. I applied Kelly's work to the most important system in our culture: the family. I believe that the lessons Kelly derives from his study of biological evolution are priceless for parents, though they were never his identified or intended audience. It is my belief that the family is an organic system, like any species, seeking not only to adapt to forces beyond its control but also to delight in the process of growing and changing in the face of external forces. The "family" is also an organism that can establish patterns and engage in practices rooted in love, justice, discipline and the respect for the dignity and individuality of each person, leading to transformations such as healing, forgiveness, or reconciliation.

Organisms are healthy and thriving when they are free to adapt and change in an environment structured by steady natural laws. Nature provides the steady laws that have always guided human evolution, such as the laws of gravity or relativity, thermodynamics or quantum mechanics, and photonics or electromagnetism. It is the family's responsibility and opportunity to establish the laws that will guide the growth of its members.

Based on Kelly's ideas, the ideal structured environment—one that breeds the greatest diversity and productivity—can be said to be one that is "in command, out of control." "In command" refers to the natural or immutable laws that create a structure in which individuals are forced to creatively adapt in diverse ways. "Out of control" refers to the freedom that allows each individual organism to respond to the immutable laws in its own way. Fixed realities, such as gravity or weather patterns, are "in command" and thereby force and guide the evolution of organisms in response to what they cannot change. The reward for creative response to natural laws is survival and the result is constant adaptation and increased diversity among all creatures. Without consistent command, there would be no necessity or inspiration for developing equally consistent patterns of steady and ingenius growth.

You can already see the fruitful application of this theory to parenting. Have we all not seen families that lack reliable discipline and consequences, producing parents and children who do not mature as well or at all in the void of structure? Although evolution teaches us that someone or something needs to be "in command" in order for individuals to learn and grow in response to that structured environment, our culture continues to experiment with or even celebrate less successful models of unstructured parenting. It is only in a strong command structure that true freedom can flourish safely and consistently. This freedom created through structure is articulated in the second half of the phrase for ideal evolution: "in command, out of control." It is within this structured and therefore protected "out of control" freedom that individuals are safest and immediately rewarded in their adaptation and diversification. Speed limits create freedom to play, walk, and drive in neighborhoods. Roads without speed limits do not create more freedom; rather, they saddle individuals with immediate fear and metabolic anxiety. We cannot be creatively and bravely "out of control" to invent new ideas and new convictions if we are burdened with the anxieties that lurk in landscapes without consistent command.

Free play, the chance to succeed or fail, a lack of micromanaging or helicopter partnering or parenting—these are the forces of freedom that are the

fruits of "out of control" parenting, setting family members free to experiment and adapt and mature. I have never spoken to a church group of
parents, at a PTA meeting, or to a book group without begging the parents
in the room to create an "in command, out of control" family system. Too
often families fail to practice "in command" discipline and thereby sabotage
the safety needed for sustained use and fruition of freedom for all members
of the family. Or families may allow anxiety to rule and refuse to practice the
"out of control" parenting that sets both parents and children free to grow,
change, and gain wisdom through experimentation and adaptation.

Families ought to create and sustain an environment that maximizes
the freedom of everyone in the family to experiment and to mature, while
simultaneously unwavering from the laws, rooted in love, of the family.
Families with laws but without freedom produce family members who are
driven by fear and conformity to avoid failure. Families with freedom but
few laws generate insecurity and lack of direction. Families without laws
or freedom heighten anxiety and self-defense. While the optimal family
structure is "in command, out of control," there are three other forms of
failure in family structure: "in command, in control"; "out of command,
in control"; and "out of command, out of control."

Patterns of Parenting in Harry Potter

When I read Harry Potter, I see in many of the characters' lives and families depictions of these very principles. In fact, there are families that
exemplify each of these successful and failing structures. Let's consider
some of the families in Harry Potter and what their patterned behavior
teaches us about spiritual parenting. What's important is that most of the
characters (with a few notable exceptions), despite the range of parenting
failures they endure, turn out as fairly functional adults. And this is true
in real life. Young people are extremely resilient. But this does not mean
that we cannot be better parents and nonparenting mentors in the lives
of young people. In comparison with an ideal or flawless system of relationships, every family is dysfunctional. But we can create patterns that
are more life-giving than those unhealthier ones in which we are perhaps
stuck today. Meditating on both Muggle and magical family systems in
Harry Potter might stir your imagination and rekindle your hope at any
age in forming a more loving, freer, and more joyful family system.

In Command, Out of Control: The Weasleys

When I wrote my book on teenagers, I had not yet read the Harry Potter
stories. If I had, I would have written at length about the Weasley family

serving as the perfect example of a successful "in command, out of control" family. No one is perfect in that household, but this fact only deepens the power and potential of learning from their example for all of us. The Weasleys are imperfect people who nonetheless structure their family in such a way that the love and commitment practiced are able to absorb infractions and release its members to learn from their mistakes and apply that wisdom to thrive in the world. Charlie isn't settled until he finds his footing with dragons in Romania, Bill marries needy and highly anxious Fluer, Percy betrays the family before repenting, Fred and George drop out of high school, Ron breaks any rule in his way, and Ginny takes orders from no one. And yet all seven children find their own identity, reconcile with their family, and eventually mature into leaders, lovers, and levers for justice in the world.

Arthur and Molly had few rules, but their leadership and their love were laws of nature at the Burrow. You could always count on Arthur to be a man of justice, curiosity, and forgiveness, no matter what stress or sadness he wrestled with at home or at work. You could always count on Molly to love her children fiercely, sacrifice everything to provide for their education, and stay up all night waiting to love them after any journey or crisis. No matter how different each child was in relation to their parents, the Weasley children never questioned their parents' commitment to social justice, equality, and honor. The children watched their family pay a price for their virtues in the social hierarchy of the wizarding world, rendering them working-poor "blood traitors" and "Muggle worshipers" who wore secondhand clothes and rarely vacationed or received gifts that were not handmade. But the paradigm for parenting was always grounded in abundance and not scarcity, with every child knowing they could invite anyone at any time into the family for food or fellowship. Even Percy's flirtation with seizing social superiority through political power was not a habit that turned into a life direction. The compass of his family's unconditional love and cherishing of social justice eventually led him out of corruption and back into the family fold.

Molly is a compelling role model for "in command, out of control" parenting because of her flaws as well as her strengths. She is not a perfect "out of control" mentor of her children. We see her struggle mightily with letting go of her kids and allowing them the freedom to grow and to be hurt in the world. Her fears hint that she borders on idolizing her family's safety. Rather than experiencing stress-free wonder at what their children might face in the world, as Arthur usually does, Molly worries and weeps at the thought of injury to or death of her children. What keeps her from idolatry is that she does, in fact, let them go forth from the Burrow, every day and every year. Unlike Narcissa, Molly puts her children on the altar and trusts in what will happen. She accepts the "out of control" role in parenting, though it pains Molly deeply to permit her children the freedom to fail or thrive.

The face of the grandfather clock in the Weasley house is a perfect symbol of the emotional pains of Molly as she practices "out of control" parenting. The categories on the clock are a comical list of the stages of stress that "out of control" parents experience. Instead of hours, the clock's face has a series of possible locations for family members, including "home," "school," "work," "travelling," "lost," "hospital," "prison," and "mortal peril." On the face of a clock, Rowling has brilliantly portrayed the primal fears on the face of a parent committed to the successful but stressful "in command, out of control" family system.

When we see the stress that abides with Molly, it is a fair question to ask whether "in command, out of control" parenting is worth the strain on parents, who are wired to worry for those they love. But conversations with teenagers over the last two decades have reminded me constantly of Winston Churchill's wise words that "democracy is the worst form of Government except for all those other forms that have been tried from time to time."[12] The same is true with parenting. The potential stress of the "in command, out of control" parent, youth leader, or godparent is, in my observations, less than the stress and anxiety that can rule entire families with less life-giving systems, as in the following Harry Potter examples.

In Command, In Control: The Malfoys

Some families choose their values and consistently articulate them to their children, verbally and nonverbally, year in and year out. These are "in command" families with purpose and direction. But "command" is a neutral power, able to generate prejudice as quickly as passion for justice. The Weasleys, guided by love and justice, practice a command driven by compassion and unconditional love, whereas the Malfoys, shackled by idolatries of all kinds, practice a command driven by pride and prejudice. And unlike the Weasleys, the Malfoys do not practice "out of control" leadership in their family.

Draco's mother communicates with him every day, even though Draco attends a boarding school in another country. Draco's father is on the board at Hogwarts and intrudes with power and money on his son's academic and extracurricular activities with a heavy hand. They are so addicted to pleasing Voldemort that they allow Draco to be pulled into their own twisted community of Death Eaters. They even let their son be used and perhaps killed by the Dark Lord. Lucius and Narcissa micromanage Draco's life in a way that Molly never tried with her seven children. The result is that Draco has little confidence in his own powers, agreeing to murder Dumbledore just to show his parents and their Death Eater friends that he too has value.

The tragic last moments of Dumbledore's life on the astronomy tower are a sad testament to the impact of "in command, in control" parenting on Draco. Never given the freedom to succeed entirely on his own or to learn on his own from real failure, Draco is a predictably rudderless and bitter adolescent, as are many teenagers from "in control" families. Dumbledore sees Draco raise a wand against him. Calmly, even after being disarmed by Draco, Dumbledore speaks these powerful words: "Draco, Draco, you are not a killer." Tearful and trembling, Draco snaps back, "How do you know? . . . You don't know what I am capable of. . . . You don't know what I've done!" The truth is that it is Draco who does not know who Draco is. And it is Draco who is in shock at things he has done to prove his dignity and worth to adults. Dumbledore knows that Draco is seeking a way out of the painful cycle of trying to earn one's worth that he had learned from his striving and scheming parents. Dumbledore knows that Draco has been trying to kill him all year in a series of fearful and failed attempts. "Forgive me, Draco, but they have been feeble attempts. . . . So feeble, to be honest, that I wonder whether your heart has truly been in them."[13] How tragic that a Headmaster knows the true and good heart of Draco beneath the bluster that his own commanding and controlling parents fail to see and love.

Children raised by "in control" parents are particularly vulnerable to accepting missions, moral or immoral, given to them by nonparenting adults, in hopes of at last feeling worthy and trusted with freedom in ways their parents have failed to permit. Dumbledore recognizes how vulnerable and soul-starved Draco is and offers him a way to get off of the path followed by other vulnerable young boys at Hogwarts, like Tom Riddle. But the unconditional love of Dumbledore is so foreign to a child raised in a family system of earning love and spending privilege that Draco cannot receive the lifeline. Dumbledore tries to offer Draco a way out. "I can help you, Draco." Breaking into tears, Draco explains his resistance: "No, you can't. . . . Nobody can. He told me to do it or he'll kill me. I've got no choice."[14] Sadly, these statements are all true. How different and infinitely less tragic Draco's life would have been if his parents had loved him enough to free him to build an identity sufficiently strong to resist evil rather than practice it.

Over the years, I have taught or mentored so many—too many—Dracos, both male and female. And when they cheat themselves, sell themselves, cut themselves, crash into the freedom of others, or injure themselves or others, I am usually left with one or both terrified and ashamed parents asking this question: "How did this happen? We did absolutely everything we could to avoid this outcome." And in my head are always the words of Yoda: "That is why you fail."[15]

Out of Command, In Control: The Longbottoms

The films leave out the tragic and tearful scenes in the books that depict Neville's visits to see his brain-damaged parents in St. Mungo's Hospital. We find out in the middle of the series that Bellatrix Lestrange tortured his parents for information about the Order of the Phoenix. They refused to disclose any information, so they were tortured and cursed into an irreversible state of dementia. Neville was sent to live with his stern and joyless grandmother. There is no clear parent to Neville, since his grandmother is portrayed as emotionally distant, and his living parents do not know who he is. He is not the orphan that Harry is, but neither has he parents who are raising him. His grandmother, most likely out of fear and grief, is very controlling, but the place or voice of parental command in his life is absent.

Neville finds direction and command from his teachers at school. The availability of mature and loving adults is usually a positive benefit of boarding school, though this stand-in role of teachers as parental command for Neville made him vulnerable to being used by Barty Jr. when Barty was masquerading as Mad-Eye Moody. Children raised in "out of command" families are often vulnerable to becoming followers of others. And "out of command" families who nonetheless exercise heavy control lead to children like Neville, who are quick to feel shame for bringing any chaos to a situation. Starving already for the stability to grow with direction or command, they fly below the radar so as not to lose the love of those in control. These children are vulnerable to strong leaders and are people-pleaser followers. For this reason, it is no surprise that Neville is an early devotee of Harry and Dumbledore's Army. And it is a testament to the healing freedom Hogwarts provides all children that over the years, Neville learns to break free from his grandmother's control and grasp his freedom to grow into a leader.

Out of Command, Out of Control: The Lovegoods

The word *quibble* derives from the Latin word *quibus*, meaning "who, what, or which," and has evolved into a term meaning "to argue, protest, or object." When Xenophilius Lovegood founds his own magazine, he calls it *The Quibbler*. He is a dreamer, a conspiracy theorist, a stargazer, a collector, and an eccentric to the extreme. He challenges all norms, in many cases simply because he is constitutionally suspicious of norms. Like his wife, he lives a life that is a constant experiment with truth and reality. Luna's mother, by all accounts, loved her husband and shared his interest in the occult and the unknown, killing herself accidentally while experimenting with a spell. It goes without saying that these two parents were not "in command," of their lives or anyone else's. But unlike any overinvolved or helicopter parent, neither were they "in control." Luna Lovegood was raised in a family of Seekers who refused to stop seeking, even in the face of truth. There is an undeniable beauty in their lives: creativity, nonconformity, and brave expression abound in the absence of loyalty to traditions or conventions. They laugh, they love, and they learn and discern more deeply than others.

After the death of Luna's mother, it is clear that her father tamed his grief heroically and withheld no love or joy from the household. In the absence of command or control from her parents, Luna is lost but loving as she moves through the world. She finds solid ground, spiritually and socially, at Hogwarts, though her unanchored curiosity leaves her open to teasing and exploitation. Like Luna, children from "out of command, out of control" families are often quite friendly with their parents, absent the tension of rules articulated or upheld. These kids are often friendly, creative, and patient with peers, absent a sense of expectation for productivity. School is often a negative experience for "out of command, out of control" children who lack the extreme intelligence of Luna, because every school function involves some degree of rules or expectations.

The strength of these family systems is unconditional love, and that is never a small blessing or insignificant force. The weakness is in making long-term commitments or other decisions that involve both choosing and unchoosing options. Decision-making is either done hastily, if passionately, or not at all. Mr. Lovegood demonstrates this flippant use of free will when he chooses to turn in Harry and his friends just to get Luna back from prison. He is an otherwise loving man who makes a passionate decision to save his daughter without thinking of the damage he would be doing to other children like his Luna. But it is not the habit of his family to consider and consent to the outcomes of choices.

It is also difficult for teenagers, especially, to define themselves in a family that's defined by dissent, deconstruction, or conspiracy theorizing. If everything is okay or everything is possible, then what is lasting and what is worthy of sacrifice? In the next chapter, I discuss the power of adolescents to participate in the moral and spiritual formation of their peers when asked and supported in so doing. Adults can build Rooms of Requirement where trusted and free teenagers can create Dumbledore's Army and do for Luna what it did for Neville and children from every kind of family system. In that cloud of well-formed and committed witnesses, Luna received command and freedom at Hogwarts and grew into a brave and committed leader and warrior in ways her passionately leaderless and pacifist father could not have imagined. Whereas chapter 7, on "Confirmation and Adolescent Faith," explains how teenagers can help form each other in ways beyond their families' systems, chapter 8, on "Godparenting," investigates how Luna's teachers became her family system.

NOTES

1. *Philosopher's Stone*, 299.

2. J. K. Rowling, *Harry Potter and the Order of the Phoenix* (New York: Scholastic, 2003), 127.

3. *Order of the Phoenix,* 834.

4. *Deathly Hallows,* 241–42.

5. Reinhold Niebuhr, *The Gifford Lectures* (Scotland: University of Edinburgh, 1939).

6. Lewis, "Weight of Glory," 34.

7. Augustine, *Confessions*, 1:1:1.

8. *Philosopher's Stone*, 299.

9. Ibid., 295.

10. Chris Columbus, "Harry Potter and the Philosopher's Stone" (Warner Bros. Pictures, 2011), film, 00:08:30.

11. "Order of the Phoenix," film, 00:35:39.

12. Winston Churchill and Richard Langworth, *Churchill by Himself: The Definitive Collection of Quotations* (New York: Public Affairs, 2008), 574.

13. *Half Blood Prince*, 585.

14. *Half Bood Prince*, 591.

15. Irvin Kershner, "The Empire Strikes Back" (Lucasfilm Ltd., 1980), film, 01:13:15.

CHAPTER SEVEN

Confirmation and Adolescent Faith

Building Dumbledore's Army

*"I'm of age, and I'm going to keep fighting
even if you've given up!"*[1]

I will never forget the day one high school student got me thinking for the first time about Confirmation and Harry Potter. There are very few explicit references to organized religion or religious rituals of any kind in the stories, much less specific rites of passage like baptism or Confirmation. There are hints of Rowling's sacramental imagination, for those well formed in Judeo-Christian Scripture and theology.[2] But ever since that insightful student shared her perspective with me, I cannot watch the films without interpreting so much of Harry's seven-book saga as preparation for the particular act of confirming his faith.

I had been showing movie clips from all seven films throughout my high school religion class titled "Theological Themes in Harry Potter." Toward the end of the course, I asked students to share their favorite film scenes. One of the last students to answer my query was a diehard Harry Potter fan. She was a proud Hufflepuff who would periodically dye her hair yellow and black throughout her years in high school to show her House pride. When I asked for her favorite scene, she beamed. She stretched out her arms as if to say "Duh!" and then squealed, "The Confirmation scene!" I stood silent. She said it with such confidence, as if the class knew what she was talking about. We were all at a loss to recall any Confirmation scene in Harry Potter. "You know!" She groaned as if everyone knew of the scene. "Come on, everybody . . . the scene with Harry and the others in Hogsmeade?" Her voice trailed off and sounded weaker as it fell into a very quiet and confused room of students. She looked left and right. Her half-open mouth and quickly blinking eyes said, "Surely someone in here knows the scene I mean." But we didn't. She then described, perfectly, the Confirmation scene. And when she was done, I was not the only person—believer or nonbeliever—that could ever watch or read the story again and not think of her passionate perspective on the meaning and practice of confirming faith throughout the seven books.

The Confirmation Scene

The particular Confirmation scene she described comes near the end of last book. Harry, Ron, and Hermione apparate to Hogsmeade, hoping to somehow sneak into Hogwarts and look for Horcruxes. But Hogsmeade is crawling with Death Eaters, and they are nearly captured. A man in the pub, who turns out to be Albus Dumbledore's brother, Aberforth, saves the trio. In this scene, Aberforth tries to talk sense into the three students but focuses mostly on Harry. He is insistent on one thing from the moment he recognizes them: "We need to think of the best way to get you out of here." But Harry cuts him off.

"We're not leaving," said Harry. "We need to get into Hogwarts."

"Don't be stupid, boy," said Aberforth.

"We've got to," said Harry.

"What you've got to do," said Aberforth, leaning forward, "is to get as far away from here as you can."

"You don't understand. There isn't much time. We've got to get into the castle. Dumbledore—I mean, your brother—wanted us—"

…"My brother Albus wanted a lot of things," said Aberforth, "and people had a habit of getting hurt while he was carrying out his grand plans. You get away from this school, Potter, and out of the country if you can. Forget my brother and his clever schemes. He's gone where none of this can hurt him, and you don't owe him anything."

"You don't understand," said Harry again.

"Oh, don't I?" said Aberforth quietly. "You don't think I understood my own brother? Think you knew Albus better than I did?"

" . . . he left me a job...I've got to -"

"Got to? Why got to? He's dead, isn't he?" said Aberforth roughly. "Let it go, boy, before you follow him! Save yourself!"

"I can't."[3]

The student recited this dialogue to all of us, almost word for word. Her classmates were amazed at how invested she was in every word of the scene.

I knew a fact about this Hufflepuff student that many of her class-mates did not know. She had recently been confirmed in the Episcopal Church—one of the few students I have ever taught who was so knowledgeable about the rite of Confirmation and authentically excited about being confirmed. I also knew that she was adopted and that no one in her home was religious. In middle school, she had sought out a local church on the internet and asked her family to allow her to go and join, which they did. Her family dropped her off and picked her up from that Episcopal church for years. More than most teenagers, her faith was decidedly her own—both in conviction and in daily practice. She beamed as she described this Confirmation scene: "This is Harry's Confirmation moment—when it all gets real! This is the totally intense scene where he has to face the skepticism of grown-ups who say they care about him but don't really care about his faith!" She was nearly manic with glee and insight. She had clearly thought about this scene a lot. "It's so dramatic! A grown-up tempts him to drop his conviction or deny his beliefs. But Harry renounces Aberforth's doubt that he is trying to push onto Harry, and he holds tight to what he knows and what he doesn't know . . ."

She's right. The scene is a standoff between the hardened heart of an old man and the brave mission of young adults who dream and believe in fighting evil with their lives. Aberforth's bitterness strangles his bravery. He refuses to hear or learn anything new from Harry about his brother. Aberforth does not want to hear from Harry about Dumbledore's hopes and plans for liberating the wizarding world from Voldemort. Harry tries to cut through the calluses on Aberforth's heart and appeals to his past as a member of the resistance against Voldemort. But Aberforth declares the power of the Order of the Phoenix dead. Having given up both the poetry and prose of resistance, Aberforth is now primal about the protection of lives. He does not want to hear about Dumbledore and Harry's mission to defeat Voldemort and insists that Harry must escape death.

"I can't leave," said Harry. "I've got a job—"

"Give it to someone else!"

"I can't. It's got to be me, Dumbledore explained it all—"

"Oh, did he now? And did he tell you everything, was he honest with you?"[4]

My student loved that last line. Her experience with adults is that they have a way of using an adolescent's lack of knowledge about the world against them in arguments. Too often, when an adolescent shares with us their truth against our sensibilities or convictions, we adults often respond by reminding the young person of all that they are not sure of. It is as if Aberforth can smell Harry's hidden questions and doubts about Dumbledore. Aberforth wants to drag Harry away from magical thinking and grand schemes to conquer Voldemort—that is, he wants to drag Harry to where he is in doubt, bitterness, and survival. Harry sounds too much like the teenage Albus not to stir Aberforth's decades-old anger with his brother.

> "I knew my brother, Potter. He learned secrecy at our mother's knee. Secrets and lies, that's how we grew up, and Albus . . . he was a natural."[5]

Harry is faced with a man who knew Dumbledore for a hundred years and who calls Albus a liar. Harry is also aware that Aberforth might be right about aspects of Dumbledore's life and character. With Ron and Hermione watching, Harry is forced by Aberforth to ask himself once more if he is sure about following the mission of Dumbledore. Harry had already learned, accepted, and initiated this mission, but only in the privacy of his heart and within the safe core of community and intimacy with Hermione and Ron. But in this moment of interrogation, Aberforth calls on Harry to confirm publicly and bravely the mission he had embarked on privately and safely. This scene is an emblem of the essence and energy of Confirmation.

> Harry kept quiet. He did not want to express the doubts and uncertainties about Dumbledore that had riddled him for months now. He had made his choice while he dug Dobby's grave, he had decided to continue along the winding, dangerous path indicated for him by Albus Dumbledore to accept that he had not been told everything that he wanted to know, but simply to trust. He had no desire to doubt again; he did not want to hear anything that would deflect him from his purpose. He met Aberforth's gaze, which was so strikingly like his brother's: The bright blue eyes gave the same impression that they were X-raying the object of their scrutiny, and Harry thought that Aberforth knew what he was thinking and despised him for it.[6]

In her breathless retelling of the scene, my student repeated the line three times for our class: "He had made his choice while he dug Dobby's grave . . ." According to my notes taken during her lesson, she went on to say, "That's what Confirmation is. You have to make the choice in your heart before you make it in public. You can't just show up and say you're ready to confirm something. You show up to Confirmation because you have already decided to be all in, and now you're ready to say to the skeptics and the grown-ups: *Yes. I mean it.*" She continued, "The bishop just plays Aberforth, really: the grown up who asks the questions that you answer to their face with your faith."

The revelation from Rowling that Harry made his decision to follow Dumbledore unto death while digging Dobby's grave is crucial to understanding how it was possible for Harry to face Aberforth so confidently. Harry's decision to embark on the mission against Voldemort even if he dies doing it is, in part, a response to the sacrificial love of Dobby. Harry was already following the mission before Dobby died. But what happens at the grave is that Harry recognizes Dobby's death as a sacrificial act of love for others, like the death of his mother. And he is moved to respond to this act with his own and entire life. Great insights for any Confirmation preparation can be taken from this grave-digging decision. The suggestion for any Confirmation process would be to ask the confirmand to encounter and ponder the life and death of Christ not just as an act of love or gift, but also as an invitation for response in kind.

Grief is the natural response to death, and Harry clearly feels that for Dobby. But because it was a sacrificial death from a selfless and intentional giver—a marginalized elf who chooses to use his freedom to serve—Harry is invited to do more than grieve. Dobby literally took the knife that could or would have stabbed others. As a recipient of the grace given to him, Harry feels called to conform his life to the values and choices of Dobby and his mother: to do for others what was done for him. All sacrificial love has this power: to call us beyond awe of sacrifice into conformity with acts of sacrifice. Dumbledore gave Harry the mission; martyrs taught Harry the means. At baptism, we become the mission. At Confirmation, we become the means.

The seven books slowly reveal the extent of the protection his mother's sacrificial blood gave Harry. But the reality is that her death and that of Dobby are what give him the vision and the power to walk away from protection and toward his own death. In the end, the death of Christ should not safely solidify us into a paradigm of protection—always a possibility when one's theology focuses too much on atonement. You have only to listen to contemporary Christian music lyrics to hear, over and over again, that Christ died for sinners. But you'll hear little about what kinds of lives we ought to live in light of this atonement and freedom. The lyrics tend to speak of the crucifixion as something Jesus did for "me" and not "us." Jesus's life, in these atonement-centered theologies, accomplished primarily the needed sacrifice for our sins; they fail to emphasize Christ's lifelong mission to challenge unjust structures, name the marginalized, heal the sick and forgotten, challenge and condemn corruption, and honor the dignity of both men and women. By defeating the power of death over us, the resurrection should drive us forth from paradigms of protection from condemnation into plans for action. Confirmation can be the process by which we both acknowledge what Christ has done for us (atonement) and respond with conformity to his way of life and love (discipleship).

I turned off the lights in the classroom and played the clip of the Aberforth scene while the confirmed student was talking and teaching from her seat. She then came up to my laptop at the front of the class, politely nudged me away from the keyboard, and took over the teaching with her enthusiasm. She explained that the book "has way more conversation than the movies," saying, "I'll just pause it and fill in what's missing, okay?" I was so blissfully sidelined in this lesson that I took a seat against the wall. She paused the scene multiple times, walking us through the Confirmation aspects of each sentence spoken. She explained to the class that a bishop asks questions of those who are being confirmed "in real life." She added, "The bishop is way nicer than Aberforth, though. Seriously." I had the students open their copies of the Book of Common Prayer to see the actual questions asked by a bishop. My teaching student pressed play again on the film.

> "How can you be sure, Potter, that my brother wasn't more interested in the greater good than in you? How can you be sure you aren't dispensable, just like my little sister?"
>
> "I don't believe it. Dumbledore loved Harry," said Hermione.
>
> "Why didn't he tell him to hide, then?" shot back Aberforth. "Why didn't he say to him, 'Take care of yourself, here's how to survive?'"
>
> "Because," said Harry before Hermione could answer, "sometimes you've got to think about more than your own safety! Sometimes you've got to think about the greater good! This is war!"
>
> "You're seventeen, boy!"
>
> "I'm of age, and I'm going to keep fighting even if you've given up!"[7]

I was so choked up hearing this student, herself an orphaned child whose clear hero and soulmate was Harry Potter, repeat the line to her classmates twice: "Sometimes you've got to think about more than your own safety." Harry was formed into this kind of mature, self-sacrificing young man over the course of years with Dumbledore. The Dursleys' abuse left Harry a lone warrior, sleeping under the stairs, with no other community offering or asking for help. He arrived at Hogwarts a hopeful but primal person, a boy bullied by his relatives and forced to cope with that rejection alone in a cupboard under the stairs. Aberforth is tempting Harry to view Dumbledore like the Dursleys: adults officially caring for Harry but deep down uncommitted to Harry's health and safety. But Harry holds fast to his impression of Dumbledore as a complicated, cryptic, but committed mentor. Harry accepts that Dumbledore was willing to die and willing to let Harry die to defeat Voldemort. The gospel readings for the Confirmation liturgy include parallel words to Rowling's scene:

> Then Jesus told his disciples, "If any want to become my followers, let them deny themselves and take up their cross and follow me. For those who want to save their life will lose it, and those who lose their life for my sake will find it."[8]

In the book and the film, you can sense Harry's confidence growing stronger with every word about the mission he received from Dumbledore. Confessing his faith strengthens it, as is the purpose and the power of the Confirmation rite. Harry's confession to Aberforth that he must be willing to lose his life in order to save anyone is a sermon on the Mark passage:

> "Your brother knew how to finish You-Know-Who and he passed the knowledge on to me. I'm going to keep going until I succeed—or I die. Don't think I don't know how this might end. I've known it for years."[9]

In a phrase that nearly took my breath away, the student said to our class, "Harry's totally right. Like, here's the thing with Confirmation: It's not the end of something. It's the beginning of believing that I know I will die, so here's how I want to live."

> "We need to get into Hogwarts," said Harry again. "If you can't help us, we'll wait till daybreak, leave you in peace, and try to find a way in ourselves. If you can help us—well, now would be a great time to mention it."[10]

Similarly to the actual Confirmation liturgy, this scene shows Harry being asked what he believes, what he renounces, and to what he will be faithful along with his friends on their epic mission. Every minute and every year at Hogwarts has formed Harry into the person who stands in front of Aberforth and declares his faith against his own doubts and the doubts of the adult world. Harry decides that he doesn't need to know or completely understand Dumbledore or the mission before he is ready to die for it. It takes years for Harry to understand his mother's gift to him, to realize that she was more than a victim of Voldemort—she was also a willing resistor and sacrifice for others.

We watch and read how Harry's understanding grows regarding the agency of sacrifice. Lupin is first to reprimand Harry for careless living, when Harry does not turn in the Marauder's Map, by reminding him that his parents died for his freedom and that he should live up to and live into this gift. Later in the narrative, Harry demonstrates the maturing of his understanding of sacrificial love in daring Slughorn to give up the Horcrux memory by saying:

> "I'm going to tell you something, something others have only guessed at. It's true. I am the Chosen One. Only I can destroy him. But in order to do so, I need to know what Tom Riddle asked you that night in your office all those years ago. And I need to know what you told him. Be brave, Professor, be brave like my mother. Otherwise, you disgrace her. Otherwise, she died for nothing."[11]

There is nothing Harry can say to prove himself to Aberforth. But Harry's Confirmation, like any true Confirmation, is not an act of certainty, but rather an act of clarity. When we train teenagers in certainty, we betray our own experience of truth and lose credibility with most young adults, who know through experience the limits of human understanding. Our call is to prepare young people to respond to sacrificial love: to help them find clarity about the life and love of Christ. And then to help them find and articulate clarity about how they want to respond to Christ's invitation to abundant life and to resurrection from every death. As Romans 12:1, one of the appointed readings for the Confirmation liturgy, directs us all, "Present your bodies as a living sacrifice, holy and acceptable to God, which is your spiritual worship."

Lessons from the Room of Requirement

Conformity gets a bad name these days. We have all heard warnings from parents, pulpits, and profiteers to avoid conformity, as if its only form is mindless ascent to unworthy or untrue externalities. And young people have heard us. The result is that the concept of identity creation through nonconformity is near dogma—for any age or generation—in the twenty-first century. Just look at the commercials aimed at baby boomers to redefine retirement or reject altogether the reality of aging. Think of the for-profit colleges and universities inviting all ages to acquire nontraditional degrees, as well as the countless commercials for vacation resorts, clothing, and cars tempting consumers to redefine, reimagine, or remake traditions or expectations. The not-so-subtle message in this cultural moment is that conformity is the enemy of authenticity.

So long as conformity is synonymous with mere replication, perhaps it is good to avoid. But there is a far richer understanding of conformity that involves learning passed-down practices of living, loving, and choosing in the pattern of Christ. Paul exhorts us in Romans 12:2, "Do not be conformed to this world," but this verse is a warning against aping the ways of the dominant culture, not a command to avoid patterns of conformity that enable us to grow into the people we are called to be through baptism. Holistic and life-giving conformity—that is, the forming and ordering of one's life in accordance with truth—is an essential skill for learning and living the way of Jesus. Paul's concern was not that disciples might conform, but rather that they might conform to unworthy or untrue things.

Teaching has proven to me over the last two decades that we have a crisis of conformity among young people. Many students of all races and classes seem allergic to invitations to conform in any way. The buzzword from consultants helping students applying to colleges or jobs or businesses looking to expand is the need to define what makes one "distinctive." The hottest word to describe marketing in our age—marketing of self or services—is "disruption." The recent tendency to stand against forms of convention as a matter of principle and courage is the darker side of the maker generation and the core of the gripe against millennials by their parents and employers. The question that arises from this cultural drive to distinguish or disrupt is clear: Are we losing the ability to practice or pass on ways or patterns of life that are tried or, for lack of a better term, traditional? Our problem—unlike the exploding and nearly uniform consumption patterns at the dawn of the suburb or the retail mall in the post–World War II period—is not that young people are conformists; it is rather that they are unwilling or unable to thoughtfully conform to passed-down patterns of reflection, prayer, or action, and this is a problem for passing on the faith.

This current maker generation of young people is clearly more collaborative than older demographic groups, and this can be a healthy development in all sectors of our society. However, this same generation of tinkering thinkers resents being assessed or graded as a group. They like to spread the work or the blame, but not the credit. Competition for selection to private or charter schools, to travel with sports teams and performance groups, and, infinitely more so, for admission to colleges or universities is causing young people to try to distinguish themselves from the herd at nearly any cost. More and more, parents are calling the schools to complain when group work or group projects are graded and all members of the group receive the same grade. Certain highly anxious parents (of all ethnic and socioeconomic groups) do not want their children's assessments yoked to a group, for fear, in their common wording, that their children will be "lost in the crowd" or "punished for the poor performance of others."[12] We are a culture that rewards those who *stand out*, not those who *stand with*.

We need to go beyond our worries about the caricature of conformity that has (rightly) become a liability to the differentiated individual of any age. The dynamism and joy in Rowling's descriptions of the community, purpose, and mutual maturation of Dumbledore's Army, with students teaching students, call me to put in a word for the power of teaching people to conform in life-giving ways. But we have to build our imagination and our lesson plans on a healthier and more holistic definition of conformity. The definition of the word *conformity* is actually more fulsome than you might think. It includes words and concepts such as "abide by," "uphold," "share," and "respect." Conformity is a glue of community: an act of learning, sharing, and passing on practices of faith. It is what Anglican ethicist Timothy Sedgwick calls "traditioning," the passing on of our convictions to the next generation,[13] where quite often the best ideas are not created in every generation, but rather cared for, shared, embodied, and transferred.

Traditioning is not an uncritical process, like handing an immutable baton from one person to the next, but rather it is a process by which we inherit inspired, holy, and catalytic texts, rituals, and practices that are both created for and re-created by every person who incarnates them into their lives. Traditioning, at its best, is like teaching and learning music. Everyone who learns to conform—to the bar, to the note, to the meter, either by sight or by ear—can then and only then express their own unique voice and sound. The liberty of self-expression and improvisation come through conforming to the rule of life that is the grammar of music.

The place where students at Hogwarts conform to truth in community is the Room of Requirement. Understanding the powerful role this room plays in the plot—and in the emotional, social, and spiritual development of each character—is crucial to understanding how the students mature from first-year classmates yelling "Leviosa" at still feathers into young adult warriors who willingly bleed and die in war. I believe that adults can create Rooms of Requirement—places where young people can learn and grow with and separately from one another—for the young people in their lives. But the Rooms of Requirement that we construct for teaching faith must be built and resourced thoughtfully, just as in the Harry Potter series. In the books, we learn that the opening and supplying of the Room of Requirement happens by magic. In our lives, it is the intentional vision, creation, and maintenance of safe spiritual places by adults that incarnates this kind of nonanxious, resourceful, and hero-making space where young people can learn, practice, and pass on their faith to their peers in community.

The Room of Requirement is more than a classroom, of which Hogwarts has many. This "Come and Go Room" is a particular learning and practice space, existing to help young people prepare for specific missions without the presence of adults. Many of the skills practiced in the room were taught somewhere else, such as the classroom, greenhouse, or Quidditch field, and mostly by adults in formal teaching experiences. But in the Room of Requirement, students bring their personal knowledge and practices together, however varied their levels of ignorance or skill may be. Part of the powerful dynamism in that space is that everyone stands in a room with others who know less than, as much as, and more than they do. As Proverbs 27:17 says, "As iron sharpens iron, so one man sharpens another." The walls between the roles of teacher and student are fluid. It is a space where students can experiment with the knowledge they already have; they can hone the skills they have already learned. They enter the Room of Requirement, with this radical difference from their traditional classrooms, in need of building a community or accomplishing a particular mission to defend against a pressing and growing evil in their world. I have argued earlier in this book that Hogwarts teaches us how to teach; the Room of Requirement teaches us how to form souls for shared and sacred missions.

Let's take a moment to think about how the Room of Requirement reveals itself to the students and how its sacred space becomes the soul of the school. Don't miss the significance in the fact that the students first learned about the room from a house-elf as well as Dumbledore— both characters who are supreme teachers in how to find, understand, and practice freedom. After getting twenty-five curious classmates to meet secretly in a crowded pub in Hogsmeade and sign their names on the Dumbledore's Army list, Harry and Hermione are stumped as to where this group can gather to practice using magic and fighting the dark arts. The dictatorial Dolores Umbridge has forbidden the use of wands and the practice of spells in her Defence Against the Dark Arts class and on the school grounds, in hopes of disabling and dispiriting any potential student revolt against the Ministry of Magic. Harry and his close friends have succeeded in gathering a resistance force loyal to Dumbledore and the common good, but they begin to wonder if the group can sustain itself under such institutional suppression.

Dobby is the one who reminds Harry of the existence of the Come and Go Room, a place Dumbledore also hinted about to Harry. According to Dobby, it is "a room that a person can only enter when they have real need of it. Sometimes it is there, and sometimes it is not, but when it appears, it is always equipped for the seeker's needs." Wandering in the hallway where Dobby suggested they seek the room, Harry and his friends pause in front of a blank wall. "Dobby said to walk past this bit of wall three times, concentrating hard on what we need."[14] Similar to the need for focus in casting a Patronus Charm, Rowling wants Hogwarts students and us, her readers, to remember the necessity to discern the deep needs that drive us so that we make better decisions and commitments.

In giving lectures on parenting over the years, I have used the Room of Requirement as an example of a place created by adults that helps people discern the difference between a want and a need. This distinction is hard for any of us at any age. But the Room of Requirement teaches, among other things, that we learn best, we grow most, and we mature best when we begin our growing by learning the difference between what we merely want and what we deeply need.

> Ron had screwed up his eyes in concentration, Hermione was whispering something under her breath, Harry's fists were clenched as he stared ahead of him.
>
> *We need somewhere to learn to fight . . .* he thought. *Just give us a place to practise . . . somewhere they can't find us . . .*
>
> "Harry!" said Hermione sharply, as they wheeled around after their third walk past.
>
> A highly polished door had appeared in the wall. Ron was staring at it, looking slightly wary. Harry reached out, seized the brass handle, pulled open the door, and led the way into a spacious room lit with flickering torches. . . .
>
> The walls were lined with wooden bookcases, and instead of chairs there were large silk cushions on the floor. A set of shelves at the far end of the room carried a range of instruments such as Sneakoscopes, Secrecy Sensors, and a large, cracked Foe-Glass that Harry was sure had hung, the previous year, in the fake Moody's office. . . .
>
> "And just look at these books!" said Hermione excitedly, running a finger along the spines of the large leather-bound tomes. . . . She looked around at Harry, her face glowing, and he saw that the presence

of hundreds of books had finally convinced Hermione that what they were doing was right. "Harry, this is wonderful, there's everything we need here!"[15]

When I teach Harry Potter readers about the church, I call it the Room of Requirement in our world. At its best, the church can be a sacred space that is a gift we could not create or ultimately control, that opens up to those who are open to it, and that does not always offer what we want but always has what people truly need. There are (or should be) few absolutely or fixed realities in a healthy church. Dynamic faith communities are constantly praying about and discerning the needs of the people they invite and sustain, and they are open and brave in decluttering, deconstructing, and defunding things that are about wants and nostalgia rather than fonts of grace to meet the true needs of souls.

In the Anglican tradition, at our best, our ecclesiology flows from our theological anthropology. The church's message has come in and through Christ. The church's metabolism is the life and love of the Holy Spirit, breathing into and bathing the world since Pentecost. The church's methods are made in response to the nature of the person, not the person's nature falsely constructed in response to the methods of the church, which is sadly often the case. Like the Room of Requirement, the healthy church is open to those who are seekers and fills its space with resources discerned as food for the needs of the soul and the world. The Great Commission is our mission in the face of a socially unjust and broken world full of dark arts. Confirmation and other formation programs within our religious communities are the Rooms of Requirement where souls form each other in the likeness of Christ—in skill, courage, and love—to participate in mission of the resurrection of all things in Christ.

To further explain what is truly positive about training souls to conform to the life of Christ and to the lives of our saints and spiritual heroes, I often share two pictures with church groups. First, I show a picture of Yoda and Luke Skywalker from *The Empire Strikes Back*. In this film, the second of the original trilogy, we see the universe in turmoil as the evil Empire has taken over the galaxy. Much of this film chronicles the exile of Luke to a small planet where he is secretly training in the Jedi arts with Yoda. In scene after scene, we see the small Jedi knight Yoda trying to teach the complex philosophy and magic of the Force. The still picture I show is of Yoda strapped to Luke's back, his arms wrapped Luke's neck, and his voice directly in Luke's ear for their lessons each day. In these training scenes, Yoda is constantly explaining things to Luke as he tries to perform the physical and mental practices of a Jedi. More than once, Luke stumbles or even falls, throwing Yoda over his head onto the ground.

I love this image of mentoring. Yoda literally ties his fate and his body to his student. He is willing to travel with Luke, strapped to Luke's back, through every lesson, constantly sharing his hundreds of years of life and learning. He answers Luke's questions and adapts his teaching to Luke's life and level of faith. This is not just teaching; this is self-sacrificing mentoring. Luke is not being asked to conform to Yoda's way of life or religion. Rather, Yoda is sharing with Luke the teachings to which Yoda has conformed his life. Yoda is passing on a tradition that was passed to him, with humility and confidence born of his own long life of experiencing the truth of what he inherited.

I then contrast the photo of Yoda on Luke's back with a scene from the iconic 1939 film *The Wizard of Oz*, starring Judy Garland. I show a still picture of Dorothy, the Tin Man, the Lion, and the Scarecrow, singing and skipping arm in arm along the yellow brick road. If you remember this scene in the film, they are singing the song "We're Off to See the Wizard." The scene captures the friendship of the travelers. They face adversity together on the brick road. They get to know each other on the brick road. They develop strong loyalty to one another. But the reality is that none of them know exactly where they are going, what the destination will look like or be like, or whether they will be able to see the person they seek. None of them have even seen the wizard, much less made requests of him or known anyone else who has. None of them have walked this path before. They have no plan except to wonder and wander toward the Emerald City and hope for the best. Dorothy is the cause of their journey and is therefore treated as the leader on the journey. But she is the foreigner in the group, knowing less than anyone else about where she is or what is possible in Oz. They found each other, but they are all lost. They have passion but no real plan. They are fast friends who have, as Paul warned against, zeal without knowledge.[16]

I show the *Wizard of Oz* picture to teachers and mentors as my image of the tragedy of mentorless teaching and learning. It is the opposite of what is demonstrated by Yoda, who whispers constantly about a way of life, love, and mission as he is strapped to Luke's back. He is bringing the tradition to a younger soul, with his flesh and voice as the bridge. He has linked himself to the student so tightly that they literally stand or fall together. In the language of the saga, Luke is not learning ideas; rather, he is learning "the ways" of the Force. The ways do not belong to Luke or Yoda; they are learned, practiced, shared, and revered as sacred.

People's lives have been saved by the ways, and other lives have been lost in the defense of them. One cannot help but think of Romans 12:2: "Do not be conformed to this world, but be transformed by the renewing of your minds, so that you may discern what is the will of God—what is good and acceptable and perfect." The Baptismal Covenant reminds us that we do not grow by making changes in our life: baptism is not a call to try to earn one's salvation or redemption. In the words of C. S. Lewis, we are not called to be nice men or good men but "new men."[17] Following Christ is not a to-do list; it is an experience of having one's life freed from death and filled with the life of God. In baptism, we are initiated into a community practicing a holistic and holy way of life fed by the Holy Spirit; a power and rule of life that causes transformation to take over like a season on the earth. As Paul states in Galatians 2:20, "It is no longer I who live, but Christ who lives in me." When we "seek first the kingdom," we find that all other aspects of our lives get caught up in the reality of the kingdom, and then "all other things will be added" (Matt. 6:33).

I do not demonize journeys rooted and routed in friendship or fellowship, such as walking the yellow brick road in optimistic ignorance. But what it means to pass on a tradition is something entirely different. It requires brave and tireless mentoring. It requires a sage sharing a way of life, not just a lesson. When I speak of conformity, I do not invite an exercise in mere mirroring or mimicking. I mean falling in love with a way of life that you have seen and experienced in a mentor and that is not your own until you wed yourself to it. What gives you the idea, the momentum, and the means is a passionate mentor who will share the way by hitching their safety to yours; someone who knows more than you, has walked this very road before, and is a lifelong student of the truth. There is a negative form of conformity that is thoughtless parroting or patterning one's life to resemble others. But there is a deeper transformative conforming that is learning and living a creed placed in your hand and heart by someone who has already taken it into their own. Confirmation at its best can be the consummation of sharing the way of truth.

The purpose of the Room of Requirement is to be a safe place to conform to truth in community with others. It is where Dumbledore's Army is training for Confirmation. It is not that students are trying to be like one another. Rather, it is a place where young people come to learn a tradition together: the skills, symbols, and wisdom of life, love, and freedom.

There is nothing short of brilliance in the selection of the passage from Ezekiel 37:1–14, about the valley of the dry bones, as the reading for the Confirmation liturgy. This passage could easily be the caption of the still photo of Yoda on the back of Luke Skywalker. The beauty of the story is that God brings the prophet to the valley and shows him the pit of death and destruction, piles of broken bones from nameless lives. But God does not invite the prophet to watch or listen to God's voice healing the scene. Instead, God tells the prophet what to say. The healing that takes place for the creation around Ezekiel does not happen in front of him; it happens through him because God gave him the words and the power to transform everything.

This passage is perfect for a Confirmation liturgy because it sends the message that we are called to find the would-be prophets in our midst and share with them the words of life. We have to know where the valleys of death are in our world: the shelters, the free clinics, the prisons, the hospitals, the brothels, the campuses, the bases, the streets, the classrooms, and the boardrooms. Good mentors know where the broken bones are— in our hearts and in our communities. We then need to form others to understand the words of God that we are trying, through our mentoring, to teach. And once we have formed the souls in our care as best we can, having first conformed our own lives to the gospel, then it is our role and vocation to stand by and allow others to prophesy. Baptism is the great prophet maker. Those called to faith formation are the prophet mentors.

> Grant, Almighty God, that we, who have been redeemed from the old life of sin by our baptism into the death and resurrection of your Son Jesus Christ, may be renewed in your Holy Spirit, and live in righteousness and true holiness; through Jesus Christ our Lord, who lives and reigns with you and the Holy Spirit, one God, now and for ever. *Amen.*[18]

NOTES

1. *Deathly Hallows*, 568.

2. One example would be the graveyard scene in *The Goblet of Fire*, where Voldemort's body is restored. On the surface, this is a terrifying scene but not a religious scene in any way. However, if one focuses on the three parts of the ceremony that reconstitute Voldemort's body, one can see the whole scene as mirroring the eucharistic rite. Peter Pettigrew pronounces three incantations over the cauldron while holding the fetal form of Voldemort: "Bone of the Father stolen, blood of the enemy unwillingly given, blood of the servant willingly given" (*Goblet of Fire*, 641). Many commentators have noted that this is a haunting reversal of the words and meaning of the eucharistic prayer: blood willingly given, bone willingly given, and servants made free and whole.

3. *Deathly Hallows*, 561–62.

4. Ibid.

5. Ibid, 562.

6. Ibid, 563.

7. Ibid., 568.

8. Mark 8:34.

9.*Deathly Hallows*, 568–69.

10. Ibid, 569.

11. David Yates, "Harry Potter and the Half-Blood Prince" (Warner Bros. Pictures, 2009), film, 01:46:34.

12. I have always admired the thoughtful use of badges in the Girl and Boy Scout cultures. It seems to me these groups have found a balance between uniformity and individual skill development and reward. The uniform is a blunt and obvious sign of the conformity of all Scouts to their code of honor. However, every uniform displays the unique work ethic and skill development of the particular Scout.

13. Timothy Sedgwick, "Anglican Ethics and Moral Traditioning," *Anglican Theological Review* 94, no. 4 (Fall 2012): 665–70.

14. *Order of the Phoenix*, 386–87.

15. Ibid., 389.

16. Romans 10:2.

17. Lewis, *Mere Christianity*, 177.

18. Collect for Confirmation, Book of Common Prayer, 254.

CHAPTER EIGHT

Godparenting

A Sirius Role

"Godfather?" sputtered Uncle Vernon.
"You haven't got a godfather!"
"Yes, I have," said Harry brightly.
"He was my mum and dad's best friend.
He's a convicted murderer, but he's broken
out of wizard prison and he's on the run.
He likes to keep in touch with me, though . . .
keep up with my news . . .
check if I'm happy."[1]

It is tempting to say that we have a crisis of godparenting across denominations in the United States, but that observation is nonetheless imprecise. The word *crisis* is best used to describe something that people have been forced to name as a problem, such as a financial crisis or a health crisis. The shameful open secret of the church's abandonment of focus and formation around godparenting does not get the attention that a crisis usually stirs. It is more accurate to describe the state of godparenting in the church as tragic. The definition of *tragedy* is that the sad event or events are, in part, avoidable. And that is true for the state of godparenting in the contemporary church. I believe godparenting is one of the least defined and supported vocations in the life of faith.

.Everyone baptized has a godparent or godparents. And informal godparents can be and are chosen by disciples every day. And yet in conversations, interviews, or consultations with churches all over this country, I have the same conversation with men and women of any age about godparenting. I ask group members to raise their hands if they are godparents. Often, nearly everyone in the room claims the title. And then I ask folks, "How is it going? Are you proud of your godparenting? Is it an active part of your faith life?" These kinds of questions are usually met with a combination of silence and shame. Rarely have I met a godparent who is pleased about or proud of their godparenting. But equally rarely have I found churches that offer ongoing education, formation, fellowship, or suggestions for godparents. Our pews and our planet are full of godparents, but there is little to no formation for this sacred role.

Most people who identify as godchildren report that they have no contact with their godparents at all. I can count on one hand the number of godchildren or godparents I have met over the years who attest to an ongoing and dynamic relationship rooted in fruitful, joyful, and enduring godparenting. We all use the term and take the picture on the day of baptism, but then we fail to form, support, and celebrate this unique relationship in the lives of our faith communities. The vocation of godparent has altered over the years, as our understanding and ritualization of baptism has changed. However, we *have* had sponsors or godparents at baptism from the very beginning of the life of the sacrament. As a vocation, it is at least as old as deacon and definitely older than priest.

Countless studies about human development and cross-generational mentoring herald the transformative power that nonparent adults can have on younger people and the equal power that being a nonparent adult in someone's life can have on you. We know it works. We know that potentially every person's life, at any age, can be enriched, stretched, and blessed by the kind of giving and receiving of love that healthy godparenting involves. And yet, as leaders and educators passing on our faith, many of us concern ourselves with things and issues other than godparenting in the lives of our faith communities. Ironically, many of us work instead on periodic programing that aims to engage multigenerational groups for mentoring and unconditional love—the very definition of the godparenting reality. Godparenthood appears to be the orphan of our biblical and historical vocations. For over a thousand years, we have had and held this role in our rituals and common law. If godparenthood did not already exist, thousands of research projects in healthy intergenerational development cry out that it should be invented. The sacred reality of godparenting is like a set of sturdy pathways toward grace and growth that we mysteriously and perhaps mindlessly choose not to walk. Herein lies the tragedy.

If you are reading this book, chances are you are one of the few people in the church and in this culture who are part of the solution: you are experiencing or practicing healthy, joyful, fruitful godparenting. But you are rare. And you know it. One of the many gifts J. K. Rowling has given to faith communities through the Harry Potter series is chapter after chapter of a saga that investigates, elevates, and celebrates nonparent relationships of godparenting, both explicitly and implicitly. You cannot read a single book in the series and not come away with the conviction that Rowling believes it takes a village to raise a spiritual child. And specifically, that every person at any age needs a strong, brave, present godparent. The two stars of the series, Harry and Voldemort, are both orphans, meaning that the only parents they will have in the world will be guardians of one kind or another who choose kinship with them. Orphans are existentially and unavoidably godchildren waiting for godparents. And the divergent destinies of Harry Potter and Tom Riddle are a stark study in the power of nonparent adults in the life of children.

The word *godparent* is mentioned over fifty times in the seven books. In a church and a culture that has largely left fallow the potentially fruitful field of godparenting, Rowling writes a narrative that grounds the human development of nearly every significant character in the love and support of formal or informal godparents. The words *priest, reverend,* or *minister* (meaning religious minister) are not mentioned once in the series, even in descriptions of the Muggle world. Her choice to write about only one formal spiritual vocation shows her deep conviction and confidence in the priesthood of all believers and the powers of the baptized to be more than sufficient to act as moral and spiritual anchors and shepherds in the lives of others.

In his seminal work *A Secular Age*, philosopher Charles Taylor writes that the modern world has lost something that was essential and normative food for the premodern human imagination. The premodern world was "enchanted," in his terminology, while the modern and postmodern world is decidedly "disenchanted." In Taylor's words:

> Almost everyone can agree that one of the big differences between us and our ancestors of five hundred years ago is that they lived in an "enchanted" world, and we do not; at the very least, we live in a *much less* "enchanted" world. We might think of this as our having "lost" a number of beliefs and the practices that they made possible. But more, the enchanted world was one in which these forces could cross a porous boundary and shape our lives, psychic and physical. One of the big differences between us and them is that we live with a much firmer sense of the boundary between self and other. We are "buffered" selves. We have changed.
>
> This is not a mere "subtraction" story, for it thinks not only of loss but of remaking. With the subtraction story, there can be no epistemic loss involved in the transition; we have just shucked off some false beliefs, some fears of imagined objects. Looked at my way, the process of

disenchantment involves a change in sensibility; one is open to different things. One has lost a way in which people used to experience the world.[2]

Charles Taylor's image of the once more porous self rings true. Even a shallow study of premodern art, architecture, and literature observes that people were fundamentally open to meanings and realities that came from outside of one's self, and also to responsibilities that came from outside. But in the modern world, Taylor argues, we live inside a buffered self, one that is more defensive, more skeptical, more self-concerned. This means it is self-contained; it sees itself as the author of its own meaning and source of its own authority.

Whether you agree with Taylor's particular explanations or imagery to explain the increasing secularity of the public square and the human soul, I hope you can agree with his general conviction that our world feels less "enchanted" by the day. Taylor's word *buffered* does well to describe the barbed-wire walls I often encounter when working with young people and young adults. They are hardened competitors trained in collaboration concerning the material world, but lonely in the ordering and understanding of their spiritual lives. How do we create physical places and digital spaces that are safe for disarming and opening the buffered self? How do we model, create, and support a community of porous souls, marked by openness to other realities, grand narratives, hero journeys, and the transcendent or divine presence?

My experience of teaching faith with Harry Potter is that the church is dying to hear better stories—stories about both faith and the world. It is not enough to read the Gospels in liturgy or even in smaller, more intimate Bible studies. It is not that the Word is not powerful enough to transform lives. But in a disenchanted world of buffered souls, we have to be honest about how hard it is for the truths of Scripture, tradition, or liturgy to break through. We need to break through the walls of the secular souls with greater consistency, and not just with biblical language or liturgical experiences. We need to be telling stories all the time to meet and challenge the lack of enchantment in our culture. Would you describe your bulletin or church website as telling stories? Would you describe your discussions or arguments about religion with family or friends at meals as storytelling? We have to admit and address the ambient skepticism that parades as maturity, authenticity, or wisdom in our time, and we do it best by telling stories. The whole of the Harry Potter series is what it looks like to talk about life, death, and resurrection in the form of a story. And we know that works.

We need more stories, more testimonies, and more enchanted sharing of our experience of seeking, naming, and knowing God. Our society of buffered souls requires a more enchanted apologetic rather than argument. We need to find and feed better storytellers in our faith communities, and godparents are the place to start. C. S. Lewis has a great line in one of his classic sermons about the need to put our convictions into narratives when sharing our faith stories in a skeptical world:

> Do you think I am trying to weave a spell? Perhaps I am; but remember your fairy tales. Spells are used for breaking enchantments as well as for inducing them. And you and I have need of the strongest spell that can be found to wake us from the evil enchantment of worldliness, which has laid upon us for nearly a hundred years.[3]

Some use words and others do not, but every person is a preacher. But are we training the baptized with this truth? We need people who can talk about their faith while they talk about everything else. Godparents, at their best, are the church's corps of storytellers. In the depth of my heart, I believe (because I have seen) how well-formed godparents can re-enchant the world of their godchildren. Theirs is a voice calling in the wilderness. But are we naming, claiming, and forming godparents to play this crucial, world-healing role?

Recently I did a survey of four or five of the best-selling manuals for congregational ministry and formation in the church. They were all full of lists, websites, online communities, and endless plans and projects for faith formation. I was overwhelmed by how many resources there are both for congregations and for faith practices at home. But in these best sellers, there was not a single reference to godparents or godparenting, much less a plan or project for them. Stunning. It is as if faith formation leaders have given up on or just forgotten about the two-thousand-year-old institution of godparenting that has been linked to baptism since the first centuries of the church and decided instead to let the church staff become the godparents for many. This is noble but unwise and unworkable.

The power of the godparenting relationship is that it is a tight circle, supported by the community, of spiritual kinship between a godparent and a godchild. It is less a ministry and more a marriage. Congregational leadership should not try to marry individuals. Rather, as with actual covenantal marriage, the role of the congregational leaders is to form folks and support them, lifelong and life-wide, in the intimate vocation between God and the married couple. Our young people need and deserve godparents, not godparenting institutions. I understand why this has happened.

But I continue to dream for a revival of the practice of the unique grace and transformation of godparenting. J. K. Rowling clearly believes in it, and so do I. In her famous Harvard commencement address in 2008, notice how Rowling describes her lifelong college friends:

> The friends with whom I sat on graduation day have been my friends for life. They are my children's godparents, the people to whom I've been able to turn in times of trouble, friends who have been kind enough not to sue me when I've used their names for Death Eaters.[4]

Even after completing the original series, Rowling went out of her way on her online website community, Pottermore, to add to the list of godparents among her characters, telling readers that Harry and Ginny are godparents to Teddy Lupin, Ron and Hermione are godparents to James Potter II, and Neville Longbottom is the godfather to Albus Severus Potter. It is as if Rowling cannot conceive of depriving any of her beloved characters or their children of godparents.

The teenagers I have worked with report in surveys that they feel buffered and lonely, even in crowds of friends in person or online. They also act as if their souls are buffered and calloused. Connecting meaningfully with other people often requires alcohol or other medicinal forces just to break down the emotional walls of insecurity and fear around their hearts. Many middle and high schools, public and private, assign *The Lord of the Flies* as standard reading for English class. Many of the students I talk to say that this tale of the cruelty of humanity present in preteen boys is not a work of fiction, but rather more of a documentary of their experience at that age. Every year, we ask our students—girls and boys—to compete against each other for every leg-up in public, charter, and private schools, from Head Start program applications through graduate school admissions. The sad result of creating warriors is that their souls have armor. It is harder to experience the grace and love of God (or of other people) if one does not have a porous self, a life open to and embracing of forces and faces outside itself.

> According to the National Study of Youth and Religion, many American teenagers inhabit a "morally insignificant universe," in which they perceive no *telos*, no larger story in which they play a part, no sense that their actions play a notable part in moving the world forward. This was especially true for mainline Protestant, Roman Catholic, and Jewish young people in the study, who showed less religious vitality, understanding, and hope for the future than their Mormon, conservative Protestant, or black Protestant peers.[5]

Godparents can be storytellers who re-enchant the world of their god-children. Because they are not the primary parents, biological or legal, there is less stress and static in the relationship between godparent and godchild. Without the duties of daily regulation that are part and parcel of parenting, godparents have more room in their conversation space with godchildren to talk about what matters and to narrate the world. They can represent a different kind of adulthood and therefore a different world than what the media, or even the primary parents, portray. Through their presence and narration of an enchanted world, the godparents can help heal the buffered self and encourage the young person to open up to other adults.

In the opening chapters of *The Goblet of Fire*, Harry wakes up from haunting dreams and a burning scar. His scar is hurting him, and he wants to tell someone about it. He worries that a burning scar has something to do with Voldemort. Harry thinks through all the people in his life and cannot think of a person who would be a knowledgeable, available, caring, and helpful listener. But then he remembers something he learned two months before.

> What he really wanted (and it felt almost shameful to admit it to him-self) was someone like—someone like a *parent*: an adult wizard whose advice he could ask without feeling stupid, someone who cared about him, who had had experience of Dark Magic. . . . And then the solution came to him. It was so simple, and so obvious, that he couldn't believe it had taken so long—*Sirius* . . . he hadn't thought of Sirius straight away. But then, perhaps it wasn't so surprising—after all, he had only found out that Sirius was his godfather two months ago.[6]

Harry seems to intuit the vocation of godparent. He trusts that his godfather is a safe person to whom he can tell stories and from whom he can ask for help without judgment. He knows that Sirius believes in magic, believes in Voldemort, and believes in the fight of good wizards that reject Voldemort's death cult. Harry and Sirius share many of the same enchanted stories of their lives and their world. But Harry finds himself stuck in fear and ignorance about the next days and weeks in his own unfolding life. He needs to talk things through with someone who can help him see realistic possibilities and help write the next chapters of his story.

The Godparenting Scene

Mentions of godparenthood appear periodically in the Harry Potter series, and there are priceless and prolific scenes depicting spiritual kinship, faith transmission, and spiritual formation between different generations. But when I lead discussions and presentations on godparenthood in Harry Potter, I always begin with a movie clip that, in my opinion, is the godparenting scene. It is perhaps not a scene you would think of in relation to godparenting, but I find in it so much of the love, bravery, and sacrifice that transformative godparenthood requires and rewards. The scene comes in chapter 4 of *The Deathly Hallows*, "The Seven Potters." We learn over the course of the books that Harry is safe from attack from any dark force or wizard while living at 4 Privet Drive because the shedding of his mother's blood proved a sacrifice powerful enough to bathe even her sister's home in magical protection. Voldemort learns of this rare protective magic over time, but he also learns that it expires when Harry becomes an adult in the wizarding world at seventeen years old. To show his loyalty to Voldemort, Snape tells Voldemort of the plan to move Harry from Privet Drive to a safe house of the Order of the Phoenix before his birthday. But the Order members are unaware of the trap waiting for them. It is their plan to meet at the Dursley home and transport Harry to a safe house in the cover of darkness.

Harry is grateful when all his friends and the members of the Order arrive at Privet Drive to escort him to safety. But Harry's mood changes when he hears the specific plan to ensure his safe arrival at the Burrow. Mad-Eye Moody explains to Harry that six of his older friends and Order members will take Polyjuice potion so as to transform into identical versions of Harry. Each impostor would then be paired with another member of the Order. Everyone was set to leave Privet Drive at the same time so that any Death Eaters would be uncertain as to which was the real Harry. Moody is clear that the dangers are real and lives could be lost. Harry protests, not wanting anyone else to die for him. But the group is utterly committed to the plan, and Harry is compelled by their resolve to let it play out. Six volunteers drink the potion, and then all six put on clothing identical to that of the real Harry Potter. The group takes off on brooms and Thestrals, only to be ambushed by Voldemort's followers. Voldemort himself is in the battle, trying but failing to kill Harry in the attached seat of Hagrid's motorcycle.

A fact unknown to Voldemort or Harry was that the core of Voldemort's wand was a sibling to the core of Harry's wand, and therefore it failed to deliver the death curse to Harry. Hagrid was able to steer through the battle in the sky and bring Harry safely out of the clouds to the Burrow, just as he had brought Harry on that motorcycle to safety at Privet Drive sixteen years before. However, in this same battle, George Weasley loses an ear from a dark curse, Hedwig sacrifices her life, and Moody—the man that had warned the group that someone might die on this mission—is killed in the attack.

At this point, you might be wondering what this scene has to do with godparenting. The answer: everything. The scene begins with a group of adults, none of whom are biologically related to Harry, arriving at the loveless home of the Dursleys for one reason: to protect Harry's life. The living room, in which Harry was not permitted to live for most of his childhood, is flooded with adults who love Harry so much that they are each willing to die for him. Six of them are willing to literally become Harry so that they might take the brunt of the threat of murder. This form of faithfulness and love goes beyond simply loving your neighbor as yourself: the community of care that arrives for Harry is an example of becoming his neighbor in solidarity with him against murderous threats. Harry was raised in this same house by two legal guardian adults who did not guard his life beyond their begrudging obedience to Dumbledore to keep him in their house. Petunia, Vernon, and Dudley rejected Harry and abused him. The family was more than thoughtless or unkind: their actions reached criminal neglect.

Yet in this godparenting scene, every adult in the room is willing to love Harry to death. They were what the Dursleys were called but failed to be: adults committed to Harry's surviving and thriving in a dangerous world. The community of protectors, made up of dearest friends and members of the Order, heal the home by putting sacrificially loving non-parent adults in Privet Drive for the first time. The Dursleys hid Harry in a cupboard to protect their own lives. The Polyjuice Potters hid their own lives in costumes to save Harry's life. This scene portrays nothing more and nothing less than a room full of godparents.

The first two questions that a bishop asks of the godparents at the moment of baptism sets the standard high for how to love your godchildren:

> Will you be responsible for seeing that the child you present is brought up in the Christian faith and life?
> Will you by your prayers and witness help this child to grow into the full stature of Christ?[7]

In Harry's case, and more than once, his godparents (formal and informal) are called to help him "grow into the full stature of Christ" by making sure he survives and grows at all.

Another reason this is a godparenting scene is that the heroic adults gathered at the Dursley home are most of the unofficial godparents of Harry Potter from throughout the series. These protectors range in age from just a few months older than Harry up to elder of the group, Mad-Eye Moody. But each of these selfless adults has played a part in Harry's spiritual development, each being faithful to the role of godparent in protecting, teaching, challenging, delivering the truth, and unconditionally loving Harry in the world. It is important to note in this scene that a significant nonparent adult from this pantheon of spiritual parents to Harry is Molly Weasley. Although not physically in the room, we learn from Rowling that Molly is waiting breathlessly, faithfully, hopefully, and prayerfully at the Burrow.

Molly is one of Harry's most faithful godparents throughout the series, mostly through her care, prayer, gifts, and letters from afar. Molly is the incarnation of Advent: she can rarely hold those whom she loves in the flesh, but she nonetheless focuses her attention, gifts, and love on the welfare of her loved ones in between reunions. Molly symbolizes that the power of a godparent is not reliant solely on being physically present with one's godchildren, though showing up is nevertheless crucial in any relationship. On the night of the broom battle, Molly is loving Harry as she always had: keeping the light on in her home, leaving the door open for all souls, keeping nourishing food ready, and watching the horizon, ready to run toward anyone walking toward her, not unlike the father of the prodigal son.

Presence and Presents

Seminary professor and faith formation expert Lisa Kimball describes one dimension of the vocation of godparenting as a balance of presence and presents.[8] It matters not how good a storyteller a godparent can be if they do not actually show up in the life of their godchildren to share and enchant their lives with testimonies and acts of love, meaning, and hope, whether it is in person or through some digital platform that brings faces together.

The three habits of the healthy and impactful person of faith are to show up, listen, and tell the truth as you understand it. In a cultural world of pictures and posts, the actual presence of a human being who shows up in your life is more rare and precious than in any other predigital generation. The godparent is not just the storyteller about a Creator and a creation made in love, but the incarnation of those truths: a life that models and mediates the grace of God. The godparent's open hands, courageous hugs, listening ears, and soulful eyes put God's love in flesh and God's presence in reach. Presence can take many forms, depending on the location and the resources of the godparent. A well-timed text, a handwritten card or letter, or a thoughtful phone call are all ways a godparent can show up in the life of their godchild. And all of these godparenting best practices (besides the use of Muggle phones) are found throughout the seven books. Molly Weasley, Mrs. Figg, Neville's grandmother—the series is packed with people who find ways to send messages to the young people in their lives to remind their adopted godchildren that their lives matter and that there are adults in the world who believe in them and who love them.

At times, listening is all that we are called to do with our godchildren. Sometimes listening is all we *can* do. In a powerful scene from *The Order of the Phoenix*, Harry and other injured members of Dumbledore's Army arrive back at Dumbledore's office after the battle at the Ministry for Magic, in which Harry's godfather Sirius is killed. Harry is in shock as he yells and breaks objects in Dumbledore's office, having just watched Sirius die in his presence.

> "I don't care!" Harry yelled at them, snatching up a lunascope and throwing it into the fireplace. "I've had enough, I've seen enough, I want out, I want it to end, I don't care anymore!"
>
> "You do care," said Dumbledore. He had not flinched or made a single move to stop Harry demolishing his office. His expression was calm, almost detached. "You care so much you feel as though you will bleed to death with the pain of it."[9]

Dumbledore does not try to fix or heal Harry's anguish. Harry continues to yell and break things as Dumbledore stands nonanxiously in the room. As the destructive outburst continues, Dumbledore adds, "You can break more, if you like. I have too many things already." Dumbledore wisely discerns that what Harry needs is a place and time to express his tortured emotions and to be heard without judgment. And Dumbledore is willing to stand in that space with Harry and pay for that space with his own possessions.

The role of presents in the godparenting relationship is tricky but worth wrestling with because of their potential power to convey love and worth. The power of giving presents is not an invitation to consumerism or consumption. Gifts can be any material thing that testifies to the attention, prayers, and love of the giver. Gifts can be outward and visible signs of kinship. There are examples of purchased gifts in Harry Potter, such as the broom McGonagall gave Harry or the Remembrall that Neville received from his grandmother. But both gifts, though perhaps costly, had a purpose or power that enabled the recipient to expand their agency and growth. This is a good standard for deciding whether to make purchases for your godchild: does the gift merely add to the material objects in their life or can it instead enable the recipient to grow in some way? New brooms for Harry were expensive, as Minerva McGonagall and Sirius Black knew well. But they allowed Harry to fly, which was one of his strongest gifts, joys, and experiences of freedom. Giving appropriate gifts that liberate godchildren and help them become more of themselves is a powerful way to show up in their lives. And giving the right gift with purpose and strategy is a sign that the godparent is listening to the life of the godchild. Neville's grandmother knew he struggled to remember things. Dumbledore knew Ron would need a Deluminator, and the Weasley twins knew that Harry needed a magic map to sneak out of Hogwarts, since the Dursleys' neglect had left Harry without a guardian's permission to visit Hogsmeade. The best gifts come from listening.

The most courageous action of a godparent is in telling truths that need to be shared. It is important that godparents share the truth *as they understand it*, admitting that at times their understanding of what is true may or may not reflect reality. But we must try to find and share truths with our godchildren—through our own spiritual disciplines and prayers—asking the Holy Spirit to purify our understanding of truth so that our words and actions can communicate truths that will set others free.

Families have so many different goals on any given day that the intentional passing on of the faith can fall off the daily to-do list. As the sacred storyteller, the godparent has a unique opportunity to have uncluttered conversations with their godchildren. The godparent can be the person who uses their presence, words, and gifts to intentionally link their godchild's life with the story of God's love and presence in the world. Listen to these intentional godparenting words of liberating truth and faith formation from Dumbledore to Harry in a moment of grief and pain over the absence of Harry's father in his life:

> "You think the dead we loved ever truly leave us? You think that we don't recall them more clearly than ever in times of great trouble? Your father is alive in you, Harry, and shows himself most plainly when you have need of him."[10]

Dumbledore dares to share the sacred truth of the communion of saints in a moment when Harry feels acute pain from the enduring wound of being an orphan. Dumbledore does more than soothe Harry's grief; he speaks the truth he has experienced in his own struggles to love and care for lost loved ones. Too often we assume that our godchildren know how to connect their struggles with the convictions of our creeds. Too often we pray *for* and not *with* our godchildren, hoping that they practice the faith while not always practicing the faith with them. In Acts 8:31, the apostle Philip asks an Ethiopian eunuch who is reading Isaiah, "Do you understand what you are reading?" He replied, "How can I, unless someone guides me?"

Prayers for the Candidates:

Let us now pray for those who are to receive the Sacrament of new
  birth and for those who have renewed their commitment to
  Christ.

Deliver them, O Lord, from the way of sin and death.

Open their hearts to your grace and truth.

Fill them with your holy and life-giving Spirit.

Keep them in the faith and communion of your holy Church.

Teach them to love others in the power of the Spirit.

Send them into the world in witness to your love.

Bring them to the fullness of your peace and glory.

Grant, O Lord, that all who are baptized into the death of Jesus
  Christ your Son may live in the power of his resurrection and look
  for him to come again in glory; who lives and reigns now and for
  ever. *Amen.*[11]

NOTES

1. *Prisoner of Azkaban*, 434.

2. Charles Taylor, *A Secular Age* (Cambridge, MA: Harvard University Press, 2007), 25, 26.

3. Lewis, "Weight of Glory," 30–31.

4. Rowling, "Fringe Benefits of Failure."

5. Andrew Root and Kenda Creasy Dean, *The Theological Turn in Youth Ministry* (Downers Grove, IL: IVP Books, 2011), 92.

6. *Goblet of Fire*, 25.

7. Service of Holy Baptism, Book of Common Prayer, 302.

8. Lisa Kimball, "Being Godparent: A Dialogical Hermeneutic Study of Godparenthood" (PhD diss., University of Minnesota, 2007), 84–88.

9. *Order of the Phoenix*, 824.

10. *Prisoner of Azkaban*, 427–28.

11. Service of Holy Baptism, Book of Common Prayer, 305–6.

CHAPTER NINE

Faith Formation
for All Ages
"All That Is, Seen and Unseen."

"Of course it is happening inside your head, Harry, but why on earth should that mean that it is not real?"[1]

I do not have many memories of my theological thoughts as a child. I can remember what my stone, Gothic, candle-crowded Catholic church smelled like. I can remember the sounds of the old church's doors creaking open or slamming shut as whispering parishioners came and went for daily or Sunday Mass, hushing their children as they entered the sanctuary. I remember the hard pews and missalettes in the pew racks proclaiming the current liturgical season with cheesy clip-art images of plants, sacramental elements, or saints staring up into the sky.[2] Well before I could read, I would grab these little booklets containing the readings and music for the season and gaze at the drawings or graphics, marveling at how their colors and symbols mirrored the colors and themes of the banners and vestments all over the church. I have searing memories of the red glass candle next to the tabernacle, the small side altar in most Catholic churches where the leftover blessed communion bread rests between services. In the Catholic church, one candle (usually with red glass) always stands next to the tabernacle, and if ever there is blessed bread inside that small golden box with a keyhole, that particular candle is lit. As young children, we were taught to always bow our heads and kneel at the railing that surrounded the small tabernacle area when walking by this lit candle. The lit candle was a sign to all that the body of Jesus was fully and objectively present in that box on the wall.

In my parents' generation and before, Catholics were taught to cross themselves whenever they walked or drove by a church, in respect for the potential real presence of Jesus inside the church walls. The belief that Jesus was physically present in particular places on earth was perhaps my strongest formed idea about God in the first decade of my life. The real presence of Christ in the Eucharist and in the tabernacles of the world's Catholic churches was the enchanting narrative, the stickiest of ideas in all my elementary religious education. I grew up across the street from the only Catholic church around. As soon as I was old enough to cross the street on my own, I would take little trips to sit before the red glass candle. Rarely did I tell anyone where I was going. I could go visit Jesus and be back home in less than ten minutes. If childhood was a game of tag, the kneeler before my local church's tabernacle was my base. Nowhere in my home or in the world felt safer or more sacred. No matter what was happening in the world, I believed I could go to a Catholic church anywhere on earth, kneel before a red candle, and know that I was as close to Christ as possible. I never opened that locked golden box. Occasionally I would witness priests opening it for extra communion bread during crowded celebrations of the Eucharist, but I could never see inside. It was enough for me to see the lit candle: that was the sign of the unseen reality of God's presence.

Although my religious memories of the first decade of my life remain largely a collection of images, sounds, and smells, there is one sentence that I remember thinking about constantly, even before I could read along in the services and before my feet could touch the church floor while I sat in the pew. I would wait in the liturgy for this phrase to be said, because hearing the sentence made me smile and filled me with ideas about God in the world. And in the Catholic church, my treasured phrase was said every week because it was a phrase from the Nicene Creed. Still to this day, it is my favorite phrase in any Christian creed. The phrase comes from the first sentence of the creed: "I believe in one God, the Father, the Almighty, Creator of heaven and earth, of all that is, seen and unseen." As a young child, the phrase "all that is, seen and unseen," was an invitation to a magical world. I was not sure what it meant, but this uncertainty was an inviting playground for my imagination. Every week, a room full of people, including the religious leaders, would all declare that there are things seen and unseen in which they all believed. It was a testimony to mystery. I loved hearing it, and I loved adding my voice to those uttering the words around me. As I got older, I learned that it was reference to things like love, forgiveness, or grace. But as a child, I simply thought it was a declarative statement that there were invisible things created by God. And I would look all around the church—at the stained-glass windows and the statues, the paintings, the pipe organ, the banners, and the cross on the altar, and wonder, Where are all the unseen things, and when will I be able to see them? That phrase was so powerful in my life that it sent me out of church, day after day, year after year, looking everywhere for signs or perhaps even glimpses of the unseen creations of God.

That phrase in the creed was my invitation into what Charles Taylor called an "enchanted world."[3] Though I was born recently enough to have lived most of my life in the postmodern world, my strong Catholic upbringing and my eager embrace of it since childhood protected me from what Taylor argues is the increasingly powerful force of secularization sweeping much of the postmodern world. The average American walking on the street next to me as a child may not have believed in any narrative of an enchanted world, but I did and still do. And that phrase in the creed was the basis for my constant formation and fortification in that conviction. The worldview that God is present, seen and unseen, in the world is the soil in which all other dimensions of Christianity grew in my life. I went to church to experience the unseen realities of God: I wanted to hear music about the unseen; I wanted to receive the sacraments to touch and taste the unseen; I was curious about the Bible to hear every word about the unseen. Having an enchanted mind created the force and set the course for experiencing God in the Christian faith. Whenever I hear an uninspiring sermon or experience a "religious person" who seems flat or disconnected from their faith, I wonder if the person has lost (or perhaps never had) an enchanted imagination.

The words, the deeds, or the decorations of church alone can never build an enchanted imagination; those seen things are only the tools and toys of the enchanted mind. It is grace that breaks through the symbols or the Scriptures and ignites our imagination. Those who have taught the faith have experienced this transformation—this baptism of the imagination—or at least seen it in others, where ideas become more like food, taken and digested into a person, making them stronger, more mature, and more hungry for the presence of God. Without a fundamental hunger for and expectation of God's presence in both the seen and unseen of life, the Christian faith is simply a set of symbols and statements. We all know people for whom the faith might linger in the mind but has lost its grip or even its connection to their imagination. They have become disenchanted disciples. The waves of secularization in our culture that public intellectuals such as Charles Taylor observe have crashed on the beaches of our hearts at different times. There is wisdom in any church that professes weekly a shared belief in the seen and unseen, for the enchanted imagination is both a gift and a responsibility. The author of the book of Ecclesiastes says it best: "God has put eternity in their hearts" (3:11 NKJV). God has designed us for enchantment. Disenchantment is rarely a result of rationality, despite what the skeptics of faith argue. More often, disenchantment is the result of a starved imagination.

Christian formation at its core teaches and trains the imagination. You can create a lifelong learner whose imagination will fuel their faith journey if you intentionally enchant the imagination of the student or peer. Effective educators in the Christian faith name and model discipleship in a world enchanted by the real presence of God. Those of us who are trying to teach and preach our faith have this challenge: How do we create a community that nurtures a belief in the experience of the seen and the unseen? How do we create communities that feed the hunger for enchantment?

Using a grand narrative like Harry Potter helps awaken the imagination of people. And the particular story of Harry Potter, with its unique invitation to enter an entire magical world parallel to our own, is tailor-made to re-enchant the disenchanted imagination. Similarly to Narnia, the magical world of Harry Potter functions as a training ground for the reader's imagination. The magical world invites the Muggle reader to enter its enchanting reality, and then sends the reader back to the Muggle world with an imagination that now hungers for enchantment. When Lucy leaves Narnia for the last time, she sobs because she will not see the Christ figure Aslan back in England. But Aslan corrects her with the truth that he is also present in all worlds outside of Narnia. He comforts her:

> But there I have another name. You must learn to know me by that name. This was the very reason why you were brought to Narnia, that by knowing me here for a little, you may know me better there.[4]

The proven power of Harry Potter to enchant the reader so forcefully explains why it is so effective in reviving the religious imagination of people. If it is true that we are wired for enchantment, then a narrative that takes the reader into an enchanted world is pitch perfect for the natural hunger of any human soul. This is why the Harry Potter series enjoys far more followers than other contemporary grand narratives such as *The Hunger Games* or the Twilight series. At their core, those stories are as much about disenchantment as enchantment, if not more so. This is the very definition of dystopian narratives. They feed as much skepticism as they feed enchantment. I have enjoyed both book series and others like them. But as an educator, I have experienced that they are less effective in feeding the enchanted imagination.

In the rest of this chapter, I share in detail the ways I have used the Harry Potter narrative to engage and enchant the spiritual imagination of people in churches, schools, and nonprofit organizations. There are stories to tell about groups of two to two hundred whose faith in God has been discovered, fed, or recovered by reading or watching Harry Potter. I have seen people's lives transformed in ways I never thought possible by Rowling's grand narrative or by any piece of art. The stories in this chapter are the reason I wrote this book.

Harry Potter for Retreat

My husband is a seminary professor, and together we were asked to run a weekend retreat for the spouses and partners of the seminary students. It is a gift of the seminary, given every year to the spouses of current seminary students. A retreat center set in the rolling hills of Virginia is reserved, every meal is a feast of comfort food, and those who are trying to love their spouse seminarians, as well as find or feed their own vocations, get a weekend to spend with one another. It is an eclectic group of people to run a retreat for, since they are not theological students or people who are preparing for full-time ministry in the church. They certainly know a lot about church, being married to people who have decided to make religious life their profession. But this group of about a dozen spouses included doctors, lawyers, teachers, stay-home moms, and a graphic designer. They varied widely in terms of levels of faith or religious curiosity. Some would have described themselves as religious; others would not. Some had children; others did not. Some were in their late twenties; others were in their early sixties.

All we assumed going into the weekend was that these folks were looking for time away from living in married student dorms on campus. We needed to build a retreat plan that would nurture and inspire the spiritual lives of men and women with widely varying levels of formal education, who were religious and not so religious, parents and nonparents, introverts and extroverts, strong Republicans and diehard Democrats, young adults and senior citizens. What we knew for sure was that this optional retreat was bringing together folks who desired some kind of renewal and inspiration. Many of the participants had to make complicated arrangements at work and at home to be free for three days, so we knew we had the buy-in for a meaningful weekend. The question was what theme or plan could speak to these vastly different souls with varied worldviews and convictions.

In many ways, the challenge we faced was similar to what churches and synagogues in the twenty-first century face every day. Increasingly, our congregations are populated by mixed relationships or households, where at least one adult and perhaps more than one child are not as keen about organized religion as the one person who brings or drags the family to church. And more and more, the reality of secularization paired with widespread cultural conviction that institutions of all kinds have failed to create safe, sane, and sacred spaces in the public square means that there is both a skeptic and a believer inside every person. Even the quaint phrase "preaching to the choir" has little truth anymore for anyone who actually spends time preaching. I find few church choirs in this country that don't have as many skeptics or even cynics as the rest of the sanctuary. Every twenty-first-century pew—even the seats for clergy or choir—is a mission field now.

After considering many different frameworks for the retreat, we decided that it was a group of people ripe for a Harry Potter–themed weekend. We had faith that the Harry Potter stories probably enjoyed more shared love among this group of people than perhaps any other set of religious or spiritual ideas. Statistically, not everyone in the room would be from the same religion or even share the value of holding a personal religion, but statistically, many would know something or perhaps many things about the Boy Who Lived.

Up until the spouses arrived at the retreat center that Friday afternoon, they were told nothing about the theme for the weekend. We watched out our conference center window as, one by one, the cars with their seminary parking stickers found parking spaces after a two-hour drive to the retreat center. The attendees had been told only to park and make their way to the charming lodge of guest rooms. After getting their keys at the front desk, they went to their assigned rooms.

And what did they find when they got there? Attached to each door was an envelope that held the schedule for the weekend, but it was not the usual schedule that one may find slid under the door at the beginning of a weekend conference or retreat. Stuck on each parchment envelope was a large color photograph of an owl, and stuck on every door was a different owl, with the envelope glued to its talons. When the guest pulled the envelope out of the owl's talons, they saw a wax seal with the Hogwarts shield. We had printed the guests' names in a Harry Potter font, along with the locations of their rooms, just as Harry's first letter arrived to a boy "in the cupboard under the stairs." Each letter was addressed to a person "in the room by elevator" or "the room near the stairs." As the guests cracked open the wax, they each found a parchment cover letter from Professor McGonagall welcoming them to a weekend at Hogwarts School of Witchcraft and Wizardry. We used a free font from the internet for McGonagall's handwriting, and we added our own quotations from the Bible about initiation and the value of fellowship and learning for the weekend. There were also classic quotations from Dumbledore about the power of community and faith. In each envelope, there was also a pack of every flavor beans as snack for later in the day. Each guest was also given a map of the retreat center, folded like and titled the Marauder's Map, on which we had renamed all the retreat buildings after those at Hogwarts.

As the guests made their way to the main hall, which we had dubbed the Great Hall, they walked by an antique birdcage with a stuffed Hedwig puppet inside. The room was dimly lit with candles, House banners hung from the ceiling, and Harry Potter movie soundtracks played softly in the background. At the center of the room was a large boardroom. At each seat was a pen to which we had duct-taped a feather, so that everyone's pen looked like a quill pen. We had a sorting ceremony where each person received a House tie, and then we pulled out House robes from our own basement collection gathered over years of costume parties and Harry Potter presentations. The table was covered with British-themed desserts and drinks in plastic goblets. Though the guests had varied levels of knowledge about the Harry Potter world, their broad smiles, loud giggles, and completely glowing and enchanted faces were a joy to behold. Many sent smartphone selfies to family and friends in real time. "I can't believe this!" both men and women squealed. "I got a Hogwarts letter!" No matter how much or how little they knew about Harry Potter, they were sure that they had entered an entire magical world and would remain there for the weekend. It dawned on them that they were going to play—all weekend—in Rowling's fantastical world. This realization alone seemed to release something in people's facial muscles.

One epidemiologist in his sixties, draped in a Gryffindor robe with his House tie perfectly knotted at the neck, grabbed my arm and said, "This has just started and it is already the most imaginative weekend I have had in years." More than one person whispered that they were going to take their Hogwarts letters home and frame them. In years of leading retreats of all ages, I had not seen such instant bonding, laughter, and a bursting sense of expectancy for a weekend of joy and revelation in just the first session of a retreat. Being at Hogwarts for an hour had already unlocked the imagination and wonder of every person present.

We opened our first session with traditional prayers for the evening from the Book of Common Prayer and then explained what the group had already figured out: they were at Hogwarts for a weekend, and we intended to stay in that fantasy world with costumes and props for three days. We explained that we intended to cover all the elements of a traditional weekend retreat: bonding exercises, creative writing and art projects, time for both sharing and silence, periodic prayers and liturgies, walks outside, discussions in small groups, shared readings, and meditating on pieces of art—though with Harry Potter ideas and experiences. Within an hour of our opening prayer, the guests were writing ideas in response to our getting-to-know-you questions with their quill pens on the parchment paper we had bought at an office supply store.

We ended the session explaining the schedule for the weekend, which would consist of a series of courses at Hogwarts. Again, our basic format was classic for a weekend spiritual retreat: we wanted to take time to get to know each other, share our life experiences, tell our stories of joy and turmoil, pray together, read inspirational texts together, and brainstorm about how to grow spirituality in our daily lives. But we framed these traditional retreat sessions as academic courses at Hogwarts.

In the session called Divination, we handed out children's books and poetry to help participants look creatively into their lives for patterns and consequences. In Transfiguration, we talked about what it means to be a person of faith and to live, learn, and love in such a way that you feel you are being transformed by the love of God in your daily life. In the Defensive Dark Arts, we faced adversity with brutal honesty, telling how we did or did not manage the Death Eaters and dementors in our lives. This session was later in the retreat schedule, allowing for hours of authentic sharing in other sessions before talking about the darkness in our lives.

We then had a session outside in the sun called Care of Magical Creatures, in which we talked about how to be spiritual and just in our use and care of the environment. The theme of this session was also the resurrection and how kite flying is an experience of resurrection: a combination of forces like wind (which you cannot control) and personal grit in running with the kite (which you can control). We talked about how we can participate in our own daily resurrections. At the end of the discussion, everyone was given a kite shaped like a dragon that we had bought online. The final activity of this session involved people trying to fly their creature kites in groups of two. I will never forget watching participants run all over the grass of a large open field, House robes flying in the wind, House ties blowing up into faces, laughter echoing through the air, and voices encouraging each other to run faster, tug harder, and watch their creatures and their hopes for healing and resurrection soar above the earth.[5] .The weekend-long conversation was a sacred quilt of words, actions, and silences, made up of Harry Potter testimonies of reading the stories, sharing of Bible verses that echoed the Harry Potter narrative, drawings and singing and poetry inspired by characters and plot twists in Harry Potter, and overheard whispers of wonder and trust for the future set aflame by a weekend at Hogwarts. There was a gentle grief in our guests' faces and fingers as each person handed back their robe and tie in our last session. I heard the words of Aslan in my heart: "This was the very reason why you were brought to Narnia, that by knowing me here for a little, you may know me better there."[6]

"We're Gonna Need a Bigger Boat"

I was asked to give a Harry Potter lecture at a small church about an hour or two away from Washington, D.C. In a village along the Potomac River, with a population of less than a thousand, this historic church stood by the only traffic light in the center of downtown. When I arrived, I saw a handwritten poster advertising my Saturday afternoon lecture, stapled to a stick of wood stuck in the ground. The downtown area was busy with people of all ages going in and out of the small shops. I saw moms with children, seniors with walkers, two ice cream stores, two nonchain coffee shops, a firehouse, a one-room library connected to the town hall, and the two-story Episcopal church—the tallest building in town. Crossing the street, I noticed more details of the church building and took note of the deteriorating doors, windows, and roof.

I found and entered an open door to a small community hall with twenty chairs in a circle and a sweet seventyish priest who lit up when he saw my face. He welcomed me with a hug like an old friend, although I had only exchanged e-mails with him. I told him I'd need a few minutes to unpack all my props to decorate the room as the Great Hall. He was eager to help set up, though clearly mystified by my birdcage with the Hedwig puppet inside, my Gryffindor tie, and the Sorting Hat under my arm. He had never read Harry Potter or seen any of the movies. But he had e-mailed me months before, saying that his parishioners requested an event about Rowling's epic and Christian theology. I asked him to set up more chairs. He never lost his smile but nonetheless took a deep breath and said he didn't think more than fifteen people would show up. It turns out his church has only a few dozen members. "Twelve folks would be a huge gathering for a Saturday lecture here," he said.

I asked him how long the poster had been up outside the church. He said the sign had been out for a week. I had seen more than a hundred people walking on the streets outside the church. "You're only planning on twelve?" I said playfully. "There are more than twelve people in line for a coffee across the street." He chuckled while shaking his head. "Oh, there's plenty o' people 'round here. But you just can't get 'em to come into church on Sunday anymore, much less Saturday." I wasn't going to challenge my host, who had been a priest in that church for thirty years. "Well," I said with a sigh, "God might surprise us today, right?" He beamed, "That's always the hope!" My arms were full, so I told him to pick a tie off my neck, since I had all four House ties draped on my shoulders. I felt his age and reserve as he awkwardly obeyed and took a piece of clothing off a woman he had just met. He picked a Hufflepuff tie. "Put it on!" I sang to him. "You look great in yellow. I have your robe in the car." I heard him whisper to himself, "Oh, my."

Thirty minutes before the session start time, we already had over twenty people in the room. The priest stood near the door in his robe and with his wand, welcoming everyone to Hogwarts (a word it took him a few tries to pronounce correctly in practicing beforehand). While I was hanging House banners from the cracked ceiling, I heard the doorbell to the church hall ring again and again and again, the priest giddy with every handshake. Later he shared that no church activity had more than thirty people show up in years. After the event was over and everything was packed up into my car, we strolled together down Main Street, and I told him that you should never put up a Harry Potter event sign up for a week and think you have enough chairs.

During the lecture, I showed movie clips from all eight films and had various activities that matched the themes. We had House Points trivia quizzes to open the event, owls with Hogwarts' acceptance letters hanging on the walls for each person that showed up, a Sorting ceremony, seating by House. I had made my signature Chocolate Frogs and asked visitors to color renditions of their spiritual heroes on index cards and trade them with other participants, just as the characters in the books had Great Witches and Wizard trading cards. This sharing of our spiritual guides was our conversation starter.

I brought robes and ties for anyone who wanted to dress up, but about a dozen people had shown up in their own costumes. The priest seemed amazed that grown-ups as well as children in his congregation had entire wardrobes of Harry Potter clothing and props. We talked about the role of a wand in the series and the types of "wands" we have in our lives, like smartphones, credit and debit cards, guns, and voter ID cards. The youngest of the attendees was an eight-year-old, dressed in her own Hermione costume, with a wand and stuffed Crookshanks cat. The oldest guest was in her late eighties. She had read the Harry Potter books to all twelve grandchildren and seven great-grandchildren. She pulled me aside after the lecture and said she had told her children to put her copy of *Sorcerer's Stone* in her coffin with her, because that book had been responsible for bonding her with every grandchild and great-grandchild in hours and hours of reading, laughter, prayer, and love. "That book is fallin' apart! But so am I! There's no reason we shouldn't take our final rest together."

I've always been amazed at the wide age range of participants in Harry Potter lectures, events, or retreats. Even the mention of Harry Potter brings people of all races, sexual orientations, and socioeconomic situations together. The magic of libraries is that anyone with patience enough to wait for weeks can read the seven books without cost. And the periodic showing of Harry Potter marathons on television opens up the series to folks who never did or never could see the films in theaters. Leaders have told me several times that they had never had a gathering in their churches as big as the ones that were Harry Potter themed. Fans don't mind at all the age of the person next to them at a Harry Potter event. Crowds from every demographic are a testimony to every reader that they are not alone in their passion for the stories.

The most profound experience of the Harry Potter lecture at the little downtown church was an activity I called Defeating Your Dementors. I have used this activity with all sorts of groups and all ages. A few years back, I decided that the best way to help people understand Rowling's intentions in creating the dementors was to construct an actual dementor and let people try to defend themselves against it. I wanted folks to have a very physical encounter with their greatest fears, as well as a physical experience of defeating them. I'd had countless conversations with people and groups about dementors as a metaphor for forces of depression and fear, but I always knew that talking about fears or healing from fears is never as powerful as experiencing fear and healing. I created a dementor with some inexpensive props I purchased at a discount store. I draped a long, black cape that was a Halloween costume over a tall, thin coat rack and hung a skull mask under the cloak. The result was a seven-foot tall dementor. I taped a large plastic container lid under the cloak to create a solid body plate, so that people would have something to hit besides the thin pole of the rack.

After defining and discussing dementors and their role in the series and in our own lives, I took the group outside to the grassy parking lot of the church. Each person had already written on an index card what dementors he or she faced: the sources of darkness and suffering that sucked the joy and air out of his or her life. On the other side, I had folks write their personal Patronus Charms: the memories, Bible verses, or images that carry them through hard times. With other groups, I have gathered up these lists of dementors and typed them into word clouds to project on the wall in front of the group, depicting the trends of dementors across genders, ages, classes, and races within the room. Even in the most diverse groups, so many of the dementors are the same: people of all ages and backgrounds have faced cancer, poverty, addictions, eating disorders, mental disorders, financial loss, food or job insecurity, anxiety, rejection, divorce . . . the lists are painful, and the stories that pour out can be such sad chronicles of the way these dementors have sucked the life out of people.

But at the darkest points of these dementor sessions, we turn to considering the forces of light in our lives that have helped us fight back. The discussion sessions on our Patronus Charms are some of the most inspiring conversations I have ever heard in faith communities. There is such joy and privilege in watching the Holy Spirit work through this authentic sharing of what has helped pull folks out of periods of darkness. I have seen sanctuaries, parish halls, and PTA meetings transform into Rooms of Requirement, where people shared their powerful and lifesaving Patronus memories, verses, lyrics, and images with other people facing the same dementors.

We know from Dumbledore that dementors cannot be killed because there is no life in them. However, they can be pushed back by memories of love—especially sacrificial love. I invited that church hall of people to walk outside to the parking lot and see the tall coat rack dementor I had stuck in the ground. The group was silent as they beheld the dementor's cloak blowing in the wind. I told them to look at their index cards and remind themselves what their personal dementors were. I then asked them to read carefully their Patronus memories or hold in their minds the Patronus ideas they had heard from the group.

In a basket, I had gathered all the equipment to fight dementors. I had ordered affordable plastic Harry Potter wands from the internet. I wrapped white duct tape around three or four volleyballs that were slightly deflated, creating a loop on each ball so that the wands could pick up the volleyballs and hurl them at the dementor. I used volleyballs because they look like white misty things moving through the air, like the Patronus animals in the series. After the group reflected on their dementors and their chosen Patronus charms, I invited each person to take a wand, pick up a Patronus volleyball on the end of the wand, and hurl volleyballs at the dementor until it is knocked over. Over the past few years, I have amassed hundreds of pictures of people participating in this activity; every group and every facial expression is priceless. Often I play the Harry Potter soundtrack on outdoor speakers. I encourage everyone to cheer for whoever is hurling the Patronus at the dementor. Folks are invited to say their Patronus memories or verses out loud or keep them to themselves. Children, parents, young adults, and senior citizens all take such care and aim at their greatest fears or sources of darkness.

This is a physical experience of naming and defeating the things that haunt you. I encourage folks who don't have strong Patronus memories to consider prayers, psalms, or hymns of their childhood. But the most powerful formation moments come when I see and hear one person sharing their Patronus ideas with another person who is facing the same dementor. Even people who know nothing of Harry Potter seem to quickly relate to the idea of a dementor and the role of some kind of charm against it. People of all sorts—with or without athletic abilities, with or without familiarity with the stories—have hit the dementor on the first try, while others have taken a bit longer to knock it down. I sometimes have to tell folks to get closer if they cannot hit the dementor, but usually the person or the group strategizes successfully. In my experience, some of the most transformative faith formation I have ever seen in any age group has taken place in parks, parking lots, hallways, and sanctuaries where I have stood up my dementor coat rack and watched souls name their darkness and defeat it in person and in community.

I will never forget one high school student who knocked down her dementor, which represented a collection of her insecurities, eating disorder, and mother's battle with recurrent cancer. She then took pictures of the funny-looking coat rack on the ground. I asked her if she wanted me to take a picture of her and the defeated dementor, but she said no. "I want pictures of the dementor defeated. I want them on my phone so whenever I feel like I am losing the battle against the darkness, I can look at this crushed dementor and remind myself to keep going." I saw that student two years after she graduated from high school, and the first thing she did was to show me the pictures of that day that were still on her phone, still reminding her that the love in her Patronus Charm is powerful enough to triumph over darkness.

Another of my memories is when one of the shyest boys in a group of teenagers was the only student not able to hit the dementor with the volleyball. The class period was almost over, and his attempts were less and less successful with every try. I knew this experience was becoming perilous for his self-esteem. A senior and captain of a varsity team, he was very popular by any adolescent measure, but he just couldn't hit the cloaked coat rack. I knew what his peers watching did not: his emotions were overcoming him. When I first asked the students to list their dementors on an index card and turn them in anonymously, this young man wrote out an answer immediately, folded his card in half, and walked it right over to me. This gesture made it clear that he wanted me to know his answer. I will never forget that scribbled sentence in his teenager-boy handwriting: "My dementor is a gay version of myself." I sat with the card for a minute, digesting the sad truth of his life: he knew he was gay, and that truth was haunting him every day and sucking the life and joy out of him. I knew his friends and his extremely conservative parents. He was correct that his current family and friend structure was not a safe place for him. I was stunned that he felt safe enough to write it to me. But there he was, trying to knock down that dementor, while we both tried to hide the intensity of the experience. His peers were cheering. His eyes were tearing. He was using every prayer and hymn and psalm called out by the crowd to inspire him. I was beginning to worry that his takeaway from this experiential learning would be that he could not, in fact, defeat his dementor. In my mind, I was scrambling for ideas to rescue the lesson.

Just then, another student walked up to me. She was a Jewish student who had not said much during the class but who saw my concern. She walked over to me and whispered in my ear. She asked if I ever had someone who was unable to knock down the dementor. I leaned over and told her that this was my first impending failure. With the wisdom of someone decades older than her, she sighed and said, "Look, here's a plan. We give him another minute or two, and if he can't do it, we'll all get our wands out and throw all the volleyballs at once. Ya know? We'll, like, blitz the dementor together. Okay?" I looked at her and smiled with relief. And then she said, "Isn't that what you call the church? Ya know, when someone can't fight something on their own and they just need more help?"

Harry Potter for Marriage Preparation

Of all the ways you can use Harry Potter, very few might dream of using it to prepare people for marriage. The internet provides many courses and strategies to prepare for marriage, but an increasing number of twenty- to thirty-year-olds in the Harry Potter generation have requested that I help them prepare for marriage. More than once, I've seen some Harry Potter figure or banner when I visit with them in their apartments or homes. I have noticed a Harry Potter key chain, piece of jewelry, or Hogwarts screen saver. I never set out to talk about Harry Potter in the marriage preparation of young adults. But with couple after couple of a certain age, Harry Potter words, metaphors, or jokes entered the conversations about love very early on in the preparation sessions. It was the couples, and not my interests, that initially brought Harry Potter into the preparation. At first I picked up the metaphors or characters that the couples introduced, using them to enrich our conversations. But over time, I have become more systematic in using the series. It is not my goal that people have Harry Potter–themed engagements, marriage counseling, or weddings, but increasingly more and more young adults already have Harry Potter–themed relationships. My bringing up Harry Potter has not proven to be an imposition, but rather an engagement with a set of ideas and themes that are already a core part of the couple's collection of heroes and convictions about right, wrong, and love.

I will say at the outset that you don't want to theme your marriage preparation this way if Harry Potter isn't a language that both people in the couple are fairly or equally fluent in. Wedding preparation is a moment for people to feel safe and equally invested in the topics of preparation. You don't want to privilege one person's passions at the expense of the other, who may feel left out or inadequate in the terms of reflection. But if you do come across a couple that shares a love of Harry Potter and is equally eager to apply some of the epic to their marriage preparation conversations, those couples will be greatly blessed by your shepherding in these terms. I have always used an excellent book called *The Marriage Journey: Preparations and Provisions for Life Together* as the core text of my marriage prep sessions.[7] But I've found that if I join that book with a Harry Potter–themed reading and discussion syllabus, it enhances the experience for the Harry Potter fan couple.

Once we agree that Harry Potter might be a fun theme for the counseling sessions, I begin by mailing the couple a Hogwarts letter from Professor McGonagall, accepting them into the Marriage for Muggles course at Hogwarts. This letter has an owl sticker on it, and an owl feather is stuck in the envelope. In the first meeting of the formal sessions, I give the couple a Harry Potter lunch box that I purchased online, containing a collection of toys and tools for the months of marriage preparation. After prayers and a time of silence, I let the couple open the lunch box and talk through the elements.

The lunch box includes objects that represent all the topics covered in a traditional marriage preparation period. I photocopy the questions at the end of each chapter of *The Marriage Journey.* You could use this method with any book you choose that has chapters and discussion questions. I cut the questions into single pieces of paper, with one question on each, like the slips of paper in fortune cookies. I put the questions in envelopes labeled for each chapter. However, I use Harry Potter fonts and stationery. I seal each chapter envelope with a wax seal from Hogwarts. I encourage the couple to read the chapters but to share the questions and their answers at other times. I suggest that they take single questions with them out to dinner or commuting or traveling. They are instructed to pick any question they want but to stick to a chapter until they are finished with it. I find this method is a great way to let the marriage prep questions reach into their daily lives of socializing, eating, and moving through their day.

The lunch box also holds two small figures of characters from the book, usually Harry and Hermione or else two female or two male characters, depending on the genders of the couple. I use the Funko plastic characters because they are designed to have huge heads connected to tiny bodies. I put them on the table in front of the couple, and we all giggle at how out of scale the heads are on the figures. I then suggest that they are a symbol of the way many folks enter marriage preparation: our heads are full of thoughts about marriage, love, and shared life, but our bodies are often less developed or involved in those ideas. I explain that marriage preparation can be a time to help the body—with its needs for sex, intimacy, physical, spiritual and financial security, identity, and unconditional love—enter the conversation about what it means to be married.

In the lunch box are also small, portable books of devotion or prayer and a schedule of when the couple must read the chapters and answer the questions. I include sets of Harry Potter matchboxes (available on Etsy) and throw in some candles with a tag including phrases from Dumbledore about the power of light and love. I encourage them to light candles every time they set aside space for marriage prep conversations, to separate and bless these sacred sessions as distinct from the rest of their days.

I also stick in the kit LEGO minifigures of Professor Lupin and Dobby the house-elf, available online. You can use pictures of these two if the LEGO figures are too expensive to purchase. I use these figures to remind couples of the greatest teachers and the greatest disciples in their lives. I preach that preparing for marriage is a time to remember the best teaching and modeling the couples have ever seen and to study the life patterns and prayers of those heroes. The brave living and wise teaching of Remus Lupin are great inspiration for remembering their best teachers, since he was rejected by society for being a werewolf but did not let this life of exile keep him from trusting or loving others. And the figure of Dobby is always a stellar example of what it looks like to love and serve one's friends no matter what one's education level or station in life. I encourage the couple to take these figures (or pictures of them) out of the box for each of their conversations about marriage and begin each session by naming at least one great teacher and one great friend to start each talk. I have learned that after the first few sessions, both people in the relationship start to share names and stories that are new to the other person. The couples usually are quick to discern the message of this practice: there are not only Lupins and Dobbys in our lives to help us mature into marriage, but there is also a Lupin and Dobby within each of us that can be formed and fueled by the practice of a strong, loving, and faithful marriage.

Quidditch Formation

The Virginia Theological Seminary was planning a rock concert a few years ago to reach out to people of all ages with a daylong picnic and a dozen bands on a huge outdoor stage. While looking at the schedule of hours and hours of music, we discerned a need for some other activities during the day. But what games, rides, or stations for playfulness would appeal to people of all ages? I suggested we should have a Quidditch tournament, based on the idea that people who were strangers to each other would play Quidditch in the morning and then be more likely to interact during the day. We sent out invitations to all the youth and young adult groups at the churches that were planning to attend the concert. We told them that all the equipment would be provided and a clinic would be offered for the first thirty minutes of the tournament on how to play Quidditch. The response was quick and energetic. Many Harry Potter readers did not even know that Quidditch can be played in real life. Others had heard of it but had never been given the chance to play.

In order to host a Quidditch tournament, you need to go online and download the rules and directions on how to set up a park or football field for Quidditch. There are many free resources online, more than you could read in one sitting. The International Quidditch Association and US Quidditch websites offer rulebooks and equipment lists as free PDFs.[8] I print the rules on small index cards so that officials can refer to them during the match. On YouTube, you can watch hours and hours of Quidditch matches held all over the world, for ages three to senior citizens.

For equipment, I purchased inexpensive decorative witch brooms for players to hold between their legs while they run. There is a lot of expensive Quidditch equipment for sale online, but I find that the affordable decorative brooms work quite well. Look for post-Halloween sales to save even more money. T-shirts are needed to separate the teams, preferably in the four colors of Hogwarts Houses. For the rings, we borrowed track-and-field hurdles from a local high school track team. We duct-taped hula hoops to the tops of the hurdles, allowing us to put the hoops at various heights, as in the films. Official Quidditch rings are available online but are very expensive. YouTube videos will show you the different uniform options for both players and officials. The most common outfit for officials is black tie and tails, along with House ties or House scarves.

There are two ways to have a Snitch. One common way is to pick a good runner, usually a distance runner, and have the person dress in all yellow. Many Snitches also paint their faces yellow. This person must have a yellow sock with a tennis ball in it in their back pocket. The Seekers of the two teams must run after the Snitch and pull the sock out of the pocket, much like the game capture the flag. If it is a young group, you should have the Snitch running in a supervised area. Kids around the world play Quidditch, though this younger version is called "Kidditch." College Quidditch teams usually let the Snitches run off the field and into buildings or downtown areas. Another way to handle the Snitch role is to get six to ten black flying discs, and spray paint a gold circle on the back of one or two of them. Enlist volunteers to run along the sidelines of your match and throw these flying discs into the air above the players on the field who are trying to throw the Quaffles through the rings. You can tell the volunteers to hold on to the golden Snitch flying discs and throw mostly blank Snitches to see how the points are playing out and even the game up if need be. The goalkeepers need real straw brooms so that the face of the broom is wide enough to block a Quaffle. For the Quaffles, it is best to use deflated volleyballs that can be gripped by people of all ages.

A major dimension of the faith formation in playing Quidditch is how you train your volunteers and referees. I try to gather the volunteers in a separate session on a separate day from the Quidditch match. In that session, we share stories about who first read Harry Potter and when. I ask folks to share their thoughts on the role of Christian themes and symbols in the stories. The purpose of this formation is to allow the volunteers to become missionaries of the spiritual meaning in the Harry Potter stories. Sure, we also go over the rules for playing Quidditch. But I emphasize the role of the referees in answering questions about why faith-based communities engage the Harry Potter stories at all. We focus on why Rowling uses the name Seeker for a Quidditch position. We talk about how every soul is a Seeker and how so many empty treasures in our world are made of gold. But the Snitch that Harry carries throughout the stories is not empty: we learn in the last book that his Snitch contains the resurrection stone. I cherish my memories of listening to folks—who only volunteered to officiate a Quidditch match and go to a meeting to learn how—share their ideas about what resurrection is in their lives and where it is hidden in the world. When you have properly formed and joyfully inspired your volunteers, the day of the Quidditch match is more than play: it is a ministry team ready to call out the Seeker in every person and inspire them to find the resurrection in every place in the world.

At the seminary rock concert Quidditch tournament, I observed what I have seen at every Quidditch match I have attended or directed: People of all ages laughing, falling down, planning plays, learning names, cheering loudly, and having the near-magical experience of running around on a broom. Flying, which is one of the most enchanting aspects of the Harry Potter stories, becomes available in a physical experience. And much like actually taking down a dementor (even if it is just a coat rack covered with a cloak), Quidditch gives people a chance to enter the enchanted world of Harry Potter. In my experience, this trip into Rowling's enchanted world enables readers and viewers to go back to their own Muggle world ready and trained in seeking, finding, loving, and serving all that is, seen and unseen.

> O Lord, you have taught us that without love whatever we do is worth nothing: Send your Holy Spirit and pour into our hearts your greatest gift, which is love, the true bond of peace and of all virtue, without which whoever lives is accounted dead before you. Grant this for the sake of your only Son Jesus Christ, who lives and reigns with you and the Holy Spirit, one God, now and for ever. *Amen.*[9]

NOTES

1. *Deathly Hallows*, 723.
2. A missalette is a seasonal publication of readings and songs for the liturgical season placed in pews in most Catholic churches throughout the year.

3. Taylor, *Secular Age*, 28.

4. C. S. Lewis, *The Voyage of the Dawn Treader* (London: Geoffrey Bles, 1952), 209.

5. I suggest using this format of Hogwarts courses for retreats. In truth, you can cover all of your non–Harry Potter retreat content and goals under the terms of Hogwarts classes. Calling your sessions "classes" adds levity but also structure and purpose to each session. Using Hogwarts terminology injects playfulness and "gamefulness" into your content and retreat metabolism. For example, you might name your session on the cultural context for your church or faith community Muggle Studies or your Bible study time Ancient Runes.

6. Lewis, *Voyage of the Dawn Treader*, 209.

7. Linda Grenz and Delbert Glover, *The Marriage Journey: Preparations and Provisions for Life Together* (New York: Church Publishing, 2003).

8. International Quidditch Association, http://iqaquidditch.org; US Quidditch, https://www.usquidditch.org.

9. Collect for the Seventh Sunday after the Epiphany, Book of Common Prayer, 216.

CHAPTER TEN

Social Activism

What Would Dumbledore Do?

"It is important to fight and fight again, and keep fighting, for only then can evil be kept at bay though never quite eradicated."[1]

I was watching cable news the morning after Donald J. Trump was elected president. Because of the bitterly divisive campaign season, which had spanned well over a year, I was not surprised to see that protests were springing up around the country within hours of the final election results. I was surprised to see that a few of those protests across the country were led by high school students. Many of the kids I saw walking out of classrooms and marching off school campuses into the streets of their cities were not even eligible to vote. By the end of the election week, there had been protests in multiple high schools, including in Des Moines, Iowa, where one public school administrator said, "Our students have the right to be heard." "The majority of students at Des Moines Public Schools are students of color," explained Phil Roeder, the district's director of communications and public affairs. "The rhetoric of this past election has caused many concerns and divisions among them, their friends and their families. The school district will not stand in the way of our students peacefully expressing their concerns."

That same week in California, Berkeley High School's entire student body—fifteen hundred students—walked out of school before 9 a.m. Three other schools in Oakland and San Jose also had walkouts, with signs and chants in favor of immigrant rights. In Santa Barbara, students at three high schools marched to the county courthouse, chanting and singing songs of unity and peace. In Phoenix, hundreds of students from multiple high schools marched to the Arizona capital. In Seattle, nearly two hundred high schoolers chanted, "Save our future." In Boulder, Colorado, over a hundred students left school to walk downtown with signs and banners saying, "Honk for Love." In Maryland, students from multiple schools marched to their downtown areas, in one case passing by a local Episcopal church that had its Spanish congregation's sign vandalized that week with the words "Trump Nation: Whites Only."

Albus Dumbledore, Community Organizer

While watching these student protests on television and hearing the passionate words of student and faculty representatives explaining themselves to the media and to the country, I had a suspicion. So I did searches on Google Images and found hundreds of press photos of many of the high school protests that week. I did not have to wade through too many photos before my hunch was confirmed. In Berkeley, I saw five T-shirts that said, "Dumbledore's Army." In Des Moines, there were two girls wearing an election season T-shirt with the words "Granger/Lovegood 2016." In Boulder, I saw four different Harry Potter Alliance T-shirts with the motto "The Weapon We Have Is Love." Three students and a teacher in Phoenix wore a shirt asking, "What Would Dumbledore Do?"

In city after city, Harry Potter T-shirts were scattered through the crowds in nearly all the high school protest marches, along with Hogwarts House clothing; a tenth grader in Oakland held a Harry Potter wand while wearing her Gryffindor robe during the student walkout. In the hours and days after the election, certain students, their teachers, and administrators were making the direct connection between Dumbledore's Army's resistance against the corrupt Ministry of Magic, Death Eaters, Voldemort, and the postelection atmosphere in America. I heard chants of support for immigrants, undocumented people, native people, women, the disabled, African Americans, those who had been sexually assaulted, the LGBTQ community, minimum wage workers, and other marginalized groups. These young people and adults found themselves in need of organizing principles and inspiring personalities for social justice in the immediate wake of the election and chose to tap into their passion for social justice with the Harry Potter narrative. The Hogwarts T-shirts, House scarves, and wands were a sign that for some, their personal and primary language system and most potent symbolism for their deepest convictions about justice were rooted or expressed in the Harry Potter stories. Something in those stories had already bonded those readers to the notion of social action and social justice. As mentioned earlier in this book, a number of international research studies in recent years have proven a connection between reading Harry Potter and increased empathy and advocacy for minority groups.[2]

When you consider what J. K. Rowling said in many interviews after finishing the series about her own convictions and how they shaped the Harry Potter storyline, it becomes abundantly clear that the core definitions and examples of evil in the Harry Potter stories are prejudice and lack of love. So it is no wonder that Harry Potter readers are ripe for movements toward social justice. Voldemort was unquestionably the villain of the seven-book saga. But he was merely an example of evil, not its source or sole force. Voldemort simply took prejudice, and its root fear of death, to a new level of darkness and destruction in the wizarding world. And Albus Dumbledore, though a master of so many forms of magic, beauty, friendship, and frolic, emerges ultimately as the direct counterforce against prejudice and lack of love, starting all the way back in his teenage victory over the Voldemort of an earlier age, Gellert Grindlewald.[3] For millions of readers of all ages, Dumbledore transforms throughout the books from a truly playful renaissance legend into a truly brave resistance leader.

Using a term from chapter 6, Dumbledore is the consummate "in command, out of control" leader. His methods in leading and nurturing a school with a culture and metabolism that raise up leaders among its members are worthy of study. A famous phrase for leadership that arose in the civil rights period of the 1950s and 1960s describes perfectly the mastery of the Hogwarts Headmaster. In a chapter of Carl Rogers's classic *Client-Centered Therapy*, titled "Group-Centered Leadership and Administration," researcher Thomas Gordon questions whether one wants to create a leader-centered group or to be a group-centered leader.[4] Dumbledore, not least evident in the formation of the Order of the Phoenix and the embrace of Dumbledore's Army, proves himself again and again as a group-centered leader. His contagious and catalytic leadership style makes him a master community organizer.

It is no wonder that T-shirts on bodies of all ages, genders, races, ethnicities, and sexual orientations at social justice rallies ask, "What Would Dumbledore Do?" For millions of readers who speak one or more of the sixty-seven languages into which the Harry Potter series has been translated across the world, Dumbledore's life and teachings are a North Star of justice and love for multiple national or ethnic contexts. In a brilliant essay on social justice messages in Harry Potter, Stanford University sophomore Sarah Quartey writes with words that speak for the global population of millennials:

> When and how did a generation of students eagerly absorbing the Harry Potter phenomenon become a force to be reckoned with? The

answer lies in social justice education leadership theory. In short, Albus Dumbledore, the headmaster of the Hogwarts School of Witchcraft and Wizardry, and others like him, cultivated an independent and powerful youth community. As a father figure, leader, and educator for young Harry Potter, Dumbledore became the mentor of an entire youth movement in J. K. Rowling's universe. But more than that, Dumbledore served as a role model for millions of children in the real world, who make up the Millennials, the generation born between the very late 1980s through 2005, during the rapid-pace change of the Internet and digital culture. Dumbledore's influence on the Millennial generation is becoming clear as youth movements like Gay-Straight Alliances storm plazas and demand justice.[5] Dumbledore is an exemplar of social justice leadership by demonstrating extraordinary feats. . . . His example should be followed in training educators and leaders of the future.

Quartey goes on to encourage social justice educators to use Dumbledore for transformative teaching in justice education:

The Harry Potter phenomenon has not just come and gone. Through the success of Harry Potter, J. K. Rowling did much more than earn a lot of money. Her character Dumbledore fundamentally shaped the Millennials and encouraged them to accomplish as much as they can. Dumbledore, being so powerful, makes it clear that youth do need social justice leaders, and that workshops and preparation education programs should be providing educators with the tools that Dumbledore has always had: the means to enable youth to fight for their own causes and the causes of others under the unified banner of their own individual strength and their power in numbers.[6]

In 2011, author and Harry Potter fanatic Lily Zalon published an artistic and moving collection of letters written by Harry Potter fans about how the stories changed their lives. The book is titled *Dear Mr. Potter: Letters of Love, Loss, & Magic.* Each letter is printed on its own page and accompanied by color photos of the fan who wrote the letter, usually dressed in some kind of Harry Potter costume. The letters, written by children to senior citizens, are addressed to J. K. Rowling, Mr. Potter, or other characters in the books or films. The book is nearly two hundred pages of testimonies from cancer patients, librarians, bullied students, grieving widows and widowers, accomplished athletes and musicians, survivors of suicide attempts, would-be writers and artists, poets, graduate students, immigrants, LGBTQ folks of all ages, parents, grandparents, godparents, and members of the armed forces. To flip through this book is to take a tour across the globe and see life after life that has been irrevocably formed and fed by the epic story of Harry Potter.

One of the most memorable letters in the collection is found in the book's introduction. It is a letter to Dumbledore, written by Andrew Slack. Slack is a legend in the Harry Potter fandom because he was the visionary who founded the Harry Potter Alliance. Slack's letter is a testament to the notion that for multiple generations of readers, Albus Dumbledore is more than just a prominent character or an avuncular figure in the stories. To millions of readers, Albus is not just an uncle or grandfather, Santa Claus, or even a superhero. He is an active coach, an engaged spiritual sage, a loving master teacher, and a contagious community organizer.

Andrew Slack writes a stirring letter to Dumbledore that is a powerful testimony to the power of Harry Potter to inspire social justice work among its readers. Keep in mind that the brainchild of Slack—the Harry Potter Alliance—has five million members in its social justice activist movement, across dozens of countries. Why should you use Dumbledore when you teach the connections between faith and social justice? Andrew Slack's letter to Dumbledore can answer that question, and it is worth quoting at length.

> Dear Professor Dumbledore,
>
> After you died, I made a vow. At first, I just lay there, my horrified eyes transfixed to the page in shock. Everything that had ever made me feel mirthful was destroyed before my eyes. Hogwarts had been invaded by Voldemort and I, a lightning struck reader immobilized on a lightning struck tower, could not get the image out of my mind: again and again, the wisest man I ever knew was forced to kneel before hoodlums and transfigured into a "rag doll" of a corpse, then cast off one of the buildings of his own school under the perverse light of the Dark Mark.
>
> . . . The story of your death changed the story of my life. When you died, I lost the person that I wanted to grow up to be, who represented all of my greatest teachers, and who not only gave me a feeling of childlike wonder and spontaneity, but a feeling of safety. When someone I loved was suffering, whether amongst my relatives, friends, or my family at Hogwarts, I looked to your strength, wisdom and your humor for solace. And then it was over . . . Suddenly Fawkes had stopped singing—the phoenix had gone, had left Hogwarts for good, just as Dumbledore had left the school, had left the world . . . had left Harry . . . and had also left me.

But even amidst these ashes of despair, something was reborn inside of me. A vow. A vow inspired by something that Harry had said at your funeral. When Harry replied to Scrimgeour's insensitive, politically motivated questions by explaining that their answers were private between he [*sic*] and his Headmaster, Scrimgeour chided him: "Such loyalty is admirable of course . . . but Dumbledore is gone, Harry. He's gone." Conjuring from his heart something you had said in his second year Harry replied, smiling in spite of himself, "He will only be gone from the school when none here are loyal to him." Confused, Scrimgeour ended by saying, "I see you are—" and Harry interrupted, "Dumbledore's man through and through . . . that's right."

I made a vow that Harry would not be the only one who would remain loyal to you, for I would, too.

Just five weeks before watching you die, I [had] an idea I felt very passionate about: a Dumbledore's Army for the real world called "The Harry Potter Alliance." . . . I was certainly struggling to make ends meet and the HPA was only an exciting possibility. But something changed within me. My greatest teacher had just died. And so I made a vow to help ensure that you wouldn't be gone. I made a vow to be Dumbledore's man through and through. And I would do it through the Harry Potter Alliance.

Thank you for our frequent visits and your continual guidance, sir. Thank you for helping me discover that strength, love, and childlike spontaneity are more powerful than magic, status, or material wealth.[7]

Slack is just one reader whose life was called to action in the real world by reading Rowling's epic. I did not include this portion of his letter because it is rare; I included it because its thoughts and feelings are not rare at all. The fact is that this letter expresses some of the exact words and intensity I have heard from countless Harry Potter fans who approach me before or after lectures, sermons, or presentations on Harry Potter and faith. And like so many followers of the Harry Potter series, what moved Andrew Slack above all else was not Dumbledore's superior intelligence or mastery of magic; rather, it was Dumbledore's belief in love that appears to move readers to emulate this love in their real lives. In the words of Dumbledore:

"That which Voldemort does not value, he takes no trouble to comprehend. Of house-elves and children's tales, of love, loyalty and innocence, Voldemort knows and understands nothing. Nothing. That they all have a power beyond his own, a power beyond the reach of any magic, a truth he has never grasped."[8]

And we see that Dumbledore's godparenting of Harry is so effective that when Harry faces Voldemort's attempt to take over his mind in *The Order of the Phoenix,* Harry's love is able to force Voldemort out of his body. Later in the book, Dumbledore explains to Harry that it was Harry's ability to love—not to hate or even to fight—that forced Voldemort out of his mind and heart. In Albus's words,

> That power [of love] also saved you from possession by Voldemort, because he could not bear to reside in a body so full of the force he detests. In the end, it mattered not that you could not close your mind. It was your heart that saved you.[9]

We learn from Dumbledore that the ultimate resistance to evil and injustice is not cunning or force. It is love. This is the message of Dumbledore. This is the message of the Harry Potter series. We will not triumph in our greatest struggles because we defeat our enemies, but because sacrificial love and resurrection have defeated death, and our enemies have no power over us. We can love here and now, and we can love after death. So in practicing love, we are victorious both before and after death. If driven by love and convinced by love that death has lost its sting, we are always free. This is the great secret of Dumbledore's levity and trust. In his words, "After all, to the well-organized mind, death is but the next great adventure."[10] Like Dobby, we experience this radical freedom at its fullest when and only when we use that freedom to serve others until they too find freedom. Rowling captures in her series the power and paradox of love in the Gospel of Luke: "Those who try to make their life secure will lose it, but those who lose their life will keep it" (17:33). If we are willing to die to ourselves—that is, to give up our fears of death—then we can live through and beyond all the deaths of our lives. Dumbledore teaches that when we truly love, we are truly free to truly live. When we serve justice, we expand our freedom and the freedom of others. In *The Half-Blood Prince,* Voldemort engages Dumbledore on the power of love:

> "The old argument," [Voldemort] said softly. "But nothing I have seen in the world has supported your pronouncements that love is more powerful than my kind of magic, Dumbledore."
>
> "Perhaps you have been looking in the wrong places," suggested Dumbledore.[11]

In Dumbledore's last conversation with Harry on the platform in King's Cross Station, Dumbledore sums up his life's commitment to practicing love as the greatest power in the world. "Do not pity the dead, Harry. Pity the living, and, above all those who live without love."[12]

An Apologetic of Justice

Christian apologetics is that field of theology concerned with defining and defending the faith through evidence, argumentation, and rational discourse. The term *apologetics* is from a Greek word meaning "to defend oneself or one's views." In one form or another, Christian apologetics began when the first followers of Jesus had to explain their experience of Christ to others. In a world in which God has created and preserved human freedom, there is always an open space in the public square and in the human heart where we can and should present evidence, consider alternate points of view, and make rational decisions about our own loyalties and actions.

In the last century, when we spoke of Christian apologetics, certain names have been mentioned again and again: writers, teachers, and pastors such as G. K. Chesterton, C. S. Lewis, and more recently, Alister McGrath, Rowan Williams, Francis Collins, and Anne Lamott. There is also a strong varsity on the attack side of religion and faith in recent years, such as Richard Dawkins or Christopher Hitchens. The internet offers the entire world as an audience for any single voice to defend or attack the Christian faith. Blogs and self-publishing have vastly broadened the number of published or posted voices debating the big questions about God and religion. You could spend multiple lifetimes watching all the videos on YouTube of brilliant people debating whether there is a God and whether Jesus of Nazareth is that God. I have seen dozens of public debates between atheists such as Dawkins and people such as Rowan Williams or other apologists for the Christian worldview. These cage fights of conviction are entertaining, but honestly, is anyone changing their views?

What is more common, in my experience, is that the masses watch or read these debates and simply feel better about their own side. These public debates and discussions are edifying to the position you already hold. And this is no small thing. Watching the mastery of our own hopes and ideas at work in the words of others can sometimes heal our insecurities. But if the goal for either side is conversion, I can only say that I know of no person in my life that was persuaded to switch their view on the existence of God by watching or reading debates on the topic.

The folks who have changed and continue to change their minds about metaphysical ideas love stories, not slugfests. They love sharing their stories and hearing the life stories of others in coffee shop conversations, bus or train talks while commuting, meals shared with family or friends, or unexpected talks at dog parks, athletic events, shoveling snow, or raking leaves with others on their street. When we do things together—and even more so, when we dare things together—we build relationships that allow people to feel as if they belong to a tribe, a neighborhood, an ethic group, or a religion. And once shared practices lead to group bonding, individuals have a context with each other in which to hear and share stories with curiosity, authenticity, and bravery. The mature relationships—begun in behavior and then bonded with belonging that comes with shared behaviors—create a space where we can reckon with one another's core beliefs, already sharing our practices and a group identity. In my life, I have watched Christian apologetics, based in gathering around practices rather than presentations or debates, produce the most deeply shared beliefs. Within the church, we could call this a Eucharist-centered or liturgy-centered model of deepening beliefs: when we gather in the practice of worship, again and again and again, we create a community identity that confesses its beliefs as a response to its practice, not the other way around.

Although the means and methods of debate have changed with digital communication, the general project of apologetics is still largely to make linguistic arguments, written or oral, that defend the claims of Scripture and the tenets of faith. Hundreds of new books, sermons, or monthly blog posts are still being inspired by the classic twentieth-century style of rational and linear apologetics in works like G. K. Chesterton's *Orthodoxy* or C. S. Lewis's *Mere Christianity*, taking on and taking apart skepticism or nonbelief one idea or one chapter at a time. Many of these apologetic works begin by arguing for the existence of God and then move on to defend Scripture and ultimately argue for the reality of miracles, the efficacy of sacraments, or the divinity of Christ. I have entire shelves of these books in my home, with cracked bindings and worn pages with folded corners and highlighted passages. I have countless bookmarks in my browser toolbar for websites and twitter feeds that produce apologetic content every hour. Ever since college, I have borrowed or bought as many apologetic works as possible, always looking for the new analogy, story, or historical discovery that might animate my next debate with skeptics of God, Scripture, or the Christian religion.

The Limitations of Tweets

Despite the bread and butter that apologetic works have been for me and for countless Christians in prior decades, teaching high school for the last twenty years has convinced me that written or spoken defenses of our faith are no longer as persuasive or contagious as they once were in the predigital culture for the predigital imagination. Although we call our current culture the information age, I have found that young people are drowning in the twenty-four-hour news cycle and prefer to escape the noise by closing their ears to information that is not directly related to their daily life. The ability to send and receive texts on smartphones has many of the young adults in my life spending the majority of their day writing their own thoughts and reading responses to those thoughts written by friends. Every day brings its necessary vocations of school or work, but every day is also one long smartphone conversation between the young adult and their chosen conversation partners. Every sentence written or read is immediately relevant in this curated orbit of voices and images.

How can other sources of news or information compete for attention and relevance against that kind of persistent personal stream of words and ideas? Reading or listening to a well-formed rational argument about whether there is a God seems a cold, irrelevant, two-dimensional parade of phrases compared with a text from a friend, a Snapchat from a romantic interest, or a notification of a like on your Facebook post. A 191-page-long copy of *Mere Christianity* doesn't even talk about Jesus until page 50. In a truth-by-tweet world, much of everything that was ever called apologetics has lost its stickiness because, among disconnects with current cultural trends, it takes too much time to consume and digest.

I applaud those brave and tireless apologists who are trying to tweet the classic arguments. But I have given up on linear and argumentative discussions of the faith. There is too much to say to define the Christian invitation to abundant life in 140 characters or less. Reducing the claims and challenges of the gospel into tweets or brief, light touches in publications or sermons succeeds only in sloganeering, and rarely even then. Some faith formation can be accomplished through tweets and posts and Pinterest. But I have not seen these new forms of communication changing minds toward faith commitments among those atheists or agnostics to whom I have ever ministered. I have seen inspiring digital discipleship, and we need more of it. Texts, tweets, and links can feed the faithful like never before. But I have yet to see these short-form communication methods succeed in moving the young adults in my life from nonbelief or theological free agency into a commitment of faith and a relationship with God—in a word, conversion.

Behaving before Believing

Modern Church historians have argued that a popular model for ministry and building a religious community prior to our contemporary times was "believe, behave, belong." The idea was that we welcomed people into our faith communities by starting with what we believe and looking for a match or partner of belief in our visitors and seekers. Once we agreed on certain core beliefs, seekers were then invited to learn and practice our traditional or ritualistic behaviors, with the eventual extension or reward of membership or belonging to our faith communities. Church and cultural historian Diana Butler Bass makes the argument this way:

> For the last few centuries, Western Christianity offered faith in a particular way. Catholics and Protestants taught that belief came first, behavior came next, and finally belonging resulted, depending on how you answered the first two questions. Churches turned this pattern into rituals of catechism, character formation, and Confirmation. At birth, Christian children were either baptized or dedicated, with sponsors and parents answering belief questions on their behalf, promising to teach them the faith. As children grew, Sunday schools and catechism classes taught Christian doctrine and the Bible, ensuring that each generation knew the intellectual content of the tradition. Eventually, children moved from Sunday school to "big church," where they participated in grown-up church practices and learned how to pray, worship, sing, give alms, and act kindly. When a Christian child reached an age of intellectual and moral accountability—somewhere between seven and fifteen—the church would offer a rite of full membership in the form of Communion, Confirmation, or (in the case of Baptists) adult-believers baptism. Believe, behave, belong. It is almost second nature for Western people to read the religious script this way.
>
> It was not always that way. About five hundred years ago, Western Christianity divided from a single church into five different major church families: Roman Catholicism, Lutheranism, Reformed Christianity, Anglicanism, and Anabaptism faith. Each group felt the need to defend itself against all the others, making clear its interpretation of the Bible and theology. Although religious diversity is common enough today, even the limited pluralism of the sixteenth century caused intense religious turmoil—including outright warfare. Competing religious claims turned into competing claims for political and economic power. Each religious group embarked on a process of ordering and systematizing its view of faith. New theologies shifted away from emphasizing Christian practice toward articulating Christian teachings, as everyone attempted to prove that their group's interpretation was true or most biblical. Religion moved increasingly in the direction of defending philosophical truth claims.[13]

You can see how this ministry model worked well with twentieth-century apologetics: C. S. Lewis, Billy Graham, or others would help you decide on your beliefs, which would lead you into collective behaviors or actions, culminating in joining churches. The linear apologetics of the twentieth century reflected and fed this believe-first model. But the continual fraying and graying of religious communities and the general decline of mainline, mainstream organized religion in the twentieth century and into the twenty-first compel us to rethink both our evangelism and ministry models. We need something better than "believe, behave, belong"; we need to find an apologetic style that draws people in with something more life-giving than a verbal or written debate about truth claims.

The newer and more successful models at work in the church today show that what communicates better in our cultural moment is a "behave, belong, believe" model. In my own experience, I have observed people who want to do things together but with little commitment at the start. A few years ago, you couldn't get a phone contract, gym membership, or apartment without at least a yearlong contract. But now, it is far more common for all kinds of industries to offer month-to-month plans lest they lose customers. People want to be able to try yoga, music lessons, online subscriptions, mattresses, apartments, or even new cars for a trial period after which they can discontinue if not satisfied. We know from research that people seek out religious communities in similar ways: folks want to show up, do or experience something meaningful, decide whether that event or experience was valuable, and only if so, then agree to try it again. After repeatedly showing up and practicing the methods and metabolism of a faith community, they start to feel like they belong.

You can hear this identity formation happening when someone changes from saying "the yoga studio" to "my yoga studio," "the gym" to "my gym," or "the church" to "our church." Folks figure out their beliefs after they feel safe, welcome, and invested in a place. All evidence of the patterns of consumption or commitment in our culture points toward the fact that behavior and belonging breed belief, not the other way around. You can see in this model that a persuasive essay or YouTube clip arguing you into a corner about belief in God is just not what twenty-first-century Americans are looking for or what will motivate them to join a community. People are looking for communities of safe and authentic practice, made up of people who take individual acts of charity or kindness and bring them to scale or to systems.

If these assumptions about what motivates people to consider conversions or renewals in their core belief systems are true, as I have observed them to be in many church contexts, then something other than the tried-and-true linear apologetics of the twentieth century and prior is needed. Our age is seeking a set of practices that respond to the trials and troubles of the current moment, not creeds of explanations or expectations for believers. People are less interested in whether there is a God than in how they should spend their disposable time.

No Longer Preaching to the Choir

In light of the contemporary patterns of attention, attendance, and membership, among the changes necessary in our ministry models are changes to our methods of preaching, which is more like missionary work than in prior decades. The phrase "preaching to the choir" has a lot less meaning when we realize that half or more of the choir members are in church first to sing, and perhaps not even out of a faith commitment at all. As for those in the pews, we know only that they have shown up. And even if they show up regularly, there is no telling whether they feel as if they belong in our communities. If the research on consumption and connection patterns is true, folks in the pews, even those who have been coming for years, are trying us out, open to greater or lesser levels of commitment and shared beliefs along the way. And it is entirely possible that they are uncertain about whether they believe the sentences of the creed or even unwilling to confess them.

I enter the pulpit every Sunday with evangelistic aims to persuade, knowing the average audience for a sermon in a church in this day and age is not a group of people who are present because they have settled or answered their deepest faith questions. They are present and practicing on a journey to find clarity on faith questions. Apologetics is no longer a sideline genre of theologians. In our current cultural moment, every sermon must be, among other things, an apologetic work of labor and love. The door to the church used to be the line between the believers and the unbelievers; it is now more of a membrane, and the line between believers and unbelievers runs right through each pew person's postmodern heart. I am drowning in the vast oceans and whitewater pace of information on the internet like the rest of us, so I know the line of belief and unbelief runs through my own heart. The verse for all of us in the church these days is perhaps Mark 9:24, in which a man seeking a miracle says to Jesus, "I believe; help my unbelief!"

I argue that we still need powerful apologetics—we need an intentional, persuasive, educated presentation in all forms of media for our faith—more than ever. Defining and defending the faith is no longer what the church does to the world. In our day, what the church does both within and without its walls and websites is what's important. As 1 Peter 3:15 says, "Be prepared to give an answer . . . for the hope that you have." But we need an apologetic style tailored to the particular hunger in humanity that our cultural context is fueling. I argue that social justice work draws people in because it is true and real and an extension of the conscience in all of us. We do not need to create a longing for justice: it is the shape of the soul. If we speak to this part of people, we will have wired buy-in for our message.

We need an apologetic of social justice action. We need to invite people to work together, pray together, and play together, and then trust that those experiences will become evidence for our convictions, just as the chapters of *Mere Christianity* built the case for Christ and the church. The Quakers have a lovely and powerful phrase that is as close to a creed as that noncreedal community can be: "Let your life speak." Churches that are growing are leading with practices and social justice actions in the world. They are clearly, joyfully, and bravely inviting all people in their bounds to take part in the healing of the world and the healing of their own hearts in the process. Let the world watch us and join us as we march, write, preach, get arrested, build houses, and mentor young people. Let our actions for justice in a jaded, classist, bigoted, violent world be our apologetics, trusting that if we invite people to join us in the healing of the world, they will immediately or eventually be curious about our beliefs and for their own convictions.

Twenty years ago, I used to give copies of *Mere Christianity* to all my seeker friends and colleagues. Nowadays, I am much more likely to invite seekers to help at my church's soup kitchen, to walk with our church group at a human rights march or gay pride parade, to come and sit with members of our church at a community meeting, or to join us as we take ride-alongs with local law enforcement. I trust that when the seeker shares an experience of reaching, marching, or praying toward social justice, the impact of that experience will become evidence for the reality and power of the God we profess. Moments of working or fighting for justice are more powerful and persuasive experiences than a debate, presentation, or sermon. In healthy justice-seeking churches, sermons are commentary on the Scriptures and on the community's epic journey to take part in the healing of the world. And the sacraments are both the fuel for and the actual experience of the reign of God we are working to expand in the world.

The reality is that the attention span of the average American is getting shorter by the hour. And I do not believe that current Christian apologists should try to jam our message into that shrinking space. The way forward, in my view, is to expand the attention span. Real curiosity, always the antecedent to discovery and commitment, is possible only with attention. But how do we expand the attention span when our culture of communication is working against us every second? We don't need a better apologetic; we need a new one. And Dumbledore's Army gives us one. I know it works because I have seen it work.

The Apologetics Scene

In *The Order of the Phoenix*, Harry, Ron, and Hermione admit to each other that the corrupted Ministry of Magic has in fact initiated a takeover of Hogwarts. They agree that Professor Umbridge has no intention of training students in Defence Against the Dark Arts, for fear that students might unite to fight against the Ministry, so they dare to invite other students to a secret meeting in Hogsmeade to plan a resistance movement. The plan is that students could be persuaded to form a secret organization in which they could learn defensive magic and prepare themselves to fight for what is right, both at school and in the wider wizarding world.

The challenge for Ron, Harry, and Hermione is real: how to unite the students against the Ministry's scheme to neuter their learning and soften their resistance to pro-pure-blood culture. Fellow students are not in agreement as to whether the Ministry of Magic was corrupt, nor do all of them think that Umbridge is intentionally refusing to teach defensive spells so that the students will not wage a war against the Ministry. Many of them are unconvinced that Voldemort has, in fact, returned. There are rumors and factions concerning the major news in the *Daily Prophet* each day, but many students, as in many high schools in any culture, don't much care about the world outside of Hogwarts. This is the diverse group of peers that Harry, Hermione, and Ron are trying to unite in order to learn Defence Against the Dark Arts and take a stand against Voldemort. Harry and his closest friends are completely convinced of the threat Voldemort and the corrupted Ministry of Magic pose to the entire world, but many of their peers are not. What form of apologetics will they employ to bridge the gap?

Shared Convictions or Shared Curiosities

Hermione quietly invites a number of other students to a secluded place called the Hogs Head, in her words, a "dodgy" pub on the outskirts of Hogsmeade. Harry is surprised when over a dozen students pile into the dusty watering hole. Harry knows the student body is all over the map concerning the anti-Dumbledore changes at the school and at the Ministry. "What have you been telling people," Harry asks Hermione. "What are they expecting?" Hermione is not sure what will happen at the meeting.

> "I've told you, they just want to hear what you've got to say," said Hermione soothingly; but Harry continued to look at her so furiously that she added quickly, "You don't have to do anything yet, I'll speak to them first."[14]

So begins the apologetic endeavor of Harry and Hermione to define the threat of Voldemort and to defend their convictions that Hogwarts is no longer preparing young wizards to use either defensive or offensive magic. Their challenge is to name and face the rumors, falsehoods, and doubts of the gathered group and try to unite them in a common purpose.

In the end, what the reader learns from Hermione is that you don't have to get a group to agree on fundamental questions in order to marshal them into collective action. You need to leave space for curiosity and not try to force consensus before building community or sharing in moral and spiritual practices. The brilliant idea in this scene is that if enough people are curious about what might be true or possible, they will take the next step to sign their names to a group—a symbolic but no less real step toward collective action. A group can agree to explore possibilities together without deciding at the outset what all the possibilities are. Hermione knows she doesn't have to get folks to agree on all the reasons for learning defensive spells. She has faith that as the group gathers and practices dark arts defense together, over time the group might come to share expectations and plans for the use of their new skills.

Harry is more anxious than Hermione because his apologetic approach is different and less appropriate to this context. Harry worries about whether he can get the students to believe his claims about Voldemort or the Ministry of Magic. He feels burdened to convince them and grows bitter and defensive when consensus on his convictions does not come together. Hermione's brilliant community-organizing mindset wants to invite peers to training, which in any case would be helpful in life, in hopes that those who train together can eventually trust each other's truths. Harry wants shared convictions; Hermione wants shared curiosity. There's tension in the scene between Harry and Hermione as their different strategies collide.

> "Well . . . erm . . . well, you know why you're here. Erm . . . well, Harry here had the idea—I mean"—Harry had thrown her a sharp

look—"I had the idea—that it might be good if people who wanted to study Defence Against the Dark Arts—and I mean, really study it, you know, not the rubbish that Umbridge is doing with us"—(Hermione's voice became suddenly much stronger and more confident)—"because nobody could call that Defence Against the Dark Arts"—"Hear, hear," said Anthony Goldstein, and Hermione looked heartened—"well, I thought it would be good if we, well, took matters into our own hands."

She paused, looked sideways at Harry, and went on, "And by that I mean learning how to defend ourselves properly, not just theory but the real spells—"

"You want to pass your Defence Against the Dark Arts O.W.L. too, though, I bet?" said Michael Corner, who was watching her closely.

"Of course I do," said Hermione at once. "But I want more than that, I want to be properly trained in Defence because . . . because . . ." She took a great breath and finished, "Because Lord Voldemort is back."[15]

Immediately the room is filled with both short screams and arresting silence. Hermione does not hide her belief in the reemergence of Voldemort, nor is she shy about using this belief to explain her passion for proper magical training. But she blesses any stake in the training, even if students only want to pass their Dark Arts exams. She is less concerned about why a student would want to join a resistance group and more focused on drawing them to join. Harry is nervous throughout this meeting because he is operating on the old model of argumentative apologetics and of the "believe, behave, belong" method in forming a faith-based community. Harry is anxious that his peers won't believe him or Hermione before they commit to collective purpose or collective resistance. But Hermione is practicing the more helpful model of faith-based community—that is, the "behave, belong, believe" model, in which you gather people around a set of practices (in this case, learning defensive spells together) and then trust that shared practice will breed a sense of belonging, which can ultimately form the foundation for trusting the group and sharing core beliefs.

Hermione's apologetic style is one based in action: if students learn a skill from Harry, they are more likely to believe him about seeing Voldemort, not the other way around. Hermione, like any effective twenty-first-century apologist, is aiming for conversion to a set of shared practices rather than a set of shared first principles. It is not that principles should not matter to contemporary apologetics; rather, in this scene in the Hogs Head, we see an example of the power of gathering around practices before gathering around shared principles. In the end, this kind of apologetics is driven by hope that *lex vivendi, lex credendi* ("as we live, so we believe"), a twenty-firstcentury reordering of centuries-old principles in our tradition.

But some students want to debate Hermione on the rumors they have heard, and their skepticism threatens the project to unite the group for learning together. They are more than curious about Harry's convictions concerning Voldemort. "Where's the proof You-Know-Who's back?" asked a Hufflepuff "in a rather aggressive voice." And other students raise similar questions about Harry's claims or Dumbledore's embrace of them. Hermione tries to refocus the room on committing to learning together. "Look," she says, quickly intervening, "that's really not what this meeting was supposed to be about—" Harry then took out his frustration on the room:

> "What makes me say You-Know-Who's back?" he repeated, looking [the students] straight in the face. "I saw him. But Dumbledore told the whole school what happened last year, and if you didn't believe him, you don't believe me, and I'm not wasting an afternoon trying to convince anyone."[16]

Harry has met the limits of "believe, behave, belong" apologetics. He can't get everyone to believe him or Dumbledore. Harry's temper, shorter than ever that year at Hogwarts, leaves him unable to move the group. Hermione rescues the mission.

> "So," said Hermione, her voice very high-pitched again. "So . . . like I was saying . . . if you want to learn some defence, then we need to work out how we're going to do it, how often we're going to meet, and where we're going to—"[17]

Hermione's approach of focusing on working together rather than believing each other's worldview is rewarded. Students ask more questions about Harry's experiences with dark magic, but Hermione does not shut down their questions. In the practice of deep listening that Hermione demonstrates, other students begin to stand up for Harry's stories and skills. As the group discussion continues, Harry's fans portray him as a hero to the skeptics in the room, prompting this response:

> "Look," [Harry] said and everyone fell silent at once. "I . . . I don't want to sound like I'm trying to be modest or anything, but . . . I had a lot of help with all that stuff . . ."[18]

Slowly, Harry starts to practice more effective community organizing by focusing on the role of others in his past triumphs. But certain members of the group push back on this message. They are looking for a leader and not looking to themselves for a potential role in a collective endeavor. Zacharias, a skeptic in the group, complains, "Well, we've all turned up to learn from him, and now he's telling us he can't really do any of it." As in many community meetings, there are voices that want a leader to solve the problem. They are leader-centered rather than group-centered in their understanding of how change happens. Hermione again refocuses the group on the next step. "Yes, well, moving on . . . the point is, are we agreed we want to take lessons from Harry?"[19]

In the end, Hermione's approach of bringing the group to agreement on learning defensive magic—agreement to "behave" together—wins. One by one, the students all sign their names to the parchment labeled "Dumbledore's Army." The students are not sure where, when, or how they will learn together. They never did have a vote or feel consensus on Voldemort's return. All these questions and divergent opinions are left respected but sidelined to make room for the mission of learning essential magical skills sooner than later, and with Harry as the leader. Some students may have joined Dumbledore's Army to fight Voldemort; others perhaps wanted only to improve their chances at high grades on the O.W.L. exam in the Dark Arts. But they are all united in the group's first action. The group can now become a solid and fertile ground in which a group identity and creed can grow.

Seeking One's Apologetic

People to whom I minister, inside the church and out, are trying to find out how to live their lives in a meaningful way. The Dursleys are described in the first line of the first book this way: "Mr. and Mrs. Dursley, of number four, Privet Drive, were proud to say that they were perfectly normal, thank you very much."[20] There is something about this first line that alerts or reminds the reader that only the incurious, defensive, and fearful aim for normalcy of the status quo in their lives. Folks of all ages tell me they are interested in actions and affiliations that feel true, joyful, or just. The internet makes us more aware than ever of the suffering and brokenness all around us. The public square is full of wounded seekers, more aware than ever of what is wrong and more disconnected than ever from institutions that used to form and feed us in what is right.

The need for apologetics that work is greater than ever in our lifetimes. The wizarding world of J. K. Rowling is much like our own. It is riddled with classism, racism, violence, and injustice that parallel today's reality. Centaurs fighting for their dignity and cultural survival are like the native peoples we see at Standing Rock and around reservations all over this country. The Giants, who cannot hide their genes, fight being ostracized by the dominant ablest culture, which sets the norms for mobility and size. Elves serve wizards as slaves for centuries, portraying the scourge of human trafficking and modern-day slavery around the world. Paternalism, colonization, or violence against Muggles by wizards for centuries led to outbreaks of persecutions against witches and wizards in multiple centuries in western civilization, portraying the cycles of postcolonial wars and retributions that we see playing out across the developing world.

The wizarding world is as overwhelmingly broken as our own. And it is no surprise that Rowling has created a magical but broken world, since we know that she was working for Amnesty International in her twenties while going home at night to write the Harry Potter books. She worked with transcripts of political prisoners smuggled out of foreign countries and received as refugees at her London office, testifying to their imprisonment and torture. Rowling greeted and listened to the nightmarish accounts of many who escaped their persecution and managed to arrive safely at Amnesty International. When I read Rowling's stories of the horrific testimonies she heard in those years at Amnesty, it is no wonder that she makes the Cruciatus Curse, the torture curse, one of the three Unforgivable Curses in her wizard world. It is impossible to think that this day job did not inform and inspire some of her night writing. Rowling speaks powerfully to the wounded Seeker because she was one while writing Harry Potter.

Rowling's personal as well as professional experience with the brokenness of the world while writing the Harry Potter stories explains why she articulates and advocates so creatively and passionately for an apologetic of social justice, sharing her faith not by arguing for it but instead by marshaling readers to "choose what is right over what is easy." You don't get your hands dirty holding one of my most cherished books, *Mere Christianity*. This moment in our culture needs our faith to go to work. And wounded seekers are literally dying to join us in anything that looks like a way out of the darkness.

Defining Social Justice Work

Rowling seals with a kiss her conviction that battling for justice is one of the foremost themes of the Harry Potter novels. Although the movies portray a different version, in the books Hermione, at long last, kisses Ron for one reason: he finally and, unprompted, shows concern for house-elves. After having returned to Hogwarts in the last book, while the battle against Voldemort rages, Ron suggests that they go down to the kitchen to allow Hogwarts's house-elves to escape. Immediately, this scene transpires:

> There was a clatter as the basilisk fangs cascaded out of Hermione's arms. Running at Ron, she flung them around his neck and kissed him full on the mouth. Ron threw away the fangs and broomstick he was holding and responded with such enthusiasm that he lifted Hermione off her feet.[21]

What is moving about Rowling's social justice convictions is that they are rooted in love, not law. Rowling portrays in the books, time and again, that characters find their way to moral clarity when they are led by love. They find what is right by choosing love as the guide. Consider Harry as early as the opening of the second book in the series: he has been punished severely, even criminally, by the Dursleys for ruining Vernon's business dinner. He is locked up and for days given only enough food to keep him alive. But the story tells us that he reserves some of all his meals to feed to Hedwig. Harry is starving that week, yet his devotion to Hedwig and her devotion to him make his choice clear and even joyful—he feeds Hedwig first.

Harry is also an example of resistance rooted in curiosity. An even earlier and subtler example of Harry's love that leads to justice is his conversation with the snake at the zoo in the first chapters of the first book. While others bang on the glass or think nothing at all of the snake, Harry stops to talk. He doesn't care that the snake is not human; instead, he asks questions and expresses sadness over the snake's captivity and shared identity as orphan and foreigner in his own house. Don't miss the symbolism that Harry's reaction to Dudley's banging on the glass results in the glass vanishing. Harry's ability and desire to love the stranger is so profound that it literally destroys the wall between species. The snake is liberated not by vengeance or violence, but by love.

Love, Marginalization, and Community

Readers of the Harry Potter books enjoy much richer and more frequent debating between Voldemort and Dumbledore on the power of love than those who watch the movies. There are also far more words between Dumbledore and Harry on the topic of love in the books than in the films. The movies appear more focused on portraying Voldemort as obsessed with dark magic and death and less interested in the rival force of love.

Here, as in multiple passages in the books, Voldemort questions Harry on the power of love:

> "Is it love again?" said Voldemort, his snake's face jeering. "Dumbledore's favorite solution, love, which he claimed conquered death, though love did not stop him falling from the tower and breaking like an old waxwork? Love, which did not prevent me from stamping out your Mudblood mother like a cockroach, Potter—and nobody seems to love you enough to run forward this time and take my curse. So what will stop you from dying now when I strike?"[22]

Part of Voldemort's mission is to prove Dumbledore wrong about the power of love. And one cannot help feel some sympathy for Voldemort's view, when one considers the unloved life he was born into. When Harry's parents were killed, Harry was soon in the presence of Snape, who loved Harry's mother more than his own life. In the minutes after Lily and James were killed, Harry was in the arms of Hagrid, flying to safety. As soon as Hagrid hit the ground in safe Little Whinging, Professor McGonagall, a woman who had been watching over this landing place for hours, met Harry, who was then held tightly by Dumbledore himself. Harry was then swaddled and left at a home bathed in sacrificial blood and thereby sealed with the most powerful magic of all, which would make it impossible for him to be harmed for over a decade to come.

Compare this ocean of embrace and love with the start of Tom Riddle's parallel reality of being an orphan. There is no doubt that life on Privet Drive was horrible for Harry, as was the orphanage horrible for Tom Riddle. But there is no denying that Harry was known, watched, guarded, and loved far beyond his understanding, in every hour of his life until and through his time at Hogwarts, whereas Tom Riddle was never embraced by anyone. It is no wonder that love seems a cruel hoax or foolish hope to Voldemort.

Rowling's belief that love fuels the more effective endeavors of social justice is not her only conviction about how justice is sought and served in both the real and the wizarding worlds. Harry's friends all share another dimension of the social justice hero: they not only love bravely but also are all outcasts in some form. They seek justice, having lived without it in some real way. Rejection, abuse, or oppression brings Harry and his close friends into a tight and trusting community of the marginalized. Ron has a garden rat as a pet because he can't afford an owl. Hermione tries to make up for a Muggle background by overperforming in the magical world. Neville's grief, awkwardness, and clumsiness make him the brunt of many jokes. Luna's oddities put her outside all other cliques at school. Seamus is Northern Irish, Dean is of African descent, and Cho is Asian. Nearly everyone who moves in the orbit of Harry and Dumbledore's Army has been on the margins.

There is unavoidable loneliness in all those students who live on the margins, which creates in them a longing for community and belonging. They cherish inclusion, while Draco and others with social capital are too busy competing with or degrading their peers to seek comfort, safety, or peace with others. Think of the dear mural of "Friends" with his name and others' listed on it that Harry sees in Luna's bedroom. The members of Dumbledore's Army are personally invested in building community because they know the isolation and pain without it. And once the army forms and the community bonds, it is ready to fight the enemies of community and justice. If Harry Potter teaches anything about seeking justice, it is that love must guide, that there is wisdom and bravery in the hearts of those on the margins, and that ultimately, these personal experiences drive action. In these stories, and in any powerful social justice movements, the personal is political.

Challenging Unjust Structures

There will always be a role for reading Harry Potter as a way to train people to fight for love-driven, nonviolent social justice work. People in power are not always right. *The Order of the Phoenix* is a long treatise on corruption and what to do when you find yourself in a corrupt system. Evil is depicted throughout the series, but this fifth book studies the systemic kinds of evil we all face. Through the *Daily Prophet*, Rowling shows that you can't always trust the news. Mad-Eye Moody's year in the bottom of seven boxes proved that people are not always who you think they are; corruption can change people you thought you knew. But what is the antidote to such a broken and corrupt world? Find friends you can trust. And then share practices of hope and justice. Invite others into your movement. With trusted friends, practice what you need to learn to fight the system and realize the need to rely on others. One of the most endearing lines in the series is when Harry, Ron, and Hermione fight the troll in *The Philosopher's Stone*. At the end of that long Halloween night, all three go to bed safely in their dorm rooms. And Rowling ends the reflection on their day by saying, "But from that moment on, Hermione Granger became their friend. There are some things you can't share without ending up liking each other, and knocking out a twelve-foot mountain troll is one of them."[23]

It is also important in social justice work to believe in the possibility of conversion among those we oppose. Rowling believes in the ability of any person to change course in their life. The most profound example in the series is Severus Snape. But Slughorn also changes his views, ultimately rejecting his persistent classism and racism to serve the Order. Aberforth battles back his bitterness and joins the Battle of Hogwarts. Draco doesn't turn Harry over to Voldemort at Malfoy Manor. And Draco's mother protects Harry by declaring him dead to Voldemort's face in the forest. Part of social justice work driven by love is the persistent belief in the potential transformation of our adversaries toward justice. Rowling speaks the boldness of her belief when Harry asks Voldemort in their final battle to show some remorse—to cease his evil on the spot. Harry fights Voldemort to the end but leaves open the possibility for remorse even in the last seconds of Voldemort's cruel and murderous life. Despite fits of rage and hatred that Harry feels for Voldemort over the years, in the end, Harry extends the hope of transformation to the man who seeks to murder him, just as Voldemort had murdered Harry's parents.

Rowling also points out something very important in social justice work: the difference between charitable works and social justice. True justice work done by schools, churches, or other community groups goes beyond bake sales. This distinction is crucial: charitable works meet basic needs and aid individuals. Think of Harry buying loads of candy off the Hogwarts Express trolley when he sees that Ron has no money or, when shopping for school supplies in Diagon Alley, giving all the free books given to him by Gilderoy Lockhart to the working-class Weasley children. This kind of immediate love and charity is present throughout the Harry Potter stories.

Throughout the New Testament, Jesus often performed acts of immediate and healing charity. But healing a leper did not and does not heal the social discrimination that makes lepers outcasts in every society. One leper being healed does not improve the experience of justice and dignity of any other leper. So many of the caustic and condemning exchanges between Jesus and the religious or secular authorities of his time display the confrontation with unjust structures, not just immediate needs of starving, sick, bleeding, or disabled people. John the Baptist and many prophets before him assaulted unjust power structures with their preaching and teaching. Discipleship requires that we do more than acts of charity. Jesus calls us to a radically different kind of discipleship—a life that is marked by care and concern for the poor and the disadvantaged, and for the systems of injustice that sustain poverty and discrimination. We are called to give more than what we have left over. And we are called to do more than give within systems that are fundamentally unfair. The scene of Jesus "cleansing the Temple" is an example of how working for social justice at times means challenging, confronting, protesting, and being aggressive toward unjust social structures.

Acts of social justice aim at the root causes of social ills, such as the need for affordable housing, quality public education, medical care, legal protection for the vulnerable in society, and a living wage, and question the proliferation of prisons and mass incarceration. These are root causes of hunger, poverty, violence, and discrimination. Social justice work begins with the premise that structural prejudice or inequality requires structural solutions. Buying someone candy, giving one or thousands of people a meal, or giving your coat to someone on the street are acts of charity. Volunteering long-term or funding campaigns against root causes is social justice. In the novels, we see the larger battle against injustice, blood purity policies, and Muggle-Magical-Creature social structures playing out and requiring far more than gold coins from Harry's vault.

One of the unfortunate developments in social justice projects with all ages is the phenomenon of "voluntourism," a recently coined term for bringing privileged people into underprivileged places to do short visits or work projects that address, at best, immediate needs for charity but do little to change the systems that cause suffering. Think of trips to Haiti, Honduras, or parts of Africa, where small groups spend a few days in an area, take thousands of pictures, engage in a project planned to last the length of their visit, and then return home. These kinds of trips are not entirely without value. More and more, we are learning how to surround these kinds of trips with intentional learning and reflection, before, during, and after the trip.

In the Harry Potter series, there is a humorous but insightful example of meaningless service work: the de-gnoming of the garden at the Burrow. Look at the dialogue around the "service" to Molly of de-gnoming the garden.

> There was a violent scuffling noise, the peony bush shuddered, and Ron straightened up. "This is a gnome," he said grimly.
> "Gerroff me! Gerroff me!" squealed the gnome. . . . It was small and leathery looking, with a large, knobby, bald head exactly like a potato. Ron held it at arm's length as it kicked out at him with its horny little feet; he grasped it around the ankles and turned it upside down.

"This is what you have to do," he said. He raised the gnome above his head ("Gerroff me!") and started to swing it in great circles like a lasso. Seeing the shock on Harry's face, Ron added, "It doesn't hurt them—you've just got to make them really dizzy so they can't find their way back to the gnomeholes."

He let go of the gnome's ankles: it flew twenty feet into the air and landed with a thud in the field over the hedge.

"Pitiful," said Fred. "I bet I can get mine beyond the swamp."[24]

The Weasleys are good people, which is why their practice of hurling howling creatures through the air is so poignant. In theory, de-gnoming is meant to help Molly and the household. But this ritual is nonetheless an act of cruelty that is forming family members. When "service" is not rooted in love and dignity, the result can be disenchantment with justice work or pure resentment for the people needing help. Consider what happened to Harry after a few minutes of engaging in this unjust service work:

Harry learned quickly not to feel too sorry for the gnomes. He decided to just drop the first one he caught over the hedge, but the gnome, sensing weakness, sank its razor-sharp teeth into Harry's finger and he had a hard job shaking it off—until—"Wow, Harry—that must've been fifty feet."[25]

This is the high price of poorly planned formation in service projects. In the end, Harry not only has practiced injustice, nurtured deafness to the cries of an oppressed creature, but also has learned resentment for gnomes. When analyzing any of our social service projects—as families, schools, Scout troops, or churches—we must ask ourselves a moral question for which our answer may have deep and perhaps even dangerous implications: despite the proliferation of great pictures for our publications, are we just de-gnoming the garden?

★　★　★

Just ten days after the election of Donald J. Trump as the nation's forty-fifth president, I traveled to Cambridge, Massachusetts, to attend the annual Harvard-Yale football game. While an undergraduate at Harvard, I had been a member of the marching band. Band alumni of all ages are always welcome to sit and play with the undergraduates. That weekend, I was asked and honored to be the "band chaplain for the day." Wearing my clerical collar and my band blazer embroidered with the Harvard bass drum logo, I spent the day talking with band members and alumni (ages eighteen to eighty-one) about their lives and current events. I asked them this question: "What's been the most spiritual thing that has happened, or did happen, to you at college?" The answers were beautiful and sometimes overwhelming: finding love, the death of a roommate, dinner with a hero, cancer, coming out, breaking up, sexual assault, forgiving my family, finding my passion, learning a new language, failing and learning to be okay with failing. This group of a hundred musical theists, agnostics, atheists, Jews, Christians, Sikhs, Muslims, Nones, Dones, and Funs had lots to say. Curiosity about big questions was alive and well, especially in those postelection days. The experience showed me that no matter what one's political convictions, the election of 2016 had truly shaken souls.

Just before the start of the game, three band members asked me to bless the ceremonial bass drum. This drum is nearly eight feet across and rests on a rack of wheels. It is one of the largest bass drums in the country. Generations ago, the band named it Bertha. It represents the heart and soul of this college band. I walked down to the drum and prepared to bless it. When the students announced to the band what was about to happen, one happy undergraduate piccolo player pushed her way forward through her band colleagues and rushed up to me. "Here!" she said. And in her hand was a Harry Potter wand. Hermione's wand, to be exact. She didn't need to tell me she was a Hufflepuff, because her hair was dyed bright yellow that day. "Here, use my wand!" I smiled back at her. I explained that although I was a huge Harry Potter fan, I would instead use a more traditional Christian blessing. "But please," I petitioned her, "join me and cast your own spell!" She looked thrilled. In a conversation with her later, I learned that she does not believe in God.

I blessed the drum and heard the student next to me whisper a spell as she waved her wand. As we walked away from the drum, my curiosity took over. "Do you always carry a Harry Potter wand with you?" She slid the wand into her blazer pocket as if she'd done it for years. "Not usually. But I've kept it near me since the morning after Trump won. It reminds me that even if the Ministry is corrupt, I can always 'choose what is right over what is easy.' It gives me hope." We walked silently for a moment in the wake of her beautiful words, then I answered, "It is our choices, Harry, that show us who we really are, far more than our abilities." She sighed, smiled, and nodded.

We kept walking side by side along the sideline. For years, I have delighted in conversations like this one with strangers that quickly become fluent in Harry Potter. But this conversation already felt unique. It felt holy. "What spell did you use on that drum?" She giggled. She stopped walking to face me and said, "I used Alohamora, of course!" For those of you who don't know, that is the spell from the books used to open things. "That's a curious choice," I said. "Why did you bless something with the spell to open?" She took a deep breath. "The whole world feels like it's closing right now. Everything. Everyone. I want things to open. I want people to open. I want everything to open."

I was so moved by what she said that when I blinked, a tear dropped down my face and she saw it. "Awww. Bring it in!" And the piccolo player gave me an awkward but sincere hug. When she pulled away, I said the first thing that came to me: "Because of resurrection, everything will open at the close." And the yellow-haired Hufflepuff beamed and said, "Amen."

Prayer for Social Justice
Almighty God, who created us in your image: Grant us grace fearlessly to contend against evil and to make no peace with oppression; and, that we may reverently use our freedom, help us to employ it in the maintenance of justice in our communities and among the nations, to the glory of your holy Name; through Jesus Christ our Lord, who lives and reigns with you and the Holy Spirit, one God, now and for ever. Amen.[26]

NOTES

1. *Half-Blood Prince*, 645.

2. Vezzali et al., "Greatest Magic of Harry Potter."

3. *Deathly Hallows*, 360.

4. Thomas Gordon, "Group-Centered Leadership and Administration," in *Client-Centered Therapy: Its Current Practice, Implications, and Theory*, ed. Carl Rogers (Boston Houghton Mifflin, 1951), 320–83.

5. The Gay-Straight Alliance Network recently changed its name to Genders & Sexualities Alliance Network; see http://gsanetwork.org.

6. "Harry Potter: Social Justice Theory Absorbed by a Generation," Static: A Site for Stanford Activists to Connect and Create, March 6, 2012, https://stnfrdstatic.wordpress.com/2012/03/06/harry-potter-social-justice-theory-absorbed-by-a-generation/Sarah Quartey.

7. Lily Zalon, *Dear Mr. Potter: Letters of Love, Loss, & Magic* (n.p.: 2011), 6–7.

8. *Deathly Hallows*, 709–10.

9. *Order of the Phoenix*, 844.

10. *Philosopher's Stone*, 297.

11. *Half-Blood Prince*, 444.

12. *Deathly Hallows*, 722.

13. Diana Butler Bass, *Christianity after Religion: The End of Church and the Birth of a New Spiritual Awakening* (San Francisco: HarperOne, 2012), 201.

14. *Order of the Phoenix*, 339.

15. Ibid., 340.

16. Ibid., 340–41.

17. Ibid., 341.

18. Ibid., 343.

19. Ibid.

20. *Philosopher's Stone*, 1.

21. *Deathly Hallows*, 625.

22. Ibid., 739.

23. *Philosopher's Stone*, 179.

24. *Chamber of Secrets*, 37.

25. Ibid.

26. Collect for Social Justice, Book of Common Prayer, 260.

Scriptures for Study

In reading this book or using it for group study you may wish to refer to these select passages of Scripture that are applicable to the Harry Potter themes discussed in each chapter.

1. From Rags to Snitches: The Resurrection of J. K. Rowling
- Psalm 23
- Matthew 28:1–10
- John 1:1–5
- 1 Corinthians 13:12
- Galatians 2:20
- Luke 24:13–35
- John 21:4–14
- John 20:24–29

2. The Bible Tells Me So: Teaching with Harry Potter Is Biblical
- Acts 1:1–11
- Acts 2:1–14
- Acts 17:16–33
- Matthew 5:1–20
- 1 Corinthians 9:20–22

3. Learning *Is* Magic: School Is the New Cool
- Ecclesiastes 3:11
- Psalm 139
- Ephesians 5:1–14

4. Do This in Remembrance of Me: The Patronus Charm Works
- Hosea 13:14
- Matthew 10:16–31
- Luke 12:1–12
- 1 John 4:7–5:5

5. Peace by Piece: Wholeness and Holiness in Harry Potter
   - Mark 14:22–25
   - Luke 24:30–35
   - Ephesians 2:14–19
   - Galatians 2:19–21
   - 1 Peter 3:15

6. Spiritual Parenting: Pride and Prejudice at Malfoy Manor
   - Exodus 20:1–17
   - Matthew 22:36–40
   - Luke 10:27–28
   - Romans 5:1–9
   - Philippians 4:8–9

7. Confirmation and Adolescent Faith: Building Dumbledore's Army
   - Ezekiel 37:1–14
   - Matthew 16:24–27
   - Romans 12:1–8

8. Godparenting: A Sirius Role
   - Deuternomy 6:6–9
   - Proverb 22:6
   - Luke 10:25–37
   - Acts 8:26–40

9. Faith Formation for All Ages: "All That Is, Seen and Unseen"
   - Leviticus 19:2
   - Joshua 1:9
   - Psalm 46:10
   - Proverbs 3:5–6
   - Colossians 1:10
   - Matthew 11:28–30
   - John 8:31–32

10. Social Activism: What Would Dumbledore Do?
   - Jeremiah 22:3
   - Isaiah 1:17
   - Proverbs 31:8–9
   - Matthew 21:12
   - 1 John 3:17
   - James 2:1–8

Index